REFL

DAILY PRAYER

REFLECTIONS
FOR
DAILY PRAYER

ADVENT **2015** TO
EVE OF ADVENT **2016**

ROSALIND BROWN
GILLIAN COOPER
STEVEN CROFT
ANDREW DAVISON
MAGGI DAWN
PAULA GOODER
PETER GRAYSTONE
MARY GREGORY
MALCOLM GUITE
EMMA INESON
JAN MCFARLANE
BARBARA MOSSE
MARK OAKLEY
MARTYN PERCY
BEN QUASH
MARTYN SNOW
JANE WILLIAMS

Church House Publishing
Church House
Great Smith Street
London SW1P 3AZ

ISBN 978 0 7151 4457 2

Published 2015 by Church House Publishing
Copyright © The Archbishops' Council 2015

The opinions expressed in this book are those of the authors
and do not necessarily reflect the official policy of the
General Synod or The Archbishops' Council of the Church of
England.

Liturgical editor: Peter Moger
Series editor: Hugh Hillyard-Parker
Designed and typeset by Hugh Hillyard-Parker
Copy edited by: Ros Connelly
Printed by CPI Group (UK) Ltd, Croydon, CR0 4YY

What do you think of *Reflections for Daily Prayer*?

We'd love to hear from you – simply email us at

publishing@churchofengland.org

or write to us at

Church House Publishing, Church House,
Great Smith Street, London SW1P 3AZ.

Visit **www.dailyprayer.org.uk** for more
information on the *Reflections* series, ordering
and subscriptions.

Contents

About the authors

Rosalind Brown is a Residentiary Canon and Canon Librarian at Durham Cathedral. Originally a town planner, her subsequent ordained ministry has included parish ministry while living for a few years in the USA, and training people for ordination. She written books on ministry and preaching, and is a published and prize-winning hymn writer.

Gillian Cooper is a writer, teacher, and Old Testament enthusiast. She has previously worked as a theological educator, a cathedral verger, and an administrator. She has recently moved to London, but still escapes whenever she can to the windswept beaches of Norfolk and Orkney.

Steven Croft is the Bishop of Sheffield. He is the author of a number of books including *Jesus People: what next for the church?* and *The Advent Calendar,* a novel for children and adults, and a co-author of *Pilgrim: a course for the Christian journey.*

Andrew Davison is the Starbridge Lecturer in Theology and Natural Sciences at Cambridge University, Fellow in Theology at Corpus Christi College and Canon Philosopher of St Albans Abbey. He is the author of *Why Sacraments?, Blessing* and *The Love of Wisdom: An Introduction to Philosophy for Theologians.*

Maggi Dawn is Associate Professor of Theology and Literature, and Dean of Marquand Chapel, at Yale Divinity School in the USA. Trained in both music and theology, her publications include five albums of songs, five books, and numerous articles and chapters. She was ordained in the Diocese of Ely, and holds a PhD from the University of Cambridge.

Paula Gooder is Theologian in Residence for the Bible Society. She is a writer and lecturer in biblical studies, author of a number of books including *Journey to the Empty Tomb, The Meaning is in the Waiting* and *Heaven,* and a co-author of the Pilgrim course. She is also a Reader in the Church of England.

Peter Graystone works for Church Army, where he oversees pioneering projects that take the Good News way beyond the walls of a church to profoundly unchurched people. One of those locations is the internet, and he edits Christianity.org.uk, which gives free, confidential, reliable information about the Christian faith. He is a *Church Times* columnist and theatre reviewer.

Mary Gregory is Rector of Kirk Sandall and Edenthorpe near Doncaster and Dean of Women's Ministry for the Diocese of Sheffield. Before her ordination ten years ago, she served as a prison governor. She is a keen walker, quilter and devoted adopter of retired rescue greyhounds.

Malcolm Guite, the Chaplain of Girton College, Cambridge, is a poet and singer–songwriter, and is the author of *What do Christians Believe?*, *Faith, Hope and Poetry*, *Sounding the Seasons: Seventy Sonnets for the Christian Year*, *The Singing Bowl* and *Word in the Wilderness*.

Emma Ineson is the Principal of Trinity College Bristol. Before that she was Chaplain to the Bishop of Bristol and was previously a member of faculty at Trinity College, teaching practical theology, gender studies and charismatic theology. Emma has also been Chaplain to the Lee Abbey community in Devon. She is a member of the General Synod.

Jan McFarlane is the Archdeacon of Norwich and Director of Communications in the Diocese of Norwich. She has served as Chaplain to the Bishop of Norwich, Chaplain of Ely Cathedral and Curate in the Stafford Team Ministry. A former speech therapist, she has a lifelong interest in communications and broadcasts regularly on local radio.

Barbara Mosse is a writer and retired Anglican priest. Prior to retirement she was a lecturer on the MA in Christian Spirituality at Sarum College, Salisbury. Earlier ministerial posts included some parish work, alongside chaplaincy experience in prison, university, community mental health and hospital. She is the author of *The Treasures of Darkness*, *Encircling the Christian Year* and *Welcoming the Way of the Cross*.

Mark Oakley is Canon Chancellor of St Paul's Cathedral. A former Chaplain to the Bishop of London and Rector of St Paul's, Covent Garden, he is the author of *The Collage of God* and various anthologies, including *Readings for Funerals*, articles and reviews, usually in the areas of faith, poetry and literature. He is Visiting Lecturer in the department of Theology and Religious Studies at King's College London.

Martyn Percy is the Dean of Christ Church, Oxford, one of the University of Oxford's largest colleges, as well as the Cathedral Church of the diocese of Oxford. From 2004 to 2014 he was Principal of Ripon College Cuddesdon. Prior to that he was Director of the Lincoln Theological Institute and has also been Chaplain and Director of Studies at Christ's College, Cambridge.

Ben Quash has been Professor of Christianity and the Arts at King's College London since 2007, and is Director of the Centre for Arts and the Sacred at King's (ASK). Prior to that he was Dean and Fellow of Peterhouse, Cambridge. He runs a collaborative MA in Christianity and the Arts with the National Gallery in London, and is also Canon Theologian of both Coventry and Bradford Cathedrals.

Martyn Snow is Bishop of Tewkesbury in Gloucester Diocese, having formally been parish priest and archdeacon in Sheffield. He has also worked with CMS in West Africa and has a particular interest in the world Church and in developing mission partnerships. Other interests include football, rugby and quiet days walking the hills.

Jane Williams lectures at St Mellitus College, London and Chelmsford, and is a visiting lecturer at King's College London. She taught previously at Trinity Theological College, Bristol.

About Reflections for Daily Prayer

Based on the *Common Worship Lectionary* readings for Morning Prayer, these daily reflections are designed to refresh and inspire times of personal prayer. The aim is to provide rich, contemporary and engaging insights into Scripture.

Each page lists the Lectionary readings for the day, with the main psalms for that day highlighted in **bold**. The Collect of the day – either the *Common Worship* collect or the shorter additional Collect – is also included.

For those using this book in conjunction with a service of Morning Prayer, the following conventions apply: a psalm printed in parentheses is omitted if it has been used as the opening canticle at that office; a psalm marked with an asterisk may be shortened if desired.

A short reflection is provided on generally either the Old or New Testament reading. In this volume for the first time, however, we are including reflections on the preferred psalms for Morning Prayer for the seven weeks starting from 11 July 2016.

Popular writers, experienced ministers, biblical scholars and theologians will be contributing to this series. They all bring their own emphases, enthusiasms and approaches to biblical interpretation to bear.

Regular users of Morning Prayer and *Time to Pray* (from *Common Worship: Daily Prayer*) and anyone who follows the Lectionary for their regular Bible reading will benefit from the rich variety of traditions represented in these stimulating and accessible pieces.

This volume also includes both a simple form of *Common Worship: Morning Prayer* (see inside front and back covers) and a short form of Night Prayer – also known as Compline – (see pp. 324–7), particularly for the benefit of those readers who are new to the habit of the Daily Office or for any reader while travelling.

The importance of daily prayer

Daily prayer is a way of sustaining that most special of all relationships. It helps if we want to pray, but it can be sufficient to want to want to pray, or even to want to want to want to pray! The direction of the heart is what matters, not its achievements. Gradually we are shaped and changed by the practice of daily prayer. Apprentices in prayer never graduate, but we become a little bit more the people God wants us to be.

Prayer isn't a technique; it's a relationship, and it starts in the most ordinary, instinctive reactions to everyday life:

- **Gratitude**: good things are always happening to us, however small.
- **Wonder**: we often see amazing things in nature and in people but pass them by.
- **Need**: we bump into scores of needs every day.
- **Sorrow**: we mess up.

Prayer is taking those instincts and stretching them out before God. The rules then are: start small, stay natural, be honest.

Here are four ways of putting some structure around daily prayer.

1 **The Quiet Time**. This is the classic way of reading a passage of the Bible, using Bible reading reflections like those in this book, and then praying naturally about the way the passage has struck you, taking to God the questions, resolutions, hopes, fears and other responses that have arisen within you.

2 **The Daily Office**. This is a structured way of reading Scripture and psalms, and praying for individuals, the world, the day ahead, etc. It keeps us anchored in the Lectionary, the basic reading of the Church, and so ensures that we engage with the breadth of Scripture, rather than just with our favourite passages. It also puts us in living touch with countless others around the world who are doing something similar. There is a simple form of Morning Prayer on the inside front and back covers of this book, and a form of Night Prayer (Compline) on pp. 324–7. Fuller forms can be found in *Common Worship: Daily Prayer*.

3　**Holy Reading**. Also known as *Lectio Divina*, this is a tried and trusted way of feeding and meditating on the Bible, described more fully on pages 6–7 of this book. In essence, here is how it is done:

- *Read:* Read the passage slowly until a phrase catches your attention.
- *Reflect:* Chew the phrase carefully, drawing the goodness out of it.
- *Respond:* Pray about the thoughts and feelings that have surfaced in you.
- *Rest:* You may want to rest in silence for a while.
- *Repeat:* Carry on with the passage ...

4　**Silence**. In our distracted culture some people are drawn more to silence than to words. This will involve *centring* (hunkering down), *focusing* on a short biblical phrase (e.g. 'Come, Holy Spirit'), *waiting* (repeating the phrase as necessary), and *ending* (perhaps with the Lord's Prayer). The length of time is irrelevant.

There are, of course, as many ways of praying as there are people to pray. There are no right or wrong ways to pray. 'Pray as you can, not as you can't', is wise advice. The most important thing is to make sure there is sufficient structure to keep prayer going when it's a struggle as well as when it's a joy. Prayer is too important to leave to chance.

+John Pritchard

Lectio Divina – a way of reading the Bible

Lectio Divina is a contemplative way of reading the Bible. It dates back to the early centuries of the Christian Church and was established as a monastic practice by Benedict in the sixth century. It is a way of praying the Scriptures that leads us deeper into God's word. We slow down. We read a short passage more than once. We chew it over slowly and carefully. We savour it. Scripture begins to speak to us in a new way. It speaks to us personally, and aids that union we have with God through Christ, who is himself the Living Word.

Make sure you are sitting comfortably. Breathe slowly and deeply. Ask God to speak to you through the passage that you are about to read.

This way of praying starts with our silence. We often make the mistake of thinking prayer is about what we say to God. It is actually the other way round. God wants to speak to us. He will do this through the Scriptures. So don't worry about what to say. Don't worry if nothing jumps out at you at first. God is patient. He will wait for the opportunity to get in. He will give you a word and lead you to understand its meaning for you today.

First reading: Listen

As you read the passage listen for a word or phrase that attracts you. Allow it to arise from the passage as if it is God's word for you today. Sit in silence repeating the word or phrase in your head.

Then say the word or phrase aloud.

Second reading: Ponder

As you read the passage again, ask how this word or phrase speaks to your life and why it has connected with you. Ponder it carefully. Don't worry if you get distracted – it may be part of your response to offer to God. Sit in silence and then frame a single sentence that begins to say aloud what this word or phrase says to you.

Third reading: Pray

As you read the passage for the last time, ask what Christ is calling from you. What is it that you need to do or consider or relinquish or take on as a result of what God is saying to you in this word or phrase? In the silence that follows the reading, pray for the grace of the Spirit to plant this word in your heart.

If you are in a group, talk for a few minutes and pray with each other.

If you are on your own, speak your prayer to God either aloud or in the silence of your heart.

If there is time, you may even want to read the passage a fourth time, and then end with the same silence before God with which you began.

+Stephen Cottrell

Monday 30 November

Andrew the Apostle

Psalms 47, 147.1-12
Ezekiel 47.1-12
or Ecclesiasticus 14.20-end
John 12.20-32

John 12.20-32

'... unless a grain of wheat falls into the earth and dies' (v.24)

In this first week of Advent, we celebrate another first: the first disciple to be called by Jesus. There were two pairs of brothers among the disciples: Andrew and Simon Peter, and James and John. Yet while three of these were especially close to Jesus, Andrew was often left out. Simon Peter is usually credited with being the first to confess that Jesus was the Messiah, yet according to John 1.41, Andrew perceived this at his first encounter with Jesus and he immediately told Simon. Both in this passage, and at the feeding of the 5,000, Andrew seems to act as a buffer between Jesus and the crowds. It seems that, like many personal assistants, he often worked tirelessly in the background while others got the glory.

Perhaps, being Simon Peter's younger brother, Andrew was used to living in someone else's shadow. Perhaps that made it easier for him, when he heard Jesus say 'unless a grain of wheat falls', not only to hear Jesus' prophetic words about his own death, but also to embrace their wider implications: that unless we are willing to lay down our small ambitions, we will never see or understand true glory. Real glory isn't about being in the spotlight all the time, but rather is about being transformed to reflect the glory of God. If that means sacrificing acknowledgement, or taking second place to someone else, it's a price worth paying.

COLLECT

Almighty God,
who gave such grace to your apostle Saint Andrew
that he readily obeyed the call of your Son Jesus Christ
    and brought his brother with him:
call us by your holy word,
and give us grace to follow you without delay
    and to tell the good news of your kingdom;
through Jesus Christ your Son our Lord,
who is alive and reigns with you,
in the unity of the Holy Spirit,
one God, now and for ever.

Psalms **80**, 82 *or* **5**, 6 (8)
Isaiah 26.1-13
Matthew 12.22-37

Isaiah 26.1-13

*'... this song will be sung in the land of Judah
... the way of the righteous is level' (vv.1,7)*

Isaiah often uses poetic metaphors to describe his vision of justice and equity. Here, high cities are brought low; in chapter 40, mountains and valleys are made level. But Isaiah not only speaks of justice; he frames it as a song to be sung, with similar themes to other justice songs sung by Deborah (Judges 5), Hannah (1 Samuel 2), and Mary (Luke 1), and the psalmists.

Songs have historically taken on an important role in situations where justice is nowhere to be found. We have songs as old as Psalm 137, and as recent as the spirituals of eighteenth- and nineteenth-century America, through which enslaved people expressed a depth of lament, a determination to survive, and a refusal to lose their human dignity. Or think of protest songs: *The Diggers Song* is famed as a seventeenth-century protest song over land rights; *We Shall Overcome* was the anthem of the labour and civil rights movements, and later a song of anti-war protest. During the years of apartheid in South Africa, resistance music was often described as a 'weapon of struggle'.

Songs can be tools of protest and change, etching on the heart the Advent longing for the world as it should be. As Isaiah calls on God to level out mountain-sized inequities, he also recognizes that a world in need of justice is a world in need of songs to sustain the soul.

Almighty God,
give us grace to cast away the works of darkness
and to put on the armour of light,
now in the time of this mortal life,
in which your Son Jesus Christ came to us in great humility;
that on the last day,
when he shall come again in his glorious majesty
to judge the living and the dead,
we may rise to the life immortal;
through him who is alive and reigns with you,
in the unity of the Holy Spirit,
one God, now and for ever.

COLLECT

9

Psalms 5, **7** or **119.1-32**
Isaiah 28.1-13
Matthew 12.38-end

Isaiah 28.1-13

'... like a first-ripe fig before the summer' (v.4)

For Ephraim, as now, figs were really a summer crop. But a few small, early figs would appear in the spring, and these were a particularly fine delicacy. Ephraim (another name for the Northern Kingdom of Israel) was a well-developed culture, a wealthy and stable society. But Isaiah saw what is true of many an empire just before its fall: a society resting on its laurels, so confident in its history and traditions that it believes nothing can assail it. Ephraim's complacency made her vulnerable to being snatched like an early fig, and 'eaten alive' by approaching enemy armies.

Just as the over-satisfied feeling after a big meal makes you want to take a little nap, so Isaiah laments that his people are so self-satisfied with their status and tradition that they cannot hear the need for change or the call to action. For cultures with a long and secure history, it seems impossible to imagine that old and beautiful buildings, ancient institutions or venerated practices might not be there forever. A sense of 'rightness' about their existence can lead to poor investments and unstable alliances, for the sake of preserving things as they are. For Isaiah's readers, the consequences were devastating. For us, too, it is important to avoid complacency about what we take for granted; our own institutions and long-held traditions may not be as solid and impermeable as we would like to believe.

COLLECT

Almighty God,
give us grace to cast away the works of darkness
and to put on the armour of light,
now in the time of this mortal life,
in which your Son Jesus Christ came to us in great humility;
that on the last day,
when he shall come again in his glorious majesty
    to judge the living and the dead,
we may rise to the life immortal;
through him who is alive and reigns with you,
in the unity of the Holy Spirit,
one God, now and for ever.

Psalms **42**, 43 *or* 14, **15**, 16
Isaiah 28.14-end
Matthew 13.1-23

Isaiah 28.14-end

'Therefore hear the word of the Lord, you scoffers' (v.14)

This short passage compares the health of society with the workmanship in a building. Just as a building is measured and tested with a line and plummet, so justice and righteousness are the qualities by which society is measured. Whatever is not properly constructed, whatever lacks a cornerstone, will be swept away by storms, and only what is upright and true will stand.

But what strikes me is that it is addressed to 'you scoffers'. Scoffing is a mode of speech that shuts down dialogue; it cuts the ground from under the feet of another person who could have been a conversation partner but instead is silenced. Life-giving conversation comes from listening, talking, considering, adjusting our viewpoint in the light of what we learn. But a scoffer is disdainful, supercilious, dismissive, someone who judges prematurely and assumes a place of superiority. Brushing off another's point of view with cruel humour may make the scoffer look 'cool' or funny, but scoffing isolates a person from friends and community, suffocating relationships and driving away goodwill.

Dialogue can open people up or shut them down, and Isaiah put his finger on what makes the difference: it is not just the content, but the spirit of conversation that makes it life-giving or deadening. The scoffers he addressed may even have been intellectually brilliant, but they brought such a negative spirit to their conversation that they had made a kind of 'covenant with death' (v.15).

Almighty God,
as your kingdom dawns,
turn us from the darkness of sin to the light of holiness,
that we may be ready to meet you
in our Lord and Saviour, Jesus Christ.

COLLECT

Friday 4 December

Isaiah 29.1-14

'... their worship of me is a human commandment learned by rote'
(v.13)

Isaiah's challenge may sound alarming to a liturgical community. When we revisit the same themes Advent after Advent, or if we daily recite the same words, learned by rote or read from a book, are our hearts far from God? Working in an ecumenical setting, I frequently hear debates between members of my congregation as to the relative value of liturgical and extempore styles of worship. Is one more heartfelt than the other? Is it more sincere to write prayers in advance, or to speak spontaneously in the moment?

Listen closely to extempore prayer, though, and you will see that it is just as much a learned and repeated pattern as liturgical worship, with language so particular to each community that you can even tell quite accurately which denomination a prayer comes from – Baptist or Pentecostal, Hillsong, Vineyard, or New Wine.

Whatever the style, repeating patterns of worship can either inoculate us against God's spirit, or cut a deep groove in our hearts. We can recite words while our hearts are disengaged, or we can discover ever-deeper layers of truth as we worship. Isaiah was not distinguishing between genres of prayer, but asking whether the community offered their prayer from the heart. Doing religion for the sake of it is worse than not doing it at all. Whatever the style, what matters is whether we are searching for God as we voice our songs and prayers in worship.

COLLECT

Almighty God,
give us grace to cast away the works of darkness
and to put on the armour of light,
now in the time of this mortal life,
in which your Son Jesus Christ came to us in great humility;
that on the last day,
when he shall come again in his glorious majesty
    to judge the living and the dead,
we may rise to the life immortal;
through him who is alive and reigns with you,
in the unity of the Holy Spirit,
one God, now and for ever.

Isaiah 29.15-end

'You turn things upside down!' (v.16)

The World Turned Upside Down was a famous English broadside ballad, published in the mid 1640s. It was written as a protest song against the attempts of the government to make Christmas a more solemn and sober occasion. At the time, Advent gave way to nearly two weeks of Christmas celebrations that continued until early January, during which time there was a ritualized reversal of social norms known as 'misrule'. Presided over by a Lord of Misrule, a child would be made Bishop for a day, masters waited upon their servants, and for a short time the world really was turned upside down. Some historians claim this provided a necessary release of tensions in seventeenth-century English society. However, a puritan faction within the government, shocked by the immoral behaviour that accompanied the celebrations, attempted to outlaw the tradition and make Christmas more 'Christ-like'.

It's easy to mistake Isaiah's call to righteousness for this kind of puritanical demand for personal holiness. But his longing for redemption was more in the spirit of Advent – less concerned with deliverance from personal sin than from systemic evil, when 'the tyrant shall be no more' (v.20). The tradition of misrule was a reminder of – and in some sense a protest against – social inequity and the abuse of power. Like the Lord of Misrule, Isaiah called for radical social and political change, and a reversal of power relationships, to turn the world right-side-up.

Almighty God,
as your kingdom dawns,
turn us from the darkness of sin to the light of holiness,
that we may be ready to meet you
in our Lord and Saviour, Jesus Christ.

COLLECT

13

Monday 7 December

Isaiah 30.1-18

*'Go now, write it before them on a tablet, and inscribe it
in a book ...' (v.8)*

Engraved into stone, pressed into clay, painted on ceramic, tooled into wax or inked onto animal skin, the written word was well developed by Isaiah's time, and has ever since had a quality of permanence. Every technological development in the production of writing has changed the way we relate to text; every change has caused alarm as well as excitement at the never-ending possibilities of speaking, reading and writing words. In the fifteenth century, the Gutenberg press led to silent reading overtaking reading aloud; later, the paperback reduced the sense of reverence for books. Turning print to pixels not only made words searchable, it changed the way we engage with text. Words on the web are more permanent than ever before, yet seem more ephemeral; they combine the visual with the aural; they have morphed from the linear arguments of traditional books to an interactive, networked engagement with words.

Isaiah captures one of the difficulties of language: that it is both our best means of communication, and at the same time always inadequate to the task. Words can weave 'illusions' (v.10) that conceal the truth, or they can take us closer to it. Perhaps it is no mistake that one of our names for Christ is 'the Word' – for in the end meaning resides neither in speech, print, nor pixels; our relationship to words constantly changes, but our faith is not ultimately anchored to words, but to *the* Word.

COLLECT	O Lord, raise up, we pray, your power and come among us, and with great might succour us; that whereas, through our sins and wickedness we are grievously hindered in running the race that is set before us, your bountiful grace and mercy may speedily help and deliver us; through Jesus Christ your Son our Lord, to whom with you and the Holy Spirit, be honour and glory, now and for ever.

Isaiah 30.19-end

'This is the way; walk in it.' (v.21)

For people of faith, taking care over decisions is a regular preoccupation, either in terms of the ethical obligations and consequences of faith, or with a more specific notion of God's personal guidance.

There might seem to be an immediate correlation between the importance of a particular decision and how much time it takes to make it. But life is not so simple. Sometimes we have the luxury of time, and a decision may be deferred until the way becomes certain, while at other times, even with a weighty matter, the right decision may be crystal clear in an instant. Far more complicated are those paralyzing moments when an urgent decision is required, but it is still unclear which way to go.

Someone once said to me that you can only steer a moving ship. When we don't know what to do, sometimes the moment of clarity about which way to go doesn't come while we are pausing and pondering. It may be that the direction will only become clear to see once we are actually on the move. Sometimes, rather than asking which way to go, we simply need to get started, trusting that the direction will become clear as we take the first steps: '... when you turn to the right or when you turn to the left, your ears shall hear a word behind you, saying, "This is the way; walk in it".' (v.21)

Almighty God,
purify our hearts and minds,
that when your Son Jesus Christ comes again as
judge and saviour
we may be ready to receive him,
who is our Lord and our God.

COLLECT

Wednesday 9 December

Isaiah 31

'[the Lord] ... does not call back his words' (v.2)

A linguistic dichotomy between fluid, poetic meanings and stable meanings is constantly in play in the words of Scripture. Studies over recent decades have opened up our understanding of the uses of language – how what is said is inflected in the way it is said; how form and content are woven together to make meaning; how some modes of language are wide open for interpretation, while the meaning of others are more tightly understood. 'We look for His coming again' begins a discussion with never-ending ramifications, but 'I will' is not only clear in its intent, but is a vow that actually changes one's status.

Isaiah reminds us of the danger of treating God as a malleable concept that we can interpret at will. God's words are not 'called back'; God does not break vows, or cheapen promises. Stable meaning, though, does not imply stasis or immovability; rather it recognizes the power of words to make something happen. Isaiah develops the theme in 55.11: 'my word ... that goes out from my mouth ... shall not return to me empty, but ... succeed in the thing for which I sent it.' A promise or a vow is a creative force that makes something happen; it has active power to bring into being what was not there before. This is supremely true of God's words, but it is true of our words also: kept promises have the creative power to change our world.

COLLECT

O Lord, raise up, we pray, your power
and come among us,
and with great might succour us;
that whereas, through our sins and wickedness
we are grievously hindered
in running the race that is set before us,
your bountiful grace and mercy
may speedily help and deliver us;
through Jesus Christ your Son our Lord,
to whom with you and the Holy Spirit,
be honour and glory, now and for ever.

Psalms 53, **54**, 60 *or* **37***
Isaiah 32
Matthew 15.21-28

Isaiah 32

'The effect of righteousness will be peace' (v.17)

'Righteousness' is a frame for this passage, which begins with a prediction of God's righteous reign and ends with a description of life in a society built on righteousness. In current parlance, 'righteousness' has rather negative overtones, summoning up the unattractive image of a holier-than-thou, self-righteous person who preaches arbitrary, restrictive rules. For Isaiah, however, righteousness is not about refraining from a list of randomly forbidden activities, but ordering society rightly with fairness and equity such that justice and peace prevail. Righteousness is active, not passive; strong, not weak.

The sense of this reading is summed up well in the often-quoted maxim of political theorist and philosopher Edmund Burke: 'The only thing necessary for the triumph of evil is for good men to do nothing.' Burke, in eighteenth-century vernacular, addressed his maxim to men, and it is often said that we should assume this included women. It is doubly interesting, then, that some two and a half millennia earlier, Isaiah regularly made a point of addressing his prophecies specifically to women, demanding the same rigorous response from them as he did from men: 'Rise up, you women who are at ease, hear my voice; you complacent daughters, listen to my speech' (v.9). Isaiah expected women to be equally responsible for their destiny, giving them as much agency as men in whether or not they will choose righteousness and usher in God's reign.

> Almighty God,
> purify our hearts and minds,
> that when your Son Jesus Christ comes again as
> judge and saviour
> we may be ready to receive him,
> who is our Lord and our God.

COLLECT

Friday 11 December

Psalms 85, **86** *or* 31
Isaiah 33.1-22
Matthew 15.29-end

Isaiah 33.1-22

'Lebanon is confounded and withers away; Sharon is like a desert' (v.9)

We often read Isaiah during Advent because he gives concrete meaning to redemption. Looking for Christ's second coming can seem disconnected from the real world, but Isaiah placed redemption in the immediate future. In predicting that the nation's immorality and spiritual unfaithfulness would be their downfall, he never divided spiritual matters from social, political or ecological issues.

His message is laced through with poetic imagery; he likens the coming disaster not only to pests destroying a harvest, but also to more comprehensive natural disasters resulting in the land withering and drying up. Sharon was an extremely fertile plain, a place of forests, flowers and lush vegetation; it must have seemed unimaginable that it could become a desert. Lebanon was famous for its beautiful cypress trees, for forests of cedars that were used in construction and shipbuilding, and for its vineyards. Could Lebanon really wither away? It is hard to tell whether Isaiah meant this poetically or literally, but more than two millennia later his words have a particular poignancy as we see devastating pollution, rapid extinction of species, severe droughts and melting ice caps, all resulting from industrial and natural disasters.

We urgently need to understand that the call to righteousness applies just as much to our relationship to the earth as it does to social relationships. The direct result of unrighteousness is not just that society fragments, but that the land itself mourns and languishes.

COLLECT

O Lord, raise up, we pray, your power
and come among us,
and with great might succour us;
that whereas, through our sins and wickedness
we are grievously hindered
in running the race that is set before us,
your bountiful grace and mercy
may speedily help and deliver us;
through Jesus Christ your Son our Lord,
to whom with you and the Holy Spirit,
be honour and glory, now and for ever.

Psalms **145** or 41, **42**, 43
Isaiah 35
Matthew 16.1-12

Isaiah 35

'A highway shall be there, and it shall be called the Holy Way' (v.8)

To modern ears, a highway in the desert may not sound like good news. We are glad of motorways when we need to get somewhere, but if you have ever crawled round the M25 on a Friday afternoon or languished in gridlocked highways around Los Angeles, a highway in the desert is the stuff of nightmares.

What did Isaiah have in mind? Not all the exiles returned to Judah, but first a large group, and later some smaller groups really did walk some 800 miles home through the desert to Jerusalem. In contrast to the 40 years of the Exodus, with their circuitous desert wanderings, Isaiah paints a picture of a safe, straight way home, where the withering of the land we read about yesterday (Isaiah 33.9) is reversed. It is a way through the desert laid about with oases of water to save them from the confusion of mirage and the beating sun; an immense pilgrimage on which no traveller would go astray; a road along which they would sing all the way home.

Troubled neither by the standstill of gridlock nor by wandering around in circles, the road home after a long, lonely exile is a way forward not backwards, a way towards a future and a hope, a way towards re-discovered identity and recovered dignity. This is the Holy Way, the highway God makes in the desert.

Almighty God,
purify our hearts and minds,
that when your Son Jesus Christ comes again as
judge and saviour
we may be ready to receive him,
who is our Lord and our God.

COLLECT

Monday 14 December

Isaiah 38.1-8, 21-22

'Set your house in order, for you shall die' (v.1)

Prophetic utterances make up much of the book of Isaiah. All prophecy arises from within a historical context, and prophecy does indeed play a part in today's reading, although it is set here within a wider account of a historical event. The cities of Judah have come under intense attack from the Assyrians, and in the midst of the crisis, the Judean king, Hezekiah, falls mortally ill. Although he does eventually recover, his septic boil being cured by the application of 'a lump of figs' (v.21), the Lord's initial prophecy through Isaiah is that the king will die and that he should prepare himself for death.

As we enter the third week of Advent, Isaiah's blunt message in verse 1 reminds us of the traditional Advent themes of death, judgement, hell and heaven (the 'four last things'). And the challenge is as relevant for us today as it was for Hezekiah: we may not die today, or tomorrow, next week or next year – but nothing in life is more certain than the fact that we *will* die, one day. One of Jesus' parables tells of a rich man whose energies were completely focused on the need for adequate storage for his crops, and his plans for a future life of ease (Luke 12.16-21). God calls him a fool and warns the man of his imminent death, shockingly reminding him of his mortality (Luke 12.20). The season of Advent offers us, too, such a bracing reminder.

COLLECT

O Lord Jesus Christ,
who at your first coming sent your messenger
to prepare your way before you:
grant that the ministers and stewards of your mysteries
may likewise so prepare and make ready your way
by turning the hearts of the disobedient to the wisdom of the just,
that at your second coming to judge the world
we may be found an acceptable people in your sight;
for you are alive and reign with the Father
in the unity of the Holy Spirit,
one God, now and for ever.

Psalms **70**, 74 or **48**, 52
Isaiah 38.9-20
Matthew 17.1-13

Isaiah 38.9-20

'O Lord, I am oppressed; be my security!' (v.14)

Despite the statement in verse 9, it is clear from the sentiments in this writing of Hezekiah that he had not, at this stage, recovered from his illness. He is writing from a very dark place and he believes he is dying (vv.10-11). The mood is reminiscent of a number of the psalms, such as Psalm 69 ('Save me, O God ... I sink in deep mire, where there is no foothold', vv.1,2), and of the response of Job to his unjust suffering ('Truly the thing that I fear comes upon me, and what I dread befalls me', Job 3.25).

Passages such as this one present a challenge to the modern reader. Hezekiah shares with the rest of the Israelite community the belief that God himself is the agent of illness and suffering (vv.13,15), and elsewhere in the Old Testament a link is explicitly made between illness and human sin (Deuteronomy 28.58-61). In its crude form, this is not a link that present-day Christianity would make. When healing a man born blind, Jesus repudiated his disciples' assumption that the man's affliction was God's punishment for sin, although he did also state that the man's blindness served God's purposes in other mysterious ways: 'Neither this man nor his parents sinned; he was born blind so that God's works might be revealed in him' (John 9.3).

This passage from Isaiah raises some profound questions, which Christians have wrestled with for generations. Does God intervene in human lives? Does he answer prayer – and if so, in what ways?

God for whom we watch and wait,
you sent John the Baptist to prepare the way of your Son:
give us courage to speak the truth,
to hunger for justice,
and to suffer for the cause of right,
with Jesus Christ our Lord.

COLLECT

21

Wednesday 16 December

Psalms **75**, 96 *or* **119.57-80**
Isaiah 39
Matthew 17.14-21

Isaiah 39

'They have seen all that is in my house' (v.4)

The longing to be liked and accepted by others is a need that transcends generations. Natural as the desire might be, however, it can lead to actions and words that we later come to regret. This appears to be the chief concern of Isaiah when he questions Hezekiah after he has enthusiastically welcomed the Babylonian delegation – who are these men? Where have they come from? What have they seen? In his response, Isaiah highlights the rashness of Hezekiah's lack of discernment, and the future problems to which it would lead (vv.5-7).

The New Testament conveys a similar message: when Jesus sent his twelve disciples out on mission, he warned them that they would be like sheep among wolves, and that they would therefore need to 'be wise as serpents and innocent as doves' (Matthew 10.16). Discernment in their dealings with 'the world' would be vital.

We all need discernment in our dealings with others. For many, Facebook and other social media sites may well be a brilliant means of communication, but the lurid newspaper headlines resulting from people's over-exposure reveal the dark side of virtual communication only too clearly. Our faith urges us to love and reach out to all, but at the same time, Jesus warns us – his present-day disciples – to be careful how much of ourselves we disclose, and to whom. Otherwise we may, like Hezekiah, find that our rash judgements rebound on us in the future.

COLLECT

O Lord Jesus Christ,
who at your first coming sent your messenger
to prepare your way before you:
grant that the ministers and stewards of your mysteries
may likewise so prepare and make ready your way
by turning the hearts of the disobedient to the wisdom of the just,
that at your second coming to judge the world
we may be found an acceptable people in your sight;
for you are alive and reign with the Father
in the unity of the Holy Spirit,
one God, now and for ever.

Thursday 17 December

Zephaniah 1.1 – 2.3

'Seek the Lord, all you humble of the land' (2.3)

The atmosphere darkens, and today's reading from Zephaniah makes grim reading. The day of the Lord is imminent, and the wrath and vengeance of God will be relentless. The universal destruction promised in the first few verses of chapter 1 is reminiscent of God's warning to Noah before the flood (Genesis 6.11-13). This time, the prophet warns that God will destroy all living creatures, with apparently no exceptions.

This message is not easy for us to hear today. What are we to make of all this distress and anguish, ruin and devastation, and how can we relate to it? The chief sin of the people seems to have been complacency, leading them to rely on the wealth and security they had acquired, rather than on God the generous giver (1.12). They have reduced God to an anaemic, powerless figurehead and will soon learn their mistake (1.13).

For Christians in the comfortable West, the danger of complacency in our faith is never far below the surface. We may wring our hands at the increasing secularization of society, but, so far at least, our right to be disciples of Christ has not been challenged. Even in times of economic downturn, many are so cushioned by their material possessions that they find it hard to express any actual *need* of God.

How acute is our need of God? And to what extent do we *really* consider ourselves accountable to him for the way we live?

> God for whom we watch and wait,
> you sent John the Baptist to prepare the way of your Son:
> give us courage to speak the truth,
> to hunger for justice,
> and to suffer for the cause of right,
> with Jesus Christ our Lord.

COLLECT

Friday 18 December

Psalms 77, **98** *or* **51**, 54
Zephaniah 3.1-13
Matthew 18.1-20

Zephaniah 3.1-13

'On that day you shall not be put to shame' (v.11)

Yesterday's warnings of general catastrophe become more specific. The city of Jerusalem itself is soiled and defiled; it has accepted no correction from God and has insisted on going her own way (vv.1-2). But then, unexpectedly, comes the promise of restoration. With the promise that the people 'will pasture and lie down' (v.13), we have moved from universal condemnation to 'the Lord is my shepherd' (Psalm 23) in a few short verses.

Our distance from the time in which this passage was written is vast, but the situation described has a depressingly familiar ring. Injustice and corruption are also rife today, not only in society at large, but also in the recent scandals that have bedevilled the Church. We are none of us immune; we share the common frailties of humanity and may often feel overwhelmed by the enormity of the scale of the darkness, both within and outside ourselves. Yet there is a promise here, restated with great reassurance, power and conviction at the beginning of John's Gospel. That promise is that, however bleak the situation may be, however impossible the possibility of healing and restoration may seem, the seeds of divine renewal lie buried within it. 'The light shines in the darkness, and the darkness did not overcome it' (John 1.5).

In what ways, and in what situations, might you be called upon to live this truth today?

COLLECT

O Lord Jesus Christ,
who at your first coming sent your messenger
to prepare your way before you:
grant that the ministers and stewards of your mysteries
may likewise so prepare and make ready your way
by turning the hearts of the disobedient to the wisdom of the just,
that at your second coming to judge the world
we may be found an acceptable people in your sight;
for you are alive and reign with the Father
in the unity of the Holy Spirit,
one God, now and for ever.

Psalms 144, **146**
Zephaniah 3.14-end
Matthew 18.21-end

Zephaniah 3.14-end

'The Lord, your God, is in your midst' (v.17)

The momentum is now unstoppable, as the prophet urges the people to exultant praise. The nation and city are addressed as 'daughter' – her close kinship to the Lord unbreakable. His forgiveness of sin is reaffirmed and his protection assured (v.15). The day of the Lord ('On that day') is now promised as a time of irrepressible joy and freedom from fear (v.16). God himself will rejoice over his people, and renew them in his love (v.17).

The problem for believers, then and now, lies in the chasm between our present experience and the promise of future renewal and restoration. We look around and wonder how that chasm can ever be breached. Those who do find the light in the darkness often do so through a crisis, or a period of intense suffering: a severe illness, perhaps, or bereavement. People taken hostage face the daily threat of violent death, and live sometimes for years in isolation, cut off from familiar relationships and their normal daily routine.

This was the reality for Brian Keenan and his fellow Beirut hostages from 1986 to 1990. In *An Evil Cradling*, Keenan describes their surprise in discovering, in the dark heart of their captivity, a new and deeper freedom within themselves.

'The Lord, your God, is in your midst' (v.17). When we are in the midst of our own darkness, how can we reach out and connect with the same freedom and light within ourselves?

God for whom we watch and wait,
you sent John the Baptist to prepare the way of your Son:
give us courage to speak the truth,
to hunger for justice,
and to suffer for the cause of right,
with Jesus Christ our Lord.

COLLECT

Monday 21 December

Malachi 1.1, 6-end

'...where is the honour due to me?' (v.6)

It is difficult for us to identify a precise situation behind the attack in this passage against various cultic abuses. We may ask questions about possible economic and social causes, but such causes were not the prophet's principal focus. For Malachi, the failures in the cultic realm and the abysmal attitudes expressed in their performance were inextricably linked to the people's relationship to the divine. The earlier narrative about the boy Samuel, the priest Eli and his two faithless sons demonstrates the same correlation (1 Samuel 2–3).

This oracle is addressed to the 'priests who despise my name' (v.6). These priests have become lax and careless: polluted food has been offered, so polluting the altar on which it has been placed, and imperfect or sick animals have been offered for sacrifice. Even earthly masters would expect better than this, says Malachi, so how dare these priests think that such inferior service is good enough for God! 'I have no pleasure in you, says the Lord of hosts, and I will not accept an offering from your hands' (v.10).

There is a world-weariness in the priests' attitude; a tendency to take shortcuts and to think that any old thing will do (vv.13-14). But this specifically focused passage has an uncomfortably wide application. What about our own 'world-weariness'? What shortcuts do we take in our spiritual lives? And can we honestly say that we always offer God our best?

COLLECT

God our redeemer,
who prepared the Blessed Virgin Mary
to be the mother of your Son:
grant that, as she looked for his coming as our saviour,
so we may be ready to greet him
when he comes again as our judge;
who is alive and reigns with you,
in the unity of the Holy Spirit,
one God, now and for ever.

Psalms **124**, 125, 126, 127
Malachi 2.1-16
Matthew 19.13-15

Malachi 2.1-16

'And what does the one God desire? Godly offspring.' (v.15)

The diatribe against Israel's priests continues. If they will not listen and give glory to God's name, then their blessings will rebound on them as curses (v.2). Their children also will be afflicted, and there is a strong echo here of the vow that God made to Israel through Moses on Mount Sinai: that the sins of the parents would be visited 'upon the children ... to the third and the fourth generation' (Exodus 34.7).

One of the sins these priests stand accused of is complacency, and again, we need to be careful we don't fall into the same trap. I once heard of a most effective sermon relating to Jesus' parable of the Pharisee and the tax-collector (Luke 18.9-14). It consisted of precisely thirteen words: 'Hands up anyone who didn't think, "Thank God I'm not like that Pharisee!"' Think carefully about this for a minute, and you will see we are caught whether we raise our hands or not! Ouch.

The situation may be specific, but the message is universally applicable. Not only priests are called to be 'Godly offspring' (v.15). All of us are called to truly revere and worship God; all are likewise called to walk with God 'in integrity and uprightness' (v.6). We are frail humans, so often blind to our true motives and desires. Our walk with God calls for honest self-examination: 'So take heed to yourselves' says Malachi, 'and do not be faithless' (v.16).

Eternal God,
as Mary waited for the birth of your Son,
so we wait for his coming in glory;
bring us through the birth pangs of this present age
to see, with her, our great salvation
in Jesus Christ our Lord.

COLLECT

Wednesday 23 December

Malachi 2.17 – 3.12

'You have wearied the Lord with your words' (2.17)

Malachi continues to build up a picture of wrongdoing that the perpetrators seek to justify – to themselves, to others and to God. God will have no more of such duplicity, and a messenger will be sent to prepare his way. The identity of the messenger is not specified here (in 3.1, although 4.5 is more specific). By the time of the New Testament, the synoptic gospels clearly identify the unnamed messenger with John the Baptist (Matthew 11.10; Luke 7.27; Mark 1.2).

And now, the thrust of Malachi's message begins to shift. Sin is still abhorrent, but the Lord's call through the prophet is a plea for a renewal of trust. It speaks to us today as it did to Israel: 'Return to me, and I will return to you' (3.7). What follows is a ringing affirmation of God's constant love for his people, as expressed in Malachi 1.2, and his longing to provide abundantly for all their needs. If they return to a position of basic trust, then they 'will be a land of delight, says the Lord of hosts' (3.12).

In today's complex world it isn't always easy for us to draw the line between responsible provision for future needs and the sort of open-hearted abandon that seems to be advocated here. But hopefully and prayerfully such discernment is possible, if we are able to see ourselves as stewards with gifts to be shared rather than owners with possessions to be hoarded.

COLLECT

God our redeemer,
who prepared the Blessed Virgin Mary
to be the mother of your Son:
grant that, as she looked for his coming as our saviour,
so we may be ready to greet him
when he comes again as our judge;
who is alive and reigns with you,
in the unity of the Holy Spirit,
one God, now and for ever.

Thursday 24 December

Christmas Eve

Malachi 3.13 – end of 4

'They shall be mine, says the Lord of hosts' (3.17)

The message continues its new trajectory from darkness towards light. The arrogant continue to question what gain there could possibly be in serving the Lord. At the same time they are set against those who revere God, those whom God claims for his possession (3.17-18). For those who despise and reject God, the day of the Lord will bring terrible judgement, but for those who revere his name 'the sun of righteousness shall rise, with healing in its wings' (4.2).

Gathering up the threads of his message, the prophet directs his hearers to the wisdom of the past. The people are urged to remember the teaching of Moses, and the anonymous messenger from Chapter 3 (see yesterday's reflection) is here named as Elijah (4.5). Jesus himself makes the connection between these two references and John the Baptist (Matthew 11.10-14).

So, as we stand on the very threshold of Christ's birth, the prophecy of Malachi points to the messengers who prepare the way for him. In Christian tradition, of course, the ultimate 'messenger' is Jesus himself, the one in whom the kingdom of God has come among us (Matthew 12.28).

Some commentators have felt that the ambiguity of the messenger's identity is a weakness in Malachi's message, but that very ambiguity can spur us to deeper levels of 'seeing' and discernment. Who – and where – are the 'messengers of the covenant' today? And would all Christians agree on who they are?

COLLECT

Almighty God,
you make us glad with the yearly remembrance
of the birth of your Son Jesus Christ:
grant that, as we joyfully receive him as our redeemer,
so we may with sure confidence behold him
when he shall come to be our judge;
who is alive and reigns with you,
in the unity of the Holy Spirit,
one God, now and for ever.

Friday 25 December

Christmas Day

Psalms **110**, 117
Isaiah 62.1-5
Matthew 1.18-end

Matthew 1.18-end

'Now the birth of Jesus ... took place in this way' (v.18)

The long wait is over, and today we celebrate with great joy the birth of our Saviour. We'll re-enact again the much-loved narrative of inns and stables, shepherds, angels, and a baby in a manger – but Matthew's account tells us nothing of this. He relates rather how these events came about. Beginning with Joseph's engagement to Mary, the storyline is much darker than that in Luke's Gospel (Luke 2.1-40) and is fraught with menace.

Entering imaginatively into the events described, we can sense the terror Mary must have felt at the likely public reaction to her unexpected pregnancy; women in her society were often stoned to death for less. Similarly, Joseph took an enormous leap of faith and obedience in standing by Mary, rather than giving her up to the process of law. Slightly later, Matthew will tell of the threat from Herod as he tries to manipulate the wise men into divulging crucial information about Jesus' whereabouts, followed by the Holy Family's flight to safety in Egypt until the death of Herod, so escaping the evil of Herod's massacre of the infants.

We rightly celebrate, but Matthew also encourages us to remember both the context – and the cost – of this joyous event. He reminds his readers that all this has happened so that the ancient prophecy might be fulfilled (Isaiah 7.14) – so we may joyfully and gratefully celebrate 'Emmanuel ... God is with us' (v.23).

COLLECT

Almighty God,
you have given us your only-begotten Son
to take our nature upon him
and as at this time to be born of a pure virgin:
grant that we, who have been born again
and made your children by adoption and grace,
may daily be renewed by your Holy Spirit;
through Jesus Christ your Son our Lord,
who is alive and reigns with you,
in the unity of the Holy Spirit,
one God, now and for ever.

Psalms 13, 31.1-8, 150
Jeremiah 26.12-15
Acts 6

Saturday 26 December

Stephen, deacon, first martyr

Acts 6

'Stephen, full of grace and power' (v.8)

If we are tempted to over-sentimentalize the story of the baby in the manger, today's commemoration of the martyrdom of Stephen shocks us into realizing just what extremes the discipleship of Jesus can lead to. Stephen is one of a group of seven men appointed by the apostles to serve the practical needs of the growing Christian community (vv.1-6). He soon finds his brief extending beyond 'waiting at tables' (v.2), and he quickly comes to the attention of those antagonistic to Christ's message. A charge of blasphemy is made, followed by Stephen's arrest, trial, and subsequent execution by stoning (Acts 6.8–8.1).

Today's passage takes Stephen's story through his call, early ministry and the false accusations made against him, and leaves him facing the council. In Philippians, Paul reminds us that an inescapable consequence of pressing on 'towards the goal for the prize of the heavenly call of God in Christ Jesus' (Philippians 3.14) will be that we, too, become enemies of the enemies of Christ. 'Only let us hold fast to what we have attained' (Philippians 3.16). Stephen achieved this triumphantly in his living and his dying, as have countless martyrs through the centuries. In this country today, the extreme of martyrdom is perhaps unlikely, although in some countries that threat is only too real. But we have no grounds for complacency, as the call to an ever-deepening discipleship is an imperative for us all.

Gracious Father,
who gave the first martyr Stephen
grace to pray for those who took up stones against him:
grant that in all our sufferings for the truth
we may learn to love even our enemies
and to seek forgiveness for those who desire our hurt,
looking up to heaven to him who was crucified for us,
Jesus Christ, our mediator and advocate,
who is alive and reigns with you,
in the unity of the Holy Spirit,
one God, now and for ever.

COLLECT

Monday 28 December

The Holy Innocents

Psalms **36**, 146
Baruch 4.21-27
or Genesis 37.13-20
Matthew 18.1-10

Matthew 18.1-10

'Take care that you do not despise one of these little ones' (v.10)

The shocking massacre of the innocent babies and toddlers in Bethlehem (Matthew 2) sounds all too familiar today. We must never grow dull to the pain of the cry of people oppressed by rulers and regimes that destroy the vulnerable for their own ends. Herod was a vicious tyrant who killed many of his own family, so what did a few babies in Bethlehem matter? A lot, in God's eyes.

Jesus survived, and we read his interaction with little children like those who could have been his playmates had he and they been left unmolested in Bethlehem. He made a young child a model for adult attitudes to God and, in a time when children had no status or power and so counted for nothing, Jesus said that whoever welcomed one such child in his name, welcomed him. He repeated that thought in a parable when facing impending death (Matthew 25.31-46). Jesus was answering a specific question about who was greatest in the kingdom of heaven and, heard on Holy Innocents' Day, his answer is a powerful indictment of all cruel abuses of power directed against vulnerable people.

Then, as now, the kingdom of heaven is present alongside all that is antithetical to it, upending all human societies' norms and values. How we treat children, indeed all powerless people, is, in God's eyes, a litmus test of discipleship.

COLLECT

Heavenly Father,
whose children suffered at the hands of Herod,
though they had done no wrong:
by the suffering of your Son
and by the innocence of our lives
frustrate all evil designs
and establish your reign of justice and peace;
through Jesus Christ your Son our Lord,
who is alive and reigns with you,
in the unity of the Holy Spirit,
one God, now and for ever.

Psalms **19**, 20
Jonah I
Colossians 1.1-14

Jonah 1

'But the Lord provided a large fish to swallow up Jonah' (v.17)

When hard lessons have to be learned, ludicrous stories of outrageous behaviour can get us to face reality. If we take them too seriously, we miss their sheer daftness, nodding piously rather than laughing, only to find the tables turned and we are laughing at ourselves.

Take Jonah. The book dates from late in the Old Testament period but is set earlier. It is not clear who Jonah is or what the book is really about. As a story it bears the hallmarks of comedy, even pantomime. We are pitched into the middle of an argument. Out of the blue, God speaks to Jonah, who lives near Joppa. When God tells him to preach to Nineveh, the capital of the enemy Assyrians, saying in effect, 'Go east, overland for 600 miles', Jonah does the exact opposite and heads west by sea for about 1500 miles towards Spain, as far as he can get from Nineveh. That is not a promising start for a prophet!

Things move fast: God hurls a storm into the Mediterranean, the ship threatens to sink and the sailors throw the cargo overboard. Meanwhile Jonah, who makes no secret of fleeing from God, sleeps on peacefully until the sailors wake him. He suggests they throw him overboard, the storm stops, the sailors turn to God, and God provides a big fish to swallow Jonah. Even though he is fleeing from God, God holds on to him.

Almighty God,
who wonderfully created us in your own image
and yet more wonderfully restored us
through your Son Jesus Christ:
grant that, as he came to share in our humanity,
so we may share the life of his divinity;
who is alive and reigns with you,
in the unity of the Holy Spirit,
one God, now and for ever.

COLLECT

33

Wednesday 30 December

Psalms 111, 112, **113**
Jonah 2
Colossians 1.15-23

Jonah 2

'Deliverance belongs to the Lord!' (v.9)

The original narrative version of the story is just verses 1 and 10. If we take the story at face value, it seems that Jonah's mind was focused admirably by being in the belly of the big fish. His battle of wills with God cooled temporarily and he prayed. Immediately, God spoke to the fish and it spewed Jonah out onto dry land.

A later editor, thinking we should know what Jonah might have prayed, inserted a psalm culled from elsewhere which uses very different language patterns but is appropriate to Jonah's situation. Jonah cried in his distress and, using the past tense, described how God heard and acted. In the belly of Sheol, the place of the dead, he implied that God, acting through the sailors, put him there. The outcome of his disobedience was that he was driven from God's sight, surrounded by water and weeds, with escape barred. His whole relationship with God was in doubt: 'How shall I look again upon your holy temple?' (v.4)

The answer to that question comes with the word 'yet' (v.6). There is mercy with God! 'Yet you brought up my life from the Pit.' He remembered the Lord, his prayer was heard, and salvation was God's gift to him. Instantly, his religious life was transformed as he promised thanksgiving and sacrifice and the fulfilment of his vow. Round One to God.

COLLECT

Almighty God,
who wonderfully created us in your own image
and yet more wonderfully restored us
through your Son Jesus Christ:
grant that, as he came to share in our humanity,
so we may share the life of his divinity;
who is alive and reigns with you,
in the unity of the Holy Spirit,
one God, now and for ever.

Psalm 102
Jonah 3 – 4
Colossians 1.24 – 2.7

Jonah 3 – 4

'... you are a gracious God and merciful' (4.2)

God is persistent and repeats his instructions. When Jonah reaches Nineveh, one word from him and the whole city, animals and all, is on its knees praying for forgiveness. Jonah furiously lashes out, quoting God's own words about his love and compassion (Exodus 34.6), explaining his dislike of God's readiness not to punish. Something is drastically wrong with Jonah.

In an episode worthy of *Jack and the Beanstalk*, God grows an instant bush to provide shade, making Jonah happy for the first time. Then God destroys the bush, turns up the sun's heat and sends a nasty sultry wind. Predictably, Jonah complains. God then hammers home the message of his compassion.

The storyteller is an animal lover, mentioning a big fish, herds and flocks who fast on the king's instruction, a worm with extraordinary munching ability, and God's worrying about the welfare of animals. Exaggeration is used to comic effect. And there this over-the-top story ends as abruptly as it started. It is less about Nineveh than Jonah in his lonely rage and reluctant discipleship. God gives him opportunities to change. Jonah obeys with bad grace and anger. We leave him sulking in the desert. Did God get to the bottom of Jonah's anger? Why choose Jonah when it would be easier to find someone less stubborn?

Is there a message of hope for us, like Jonah, in our worst moments?

COLLECT

God in Trinity,
eternal unity of perfect love:
gather the nations to be one family,
and draw us into your holy life
through the birth of Emmanuel,
our Lord Jesus Christ.

Friday I January
Naming and Circumcision of Jesus

Psalms **103**, 150
Genesis 17.1-13
Romans 2.17-end

Romans 2.17-end

'... real circumcision is a matter of the heart' (v.29)

The reading from Paul's letter to the Romans makes for a sobering start to the new year. We celebrate the naming and circumcision of Jesus, whose name points to his saving his people from their sins (Matthew 1.21), by hearing a damning condemnation of people who rely on God's law and boast of their relationship with God while undermining it by the way they live.

We have dropped in on Paul's extended argument about the role of the law, given in the Old Testament as the expression of obedience to and worship of God. Paul wrote in the context of the gospel being proclaimed in a multi-cultural Church comprising both Jews, for whom the law was part of their heritage, and gentiles, for whom it was not. Much had changed very quickly since Jesus's death, resurrection and ascension. Paul wrote to Christians, people bearing the name of Christ, who was himself born under the law. So it was not enough to dismiss the law; he had to find its proper place in this new world of Christianity.

Paul's crucial conclusion, in this short extract from a longer argument, is that what matters is not what happens to male bodies but to all our hearts. To be circumcised is to be marked forever as God's. On New Year's Day, when we remember Jesus's naming and circumcision, we can offer our hearts to be circumcised, set aside for God.

COLLECT

Almighty God,
whose blessed Son was circumcised
in obedience to the law for our sake
and given the Name that is above every name:
give us grace faithfully to bear his Name,
to worship him in the freedom of the Spirit,
and to proclaim him as the Saviour of the world;
who is alive and reigns with you,
in the unity of the Holy Spirit,
one God, now and for ever.

Psalm **18.1-30**
Ruth 1
Colossians 2.8-end

Ruth 1

'Do not press me to leave you' (v.16)

Ruth's story is of a struggling family facing timeless issues: political instability, famine, loss of inheritance, exile, childlessness, multiple bereavements, lack of marriage prospects, economic insecurity and racial tension (Moabites were barred from Israelite cultic assembly). Biblically, foreigners were considered as defenceless as the widow and orphan and were not to be oppressed. The law spelled that out in theory; we meet people trying to live that faithfully in practice.

This story is about being unsettled. People were in transition: there are 21 travel words. Five verses summarize ten years of history and introduce six people, three of whom die in unexplained circumstances leaving vulnerable widows. Although God does not speak, there are resonances of God's bigger story: Naomi, like Job, lost all her family, while Orpah and Ruth were childless for ten years, like Sarah who, after ten years, gave her maid to Abram to bear a child.

Naomi's determination to find husbands for Orpah and Ruth drives the action. Orpah is not judged for leaving. Thinking God was against her and wanting to be called 'Bitter' not 'Pleasant' (v.20), Naomi tried to send Ruth away too. But Ruth, having seen something very compelling in Naomi's faith, demanded that this exhausted woman introduce her to her God. That took enormous courage from both of them. These are people like us, like people around the world, holding on to faith in God in difficult circumstances supported by each other. God is nevertheless silently present.

Almighty God,
who wonderfully created us in your own image
and yet more wonderfully restored us
through your Son Jesus Christ:
grant that, as he came to share in our humanity,
so we may share the life of his divinity;
who is alive and reigns with you,
in the unity of the Holy Spirit,
one God, now and for ever.

COLLECT

37

Monday 4 January

Psalm **89**.1-37
Ruth 3
Colossians 3.12 – 4.1

Ruth 3

'May you be blessed by the Lord, my daughter' (v.10)

We miss the story of Ruth meeting Boaz, the kinsman with the duty to buy back the land Elimelech had previously sold to ensure the family's survival, thus keeping it in the family. Now we meet Naomi plotting a classic seduction – to 'uncover someone's feet' had decidedly sexual connotations.

Naomi sends Ruth off in her best clothes and perfume to face a big risk: Ruth could easily have been raped or, if discovered by others who would know exactly what her actions meant, put to death. Her pressing the boundaries of respectable actions illustrates the extreme risks poor women had to take in order to survive.

Ruth, going further than Naomi told her to, seized the opportunity that presented itself. It is probably an understatement to say that Boaz, in his half-awake, semi-drunken ('contented') state, was surprised to find a woman at his feet in the middle of the night proposing marriage. Yet he acted honorably, explained that she did not know the whole story, and blessed her.

We can imagine the scene when Ruth got home. Naomi probably hadn't slept a wink all night. She cautioned Ruth not to push the pace too fast but to let the requirements of the law be worked out. Burned out Naomi was still able to mentor Ruth in the ways of the God she had chosen to serve.

COLLECT

Almighty God,
in the birth of your Son
you have poured on us the new light of your incarnate Word,
and shown us the fullness of your love:
help us to walk in his light and dwell in his love
that we may know the fullness of his joy;
who is alive and reigns with you,
in the unity of the Holy Spirit,
one God, now and for ever.

Ruth 4.1-17

'... a restorer of life and a nourisher of your old age' (v.15)

Boaz acted as promised to maintain Elimelech's name, redeeming the land and assuming the duty to marry Ruth in a Levirite marriage where a family member married a widow to perpetuate the family name. The editor explained the ancient custom of exchanging sandals for his later readers.

Perez (v.12) and the genealogy that ends the book of Ruth (vv.18-22) are important in locating this family's story in the history of the people of God. Perez was Tamar's son by her father-in-law, Judah (Genesis 38). That sorry story is the only other recorded Levirite marriage. Tamar had to take the initiative and was mistaken for and nearly killed by Judah as a prostitute, yet her son is named in Jesus's genealogy (Matthew 1.3). Salmon is described (Matthew 1.5) as father of Boaz by Rahab, a prostitute who saved Joshua's messengers and, like Ruth, a foreigner who abandoned her gods for Israel's God.

This abbreviated genealogy of King David (and thus of Jesus) relies on three women whose unconventional stories show them as more faithful than many men in preserving the faith of Israel, if necessary going outside the law to do so. Listen to the genealogies! God can redeem dubious events in our past; we need not be bound by them. The women pray a lovely blessing for Naomi, describing the Lord as 'a restorer of life and a nourisher of your old age' (v.14). How and where is the Lord your restorer of life and nourisher of old age? A redeemer of your past?

God our Father,
in love you sent your Son
that the world may have life:
lead us to seek him among the outcast
and to find him in those in need,
for Jesus Christ's sake.

COLLECT

Wednesday 6 January

Epiphany

Psalms **132**, 113
Jeremiah 31.7-14
John 1.29-34

John 1.29-34

'I myself have seen and testified that this is the Son of God' (v.34)

The dictionary describes 'epiphany' as a moment of sudden and great revelation or realization. Epiphanies stop us in our tracks and may turn our lives around. We cannot cope with too many real epiphanies in our lives, but when they occur, they can be world-shattering. In the coming Epiphany season we recall the epiphanic revelation of Jesus Christ to different people: from Magi to wedding guests and three disciples on a mountainside.

John the Baptist was already baptizing in anticipation of the Messiah's coming but had not yet identified Jesus. When he saw Jesus approach, he had an epiphany, recognizing and announcing him as the Lamb of God. In describing his vision when God revealed Jesus as the Son of God on whom the Holy Spirit rested, John moved instantly from 'I myself did not know him' (v.31) to 'I myself have seen and testified that this is the Son of God' (v.34). Epiphanies do that to us.

Today, when we celebrate Epiphany, is a good day to slow down and recall times when God has stopped us in our tracks and redirected our lives, or pray that he will do so. John goes on to tell of epiphanies for various people who became Jesus's disciples. In the Collect's phrase, he and they saw face to face and came to know by faith; we pray that as we know by faith, we will come to behold face to face.

COLLECT

O God,
who by the leading of a star
manifested your only Son to the peoples of the earth:
mercifully grant that we,
who know you now by faith,
may at last behold your glory face to face;
through Jesus Christ your Son our Lord,
who is alive and reigns with you,
in the unity of the Holy Spirit,
one God, now and for ever.

Psalms **99**, 147.1-12 *or* **78.1-39***
Baruch 1.15 – 2.10
or Jeremiah 23.1-8
Matthew 20.1-16

Jeremiah 23.1-8

'The days are surely coming, says the Lord' (vv.5,7)

Jeremiah takes us to the traumatic period after the Babylonians first conquered Judah in 597 BC. Over the next 15 years the remaining people were deported into exile or abandoned to eke out survival in Jerusalem's ruins. The theological challenges were as great as the physical survival challenges: the temple was destroyed, the supposedly eternal Davidic dynasty terminated, the land given by God to the people occupied by foreign enemies. Had God neglected and failed them, or been powerless to help?

No! said the prophet. It was all much more complex than that. Jeremiah claimed the Lord's action in this ending of the people's occupation of the land given to them (Jeremiah 21.5-7; 23.3,8). The people's sin and the failure of their leaders had precipitated this disaster. The kings of Judah had scattered God's people, God's sheep. However, God was also involved, and the element of divine punishment driving them into exile reminds us never to lose sight of God's holiness and his call to his people to be holy.

God's involvement meant that this fate was not permanent, as it would be if only the leaders of nations were responsible. God alone could promise salvation. God was, and is, as determined to bless as to judge. God had salvific plans in mind and would do vastly greater things (v.8). The good news is that God is always doing something new.

Creator of the heavens,
who led the Magi by a star
to worship the Christ-child:
guide and sustain us,
that we may find our journey's end
in Jesus Christ our Lord.

COLLECT

41

Friday 8 January

Psalms **46**, 147.13-end *or* **55**
Baruch 2.11-end
or Jeremiah 30.1-17
Matthew 20.17-28

Jeremiah 30.1-17

'I am with you, says the Lord, to save you' (v.11)

Throughout Jeremiah, fragments of hope intertwine with judgement. Chapters 30 and 31, however, express sustained hope for the future restoration of God's exiled people. The context is specifically Judah in the sixth century BC, but the principle that God's purposes for his creation are good and life-giving transcends the centuries.

Following a promise of complete restoration (vv.1-3), a vivid description of men suffering as though in childbirth emphasizes the terror of events when Jerusalem fell. Even amidst that distress there was promise of rescue (v.7), yet it was not unconditional. It would take time, during which the people would experience disciplinary correction as a consequence of their living in ways unreflective of the holiness of their God (v.11). There were implications for the people's future way of life, which was to be one of service to God (v.9), in contrast to their past futile chasing after worthless lovers (v.14). In the sweep of the biblical story, this service to God was the purpose for which they were created and saved. God was restoring them to the life-giving reason for their very existence.

There is then a description of the hopelessness of their situation using metaphors of incurable hurt and terminal illness. Only God, a good physician, could heal, and God's healing took on a public dimension when their captors were themselves captured. In their distress the people could only think of their present suffering, but God's ways always have a future.

COLLECT

O God,
who by the leading of a star
manifested your only Son to the peoples of the earth:
mercifully grant that we,
who know you now by faith,
may at last behold your glory face to face;
through Jesus Christ your Son our Lord,
who is alive and reigns with you,
in the unity of the Holy Spirit,
one God, now and for ever.

Psalms 2, **148** *or* **76**, 79
Baruch 3.1-8
or Jeremiah 30.18 – 31.9
Matthew 20.29-end

Jeremiah 30.18 – 31.9

'... you shall be my people and I will be your God' (30.22)

In 597 and 587 BC the Babylonians devastated Jerusalem, leaving it a bloody, ruined wasteland occupied only by the poorest of the poor who scrabbled for existence. For 60 years it was desolate and uncared for (30.17). Eventually, God used Cyrus, a Persian king, to restore the people but, unlike Isaiah (45.1), Jeremiah did not name him. Instead Jeremiah anticipated the effect of that restoration on the people and on God.

The people's relief at their healing and deliverance was as nothing compared to the Lord's thrill and joy at the restoration of their relationship to him, their creator and their God. We hear vivid descriptions of God's revelling in their songs, dances and merrymaking, their watchmen calling people to pilgrimage and worship. God exhorts them to see and celebrate noisily all he is doing: bringing the people back from exile in the north, gathering them from across the world, caring for the blind, lame, women in labour (an image of dread in yesterday's reading is transformed to one of hope) and consoling those who weep. Significantly, they were also to behold the wrath and storm of the Lord amidst the restoration. Hindsight was needed for them to understand.

Psalm 23 is echoed in the tender way Jeremiah describes God's leading and provision for his people – if the Psalm expresses human trust in God, Jeremiah (31.9) describes God's perspective: God glories in them as in us, the body of his beloved Son.

> Creator of the heavens,
> who led the Magi by a star
> to worship the Christ-child:
> guide and sustain us,
> that we may find our journey's end
> in Jesus Christ our Lord.

COLLECT

43

Monday 11 January

Psalms **2**, 110 *or* **80**, 82
Genesis 1.1-19
Matthew 21.1-17

Genesis 1.1-19

'Let there be light' (v.3)

When and why do we tell stories of origins?

I was once helped to appreciate the story of creation by imagining Noah telling it to his family in the dark confines of the ark, when their world had been all but completely destroyed. It's a story that speaks to us most powerfully of all when we doubt our world and ourselves, when darkness and chaos seem in the ascendant.

In the season of Epiphany, at the darkest time of the year, it makes sense to hear once again the story of how light came out of darkness, and of how the waters of chaos were made to yield every kind of life by the infinitely creative power of God.

As we are told in that other great story of beginnings, the Prologue to John's Gospel, Jesus, the light of the world, entered into the world's deepest darkness and yet kept on shining. As the yearly recollection of Jesus's baptism reminds us, the Son of God went into the water of the Jordan in solidarity with our sin and emerged to an open heaven that showered promise and delight. The new creation was afoot.

No chaos is greater than God's power to make. If God can make the world even *ex nihilo* – from nothing – then God can heal the world, however catastrophically it seems to be falling back into chaos.

COLLECT

Eternal Father,
who at the baptism of Jesus
revealed him to be your Son,
anointing him with the Holy Spirit:
grant to us, who are born again by water and the Spirit,
that we may be faithful to our calling as your adopted children;
through Jesus Christ your Son our Lord,
who is alive and reigns with you,
in the unity of the Holy Spirit,
one God, now and for ever.

Genesis 1.20 – 2.3
'God blessed them' (1.22,28)

So far in Genesis, the main three things God has done are to *utter*, to *see*, and to *name*.

God utters in what is probably best understood (grammatically) as the 'jussive' tense. We don't have an exact equivalent in English to this Hebrew form, which is why we have to add the auxiliary word 'let' to the word 'be': 'let there be'. The jussive is a sort of command, but a command based on desire. God *wants* all of these abundant and particular things – 'each according to its kind' – to *be*. Creation is an activity of desiring; God's love is its motor.

Then God sees what he has made. God is a sort of 'recipient' of the creatures that have been brought to being by his utterance inasmuch as they now appear to God. This is a first step towards something like a relationship with them.

Then, in a third aspect of God's primal work of making, there comes a further step towards the realization of reciprocity: God calls his creatures by *name*. This is a conferring of identity and of dignity on them.

Yet that is not all. In today's passage, at the point when not just 'mineral' and 'vegetable' but 'animal' creatures spring into being, there is a huge development. A new verb appears: God *blesses*, and this same blessing will soon be extended to the first humans too (1.28). No greater confirmation is needed that this world is made by and for love. It is 'very good'. Blessing is its crown.

Heavenly Father,
at the Jordan you revealed Jesus as your Son:
may we recognize him as our Lord
and know ourselves to be your beloved children;
through Jesus Christ our Saviour.

COLLECT

Wednesday 13 January

Genesis 2.4-end

'... pleasant to the sight and good for food' (v.9)

Gratuity is under threat in our world. We are trained in more and more aspects of our lives to justify our expenditure – of effort, of time, of money – in ways that are quantifiable and goal-oriented – that are, in other words, narrowly utilitarian.

In this passage, Adam is invited into God's delighted work of naming the creatures. He is a participant in the generous dynamic of blessing that is at creation's very source. He finds himself surrounded by a world of trees, planted by the Lord God, and these God-given trees are *first* described as pleasant to the sight, and only *second* as good for food.

Perhaps there is a hint here of what our world has lost. The pleasure of the eyes may not be a bare necessity of life, but when our only priority is with how we can make things work to serve our needs, we make lives that are hard to live and impossible to enjoy. The gratuitous 'excess' in things is not just some trivial 'icing on the cake' compared with the mechanics of production and consumption, it is a witness to why it is worth producing and consuming at all. We can live in a way that corresponds to this 'excess' in things by enjoying and not just using them.

Adam and Eve changed their relationship to that 'gratuitous' tree that was not for their use when they began to suspect it might do something for them.

COLLECT

Eternal Father,
who at the baptism of Jesus
revealed him to be your Son,
anointing him with the Holy Spirit:
grant to us, who are born again by water and the Spirit,
that we may be faithful to our calling as your adopted children;
through Jesus Christ your Son our Lord,
who is alive and reigns with you,
in the unity of the Holy Spirit,
one God, now and for ever.

Thursday 14 January

Genesis 3

'And the Lord God made garments of skins ... and clothed them' (v.21)

One of the greatest skills of parenthood is how to reprimand your children while letting them know that you will *never not love them*, that you will never abandon them. (The counterpart to this is not letting your assurance that you love them, come what may, make them think that they can ignore you when you scold them!)

Here, God casts these two freshly minted human creatures out of the garden, placing a fiery sword to tell them they cannot undo the devastating consequences of their first greedily self-interested action. At the same time, however, he busily makes them clothes, like a parent wrapping her child up warm against the cold. They will not be left comfortless.

These clothes are not just a comfort, though, nor even just a practicality; they are a mark of the sin that made them necessary. They are a covering for shame, a sort of hiding. For perhaps as bad as the disobedience that led to the eating of the fruit was the desire to conceal that action.

Nevertheless, read with eyes that have also read the Gospels, the clothing of skins that God makes here with his own hands can also function as a sign of something else: the robes of Christ's glory that will take longer to stitch, and that cost infinitely more, but which God begins preparing for his children from the moment Adam and Eve fall.

Heavenly Father,
at the Jordan you revealed Jesus as your Son:
may we recognize him as our Lord
and know ourselves to be your beloved children;
through Jesus Christ our Saviour.

COLLECT

47

Friday 15 January

Psalms **67**, 72 *or* **88** (95)
Genesis 4.1-16, 25-26
Matthew 22.15-33

Genesis 4.1-16, 25-26

'... am I my brother's keeper?' (v.9)

The pattern of God's parental concern continues here when the sin in question is murder. Indeed, more than murder, it is fratricide. Cain and Abel are the first humans to enter that hothouse of human kinship, the sibling relationship. Jealousy flourishes where there is closeness. Sibling relationships are ones in which comparisons can be made easily and frequently, and in which they hurt more because we care more about them.

This may not absolve Cain, but it does leave room for understanding him. He also seems to care about what God thinks of him and his offering. In this respect, he is a good example of how the corruption of the best is the worst. The desire to be acceptable to God becomes enraged disappointment when it is frustrated. God deals out both punishment and 'cover' at the same time, as he did to Cain's parents. Cain must wander the earth, but no one is to touch him.

Meanwhile, Abel lives on in a different way, 'laid down' as a different sort of sign. His legacy too is protected by God, and his blood remains vocal, proclaiming a message that Jesus will one day confirm and amplify. We are our brother's keeper. More than that, however, our 'brothers' are not just those whom we are used to fraternizing with; they are 'everyone who does the will of God'. Or maybe even those who have been left half-dead by robbers at the sides of the roads we like to pass along.

COLLECT

Eternal Father,
who at the baptism of Jesus
revealed him to be your Son,
anointing him with the Holy Spirit:
grant to us, who are born again by water and the Spirit,
that we may be faithful to our calling as your adopted children;
through Jesus Christ your Son our Lord,
who is alive and reigns with you,
in the unity of the Holy Spirit,
one God, now and for ever.

Psalms 29, **33** or 96, **97**, 100
Genesis 6.1-10
Matthew 22.34-end

Saturday 16 January

Genesis 6.1-10

'... they took wives for themselves of all that they chose' (v.2)

'Kindred and affinity' remain a big issue for Genesis as the story moves on. We are told that the 'sons of God' (v.2) were attracted by the daughters of men, and that they procreated.

There is no decisive answer to who these 'sons of God' were, nor to whether the mysterious 'Nephilim' (v.4) were their offspring, nor to what the Nephilim are meant to have looked like (probably very big!). However, in the context of this evocation of a rising wickedness on the earth, the overall impression is that something is seriously out of control in human relationships.

Genesis is exploring the dangers of relations with those who are radical outsiders; whose 'otherness' is so extreme as to exclude genuine mutuality. It knows that the opposite path can be a problem too (elsewhere, in the story of Lot and his daughters, it explores the dangers of relations with those who are not 'other' enough). Here, though, the problem is excessive distance.

Knowing how to manage otherness in relationships is a perennial human challenge, and remains contemporary – even though to 21st-century readers the world of Genesis 6 may seem wildly strange. Sexual intercourse without mutuality – with an 'other' who is and will remain alien to you – is a high-risk game with destructive potential.

Heavenly Father,
at the Jordan you revealed Jesus as your Son:
may we recognize him as our Lord
and know ourselves to be your beloved children;
through Jesus Christ our Saviour.

COLLECT

Monday 18 January

Genesis 6.11 – 7.10

'... after seven days the waters of the flood came on the earth' (7.10)

We have had it drummed into us so often that 'the animals went in two by two' that we can find ourselves surprised that some animals went in by *fourteens*. Seven pairs of all those animals considered clean were preserved in the ark (7.2), seven being a great, sacred number in the Bible, one that always signifies something special.

This is not the only time that the number seven appears in today's passage. There is also an intriguing suggestion that the animals, and Noah (with his family), were required by God to go into the ark seven whole days before the first raindrops began to fall. Why? Was it a time of prayer? Or of adjusting to their new circumstances? We are left to imagine.

From a Christian point of view, seven is special too, but it is not so much a number of *completion* as a number of *preparation*. The seven days of creation are followed by the eighth day of new creation, in Christ. Christ rises on the eighth day – the day *after* the Sabbath. This is why many baptismal fonts and baptistries have eight sides, because baptism achieves the new creation of Christians.

The flood has been seen as a figure or anticipation of baptism. So perhaps we can see the eighth day, the day on which the rain began, as the beginning of a new and gracious world as much as the ending of an old and wicked one.

COLLECT

Almighty God,
in Christ you make all things new:
transform the poverty of our nature by the riches of your grace,
and in the renewal of our lives
make known your heavenly glory;
through Jesus Christ your Son our Lord,
who is alive and reigns with you,
in the unity of the Holy Spirit,
one God, now and for ever.

Psalms **132**, 147.1-12
or **106*** *(or* 103)
Genesis 7.11-end
Matthew 24.15-28

Genesis 7.11-end

'... and the Lord shut him in' (v.16)

'The last one to leave, lock up!' Genesis offers us an interesting variation on this common-or-garden line. The place being left is the world as a whole: a world that has gone to the bad. The place being locked up is not the place being left (that old world, with its ubiquitous and relentless wickedness) but a new place that is detaching itself from the old – separating itself off and floating away towards an unknown new beginning.

So it is the place being entered, not left, that is locked up. It is, perhaps, being locked up for its own safety, and to ensure that the break is real. Meanwhile, the place being left doesn't need locking up, as it has nothing in it worth preserving. It is left with its floodgates open, ready to be swallowed up by the resurgent chaos.

God is the one with the keys. Which side of the door do we imagine God to be on, as he shuts Noah in? God will travel with the holy remnant within the ark, preserving them for the new future. In this sense God is 'in', but God is also at work in the deluge and in the swirling waters, remaking a world for the ark to come aground on. If the ark is read as a type of the Church, then God is both the sustainer of its inner life, and also an agent from without, preparing things that it will come up against, and that invite it to open its doors.

Eternal Lord,
our beginning and our end:
bring us with the whole creation
to your glory, hidden through past ages
and made known
in Jesus Christ our Lord.

COLLECT

Wednesday 20 January

Psalms **81**, 147.13-end
or 110, **111**, 112
Genesis 8.1-14
Matthew 24.29-end

Genesis 8.1-14

'... it went to and fro until the waters were dried up from the earth' (v.7)

No one seems to have expected the raven to return, in the way that the dove was expected to. The dove had to come back twice, until finally (on the third occasion) there was enough land for her to settle on.

The raven could fly for longer than the dove without getting tired. As a carrion bird, it could sustain itself from the floating corpses of the drowned creatures of the earth. So why does Noah send it out, as well as sending out the dove? In rabbinic commentary, the raven feels aggrieved about this, fearing that Noah means to destroy it and deny it a future in the new creation. After all, because they are unclean animals, there is only one pair of ravens on the ark. So if one of them dies, there will be no more ravens *ever*. By contrast, there are seven pairs of doves...

St Jerome also thought it was being excluded, seeing the raven as a 'foul bird of wickedness', symbolizing the evil expelled at baptism.

Neither Jerome nor the rabbinic raven appreciate that God's intention seems to be to preserve both clean and unclean together. The raven and the dove are not in competition. They both have a mission and will both have a place repopulating the new creation – which will be no utopia even though the world has been cleansed. And one day, it is ravens that will perform the holy task of feeding another 'expelled' figure, Elijah, in the wilderness.

COLLECT

Almighty God,
in Christ you make all things new:
transform the poverty of our nature by the riches of your grace,
and in the renewal of our lives
make known your heavenly glory;
through Jesus Christ your Son our Lord,
who is alive and reigns with you,
in the unity of the Holy Spirit,
one God, now and for ever.

Psalms **76**, 148 *or* 113, **115**
Genesis 8.15 – 9.7
Matthew 25.1-13

Genesis 8.15 – 9.7

'... be fruitful and multiply' (8.17)

The world after the deluge is the 'reboot' of creation. It reminds us that God is a God of second chances. Just as he creates the world anew after the flood, so he shows himself prepared to reboot things on numerous successive occasions. When the people of Israel prove themselves unworthy of the covenant that God gave them after saving their lives in Egypt, and they make a golden image to worship instead, God does not end the story. Moses smashes the great stone tablets of the covenant in pieces, but God summons him back up the mountain, and the law is issued again. When the social injustice and the neglect of worship in the kingdoms of Israel and Judah lead to their invasion by a foreign power and the destruction of the temple, then after a long, soul-searching time in exile in Babylon, the news comes that they can return to their own land and rebuild a new temple. They have a second chance, a second temple.

Christians have grounds for thinking that God's grace may extend even beyond second chances. The going forth of Noah and his family from the ark is like a foreshadowing of Pentecost. After the Ascension, the disciples of Jesus were crouched together in fear and in hiding, but at Pentecost, the doors were blown off their hiding place, and they were empowered to go out and begin planting the seeds of a new future in confidence and joy. New creation happens all over again.

Eternal Lord,
our beginning and our end:
bring us with the whole creation
to your glory, hidden through past ages
and made known
in Jesus Christ our Lord.

COLLECT

Friday 22 January

Psalms **27**, 149 *or* **139**
Genesis 9.8-19
Matthew 25.14-30

Genesis 9.8-19

'... never again shall all flesh be cut off' (v.11)

The so-called Noahic Covenant is the first great covenant of God with human beings. It is of huge importance for understanding what will become the characteristic pattern of God's dealings with his world, and especially with humanity. It establishes the very foundations of the world in which all subsequent covenants will unfold – the Abrahamic, the Mosaic and the Davidic, and then eventually the Christian 'new covenant' in Christ's blood. It says: 'I will not give up on this world, whatever wrong turns it takes. I will work within this world, paying whatever price is necessary in order to sustain, redeem, and transform it for a better future.'

A Christian account of history may want to begin with the idea of covenant, reading history as punctuated by a series of covenantal moments in which some sense of 'significant form' in historical process is affirmed. The revelation of God takes place through intensive disclosures of the divine presence at certain points in the temporal series.

We might say that covenants are like 'Amens'. Amen derives from a Hebrew root that signifies *reliability*. Like the covenant with Noah and all its various successors through time, Amens are strung out through history as points of intensity and recognition. Even if it may sound like a conclusion, Amen is never just said *once* – not, at least, by us creatures in history. Yet it points to a conclusive truth: that God is faithful.

COLLECT

Almighty God,
in Christ you make all things new:
transform the poverty of our nature by the riches of your grace,
and in the renewal of our lives
make known your heavenly glory;
through Jesus Christ your Son our Lord,
who is alive and reigns with you,
in the unity of the Holy Spirit,
one God, now and for ever.

Psalms **122**, 128, 150 *or* 120, **121**, 122
Genesis 11.1-9
Matthew 25.31-end

Saturday 23 January

Genesis 11.1-9

'... let us make a name for ourselves' (v.4)

Over 54 per cent of the world's population lives in cities at the time I am writing this, and by 2050 this proportion is expected to increase to a phenomenal 66 per cent.

Cities are perhaps the most distinctive phenomenon of modernity: mechanized, diverse, anonymous and morally ambiguous. At one level they are magnificent reflections of human aspiration and technical capability. They are places of intense endeavour and creativity. However, they are also places of intense alienation and individualism, as their human occupants find themselves forced to compete for goods, for space, for recognition, for security.

T.S. Eliot insisted in his *Choruses from the Rock* that in order for our cities not to be wastelands, we must persist in asking the question: 'What is the meaning of this city?' Do our own creative endeavours participate in God's? The opening chapters of Genesis show God separating and also gathering: 'Let the waters under the sky be gathered together ...' (Genesis 1.9). Gathering is God's job, and when we gather – as we do in our cities – we will only create something that can endure and be fruitful when we do it with God's help.

'Unless the Lord builds the house, those who build it labour in vain. Unless the Lord keeps the city, the guard keeps watch in vain.'
 (Psalm 127.1)

COLLECT

Eternal Lord,
our beginning and our end:
bring us with the whole creation
to your glory, hidden through past ages
and made known
in Jesus Christ our Lord.

Monday 25 January

The Conversion of Paul

Psalms 66, 147.13-end
Ezekiel 3.22-end
Philippians 3.1-14

Philippians 3.1-14

'Christ Jesus has made me his own' (v.12)

Here, in a few personal, profound and moving verses, Paul lays out the paradoxical heart of the gospel: that it requires from us nothing and everything.

The Philippians are clearly being bothered by people who are urging these Gentile converts to ensure their salvation by undergoing circumcision. They are being encouraged to believe that human beings can do something that will win them privileges from God.

So Paul reminds them that he himself had already, in theory, done everything that a human being could do and that, the minute he encountered Jesus, he saw the tawdriness of all the bargains he thought he had made with God. God opened up his arms to Paul, as he did to the Philippian Christians, before they did anything to deserve it. God's love and acceptance of us is free.

Paul is vehemently sure that our feeble attempts to regulate God are useless. He is equally sure that, once we meet the love of God in Christ Jesus, we will want to do everything in our power to come closer and closer to God. Nothing will be too much trouble, not because we are trying to prove our worthiness to God, but because nothing else in the whole of life is half as valuable or glorious. God requires nothing from us, and so we long to give God everything.

COLLECT

Almighty God,
who caused the light of the gospel
to shine throughout the world
through the preaching of your servant Saint Paul:
grant that we who celebrate his wonderful conversion
may follow him in bearing witness to your truth;
through Jesus Christ your Son our Lord,
who is alive and reigns with you,
in the unity of the Holy Spirit,
one God, now and for ever.

Psalms 34, **36** *or* **132**, 133
Genesis 13.2-end
Matthew 26.17-35

Genesis 13.2-end

'Abram called on the name of the Lord' (v.4)

At the start of our passage, Abram returns to the place where God's promise was first given (see Genesis 12.7-8), retracing his steps. Standing at the exact place where God had shown him the land he was to have, Abram prays at the altar of promise.

There, at this numinous spot, Abram and Lot make a bargain, and Abram shares the land that is not even his yet. It is a fascinating insight into what the promise of land actually meant to Abram: it is not about possession or status, but about safety and provision. Quite pragmatically, Abram sees the land in terms of how much life it will support; he sees that there is room for him and Lot, that there is enough to share.

God's promise to Abram has not made him possessive and greedy, but trusting. As Lot's senior, Abram had the right to first choice of which part of the land he would have, but he waives his rights, and allows Lot to choose first, so great is his trust in God. So Lot takes his time, and looks around, and chooses shrewdly, looking out for fertile pastures and good water supplies – all the things a sensible farmer will need. What he cannot see, of course, is the hearts of the inhabitants.

Abram, on the other hand, doesn't even look up until God guides his vision. And then he sees the faithfulness of God.

Almighty God,
whose Son revealed in signs and miracles
the wonder of your saving presence:
renew your people with your heavenly grace,
and in all our weakness
sustain us by your mighty power;
through Jesus Christ your Son our Lord,
who is alive and reigns with you,
in the unity of the Holy Spirit,
one God, now and for ever.

COLLECT

Wednesday 27 January

Genesis 14

'... the Lord, God Most High, maker of heaven and earth' (v.22)

Now Lot discovers that his entirely sensible choice of some land for himself was perhaps not quite so sensible after all. He finds that his lush pasture land is in the middle of a war zone, as a coalition of vassal-kings choose this moment to rebel, and Lot, like many another innocent victim before and since, is caught up in the repercussions. He and his family are captured and carried off.

Abram, living peacefully in the land that Lot rejected, does not leave Lot to his fate, but rides into a battle that he should have lost, given that he has no experience and his opponents have already shown their mettle against a much stronger foe. Abram is obviously aware that he owes his victory to God, because when the time comes to take spoils, he refuses. He wants it absolutely clear that he depends only on God.

In the midst of these negotiations stands Melchizedek, a king who had had no part in the foregoing battles, and who is described as a 'priest of God Most High' (v.18). The god he serves is acknowledged by all the other kings as the chief god, and Melchizedek now makes the imaginative leap to recognition that this is Abram's God. Abram reinforces this as he describes God: he is not only the 'Most High'; he is also the creator of all. No wonder no other gods can conquer the one who is their maker.

COLLECT

Almighty God,
whose Son revealed in signs and miracles
the wonder of your saving presence:
renew your people with your heavenly grace,
and in all our weakness
sustain us by your mighty power;
through Jesus Christ your Son our Lord,
who is alive and reigns with you,
in the unity of the Holy Spirit,
one God, now and for ever.

Psalms **47**, 48 _or_ **143**, 146
Genesis 15
Matthew 26.47-56

Genesis 15

'Know this for certain ...' (v.13)

So far, since God first spoke to Abram and set him going on his journey, Abram has done what God told him, faithfully. He has behaved as a servant should, and followed orders, and he has prospered. But now, suddenly, there is a new level of honesty between God and Abram, and as Abram reveals more of his true self, so he learns more about God.

Abram tells God what he really feels: nice as God's promises of land and protection are, they are hollow to Abram because he has no son. So even if God does indeed give him everything, he knows that the gift will be temporary, not his to pass on.

The solemn and frightening ritual that follows assures Abram that God has put his own reputation and honour at stake in this promise he has made. Abram will never forget the 'deep and terrifying darkness' (v.12) in which God came to meet his greatest fear.

God's covenant with Abram is entirely one-sided: nothing is asked of Abram in return for what God promises. So Abram learns that we do not need to bargain with God. It is not that God did not know before this that Abram wanted a son, but perhaps that Abram didn't know that it was all right not just to obey God, but also to show God the truth about himself.

God of all mercy,
your Son proclaimed good news to the poor,
release to the captives,
and freedom to the oppressed:
anoint us with your Holy Spirit
and set all your people free
to praise you in Christ our Lord.

COLLECT

Genesis 16

'The angel of the Lord found her' (v.7)

The God of Abram does not belong to Abram: he is not on Abram's 'side'. Although God has chosen Abram, it does not mean that he has rejected others. Ishmael is not the son God promised to Abram and Sarai, but he is still deserving of God's protection.

The relationship between Sarai and Abram is hardly exemplary. In chapter 12, for example, Abram puts his own security and wealth above his relationship with Sarai. And here in chapter 16, Abram and Sarai are rowing. It isn't clear whether Sarai has been told of God's promise of a son, but whether she has or not, she is too forceful a woman to wait around while decisions are taken out of her hands.

She does what she considers necessary in order to have a child, and then bitterly regrets it. She thought a child was a commodity to be procured, not the symbol of a relationship. So when she is faced with an unexpected outcome, she instantly acts to get rid of what is making her uncomfortable, even if that is a vulnerable, pregnant young woman, bearing the child Sarai imagined she could simply make her own. Abram doesn't come too well out of this tale, either.

But for Hagar, defenceless against her mistress, abandoned by her master, dying in the wilderness, God sends an angel and a promise of her own, and she knows that she, like Abram, has spoken with God.

COLLECT

Almighty God,
whose Son revealed in signs and miracles
the wonder of your saving presence:
renew your people with your heavenly grace,
and in all our weakness
sustain us by your mighty power;
through Jesus Christ your Son our Lord,
who is alive and reigns with you,
in the unity of the Holy Spirit,
one God, now and for ever.

Psalm **68** *or* **147**
Genesis 17.1-22
Matthew 27.1-10

Genesis 17.1-22

'... walk before me, and be blameless' (v.1)

Suddenly, God calls for a new start between himself, Abram and Sarai. The text does not say that God dislikes what Abram and Sarai did to Hagar, but it is surely hard to read this narrative in any other way.

Up till now, God has made unconditional promises to Abram, but now a new level of formality and accountability has entered into the relationship. Abram is to be 'blameless' (v.1), and the symbol of the covenant between God and Abram is to be cut into Abram's very flesh, and the flesh of all the male descendants who will result from God's promise. There could hardly be a more graphic way for God to remind Abram that the promised child is to be of God's provision, not born of the cruel and destructive ideas of Abram and Sarai. Even their names have to change: they are now Abraham and Sarah, no longer the people who connived at the abuse of Hagar, but people under a solemn promise to God, held accountable.

For the first time, Abraham does not believe God. There is a new level of separation between Abraham and God. When Abraham suggests that God should simply transfer the promise to Ishmael, he is implying that God cannot do what he has promised and is trying to get God to admit that what Abraham and Sarah did wasn't such a bad idea after all.

God of all mercy,
your Son proclaimed good news to the poor,
release to the captives,
and freedom to the oppressed:
anoint us with your Holy Spirit
and set all your people free
to praise you in Christ our Lord.

COLLECT

61

Monday 1 February

Psalms **57**, 96 or **1**, 2, 3
Genesis 18.1-15
Matthew 27.11-26

Genesis 18.1-15

'Is anything too wonderful for the Lord?' (v.14)

Rublev's famous icon of the Trinity starts from this visit of the three mysterious strangers to Abraham. While this is certainly reading Christian theology back into Genesis, there is undoubtedly something very odd about the syntax in this chapter when it talks about the three visitors. Verse 1 says that 'the Lord' appeared to Abraham, but that when he looked up, what he saw was 'three men standing near him'. He addresses them as 'My lord', in the singular and, later on, when Sarah laughs, it is again 'the Lord' (v.13) who queries her scorn. No wonder Rublev picked this up as an allusion to the God who is both three and one.

However, it is not just the peculiar alternations from singular to plural; there is also a theological impetus here. Abraham believes that he is the one offering hospitality to the visitors, but in fact, he is encountering the generosity of God. He and Sarah have reached the end of their hopes of having a child of their own, but God has not reached the end of what is possible for God.

Here is the God who brought creation out of nothing, life out of death, healing and transformation for all who gather at the hospitable table spread by the cross and resurrection. Don't laugh when this God offers the impossible.

COLLECT

God our creator,
who in the beginning
commanded the light to shine out of darkness:
we pray that the light of the glorious gospel of Christ
may dispel the darkness of ignorance and unbelief,
shine into the hearts of all your people,
and reveal the knowledge of your glory
      in the face of Jesus Christ your Son our Lord,
who is alive and reigns with you,
in the unity of the Holy Spirit,
one God, now and for ever.

Tuesday 2 February

Presentation of Christ in the Temple

Romans 12.1-5

'Be transformed by the renewing of your minds' (v.2)

When the Son of God, the second person of the Trinity, comes to live with the people who were made through him, he does not think too highly of himself, to use Paul's phrase in verse 3. He is vulnerable, dependent upon his parents, without any means to communicate, except through gurgles and cries. The Word of God humbles himself to silence.

The Son 'conforms' himself to this world so that we can be free from such deforming conformity; but it is indeed a complete revolution of our understanding to see God at work in this strange way. This truly does require a 'renewing of our minds', to see the power of God in the baby held up by Mary and Joseph. It is only as we allow our whole way of thinking to be reformed around the action of God in Christ that we can begin to see what God is like and, by extension, what we are truly like.

It is a strange paradox that God comes to share the human life so that we can share the divine life, but when we do, we find it is a life of humility and self-giving, not at all how we imagined divinity. As we become more and more like God, so we are more and more ready to 'present' ourselves, to God and to each other.

Almighty and ever-living God,
clothed in majesty,
whose beloved Son was this day presented in the Temple,
in substance of our flesh:
grant that we may be presented to you
with pure and clean hearts,
by your Son Jesus Christ our Lord,
who is alive and reigns with you,
in the unity of the Holy Spirit,
one God, now and for ever.

COLLECT

Wednesday 3 February

Psalm 119.1-32
Genesis 19.1-3, 12-29
Matthew 27.45-56

Genesis 19.1-3, 12-29

*'... the outcry against the people has become great
before the Lord' (v.13)*

Poor Lot: he is always needing to be rescued. He may have many virtues – ready hospitality, courtesy, bravery in protecting his guests – and all the blessings of family that Abraham so longs for, but Lot is still not the hero of the story. The local men demonstrate graphically that God's judgement on them is justified. Given Lot's anxiety about leaving the visitors in the town square overnight, Lot probably knew his neighbours uncomfortably well, and was probably aware that he was going to need to move house sometime soon. Perhaps he had already picked out the nice little city of verse 20 as a possibility.

It doesn't look like the two strangers really need Lot's protection. There is a ruthless efficiency to them that is chilling. They save themselves and Lot's daughters from attack, and they haul Lot and his family to safety, ignoring all their hesitations.

Verse 13 reiterates what was said in the previous chapter, that God is responding to human complaints against Sodom and Gomorrah (Genesis 18.20). People have cried out to God, for protection? In anger? In fear? Simply demanding justice? But that does not make this a comfortable story to read. It makes us examine our own calls to God for justice. What do we really want or expect God to do? If we are truthful, a bit of fire and sulphur-throwing is sometimes nearer to what we want from God than the way God ultimately chooses, the way of the cross.

COLLECT

Almighty God,
by whose grace alone we are accepted and called to your service:
strengthen us by your Holy Spirit
and make us worthy of our calling;
through Jesus Christ your Son our Lord,
who is alive and reigns with you,
in the unity of the Holy Spirit,
one God, now and for ever.

Psalms 14, **15**, 16
Genesis 21.1-21
Matthew 27.57-end

Genesis 21.1-21

'Do not be afraid' (v.17)

Red letter day. For a few brief verses, Sarah is happy. It doesn't last, of course; happiness doesn't seem to be a natural condition for Sarah. Although she now has all she thought she wanted, and is assured that her son is upheld by God's promise, yet she cannot bear to share anything, not even happiness, with another. Apparently, she still doesn't trust God; she still feels she has to take things into her own hands, however disastrously it went the last time she did that.

It is, in a way, consoling to see this massively dysfunctional family at the heart of God's action. Abraham is a hero of faith, but he still allows his wife to drive him to an action he knows to be wrong. Neither he nor Sarah seems to think at all about what Isaac will feel as his brother and playfellow is taken away. God does not need perfect people with whom to work. Our very imperfections emphasize the simple truth that we are wholly dependent upon God, justified by God's faithfulness, not by our own actions.

As Abraham and Sarah squabble over how to make the faithful God keep his promises, Hagar plumbs the depths of that faithfulness. Her son grows up in the wilderness, given all that he needs by the hand of God, sheltered from human cruelty and faithlessness.

God of our salvation,
help us to turn away from those habits
which harm our bodies and poison our minds
and to choose again your gift of life,
revealed to us in Jesus Christ our Lord.

COLLECT

Friday 5 February

Psalms 17, 19
Genesis 22.1-19
Matthew 28.1-15

Genesis 22.1-19

'God himself will provide the lamb' (v.8)

The narrative of the sacrifice of Isaac is often called a 'type' of the atonement. Here we see a father, prepared to offer up his son, without question, although everything he is and hopes for depends upon this son, and everything he knows or feels about God is bound up with the child.

There are echoes here that are profoundly helpful in our understanding of the way of the cross, particularly if we see Jesus not only as God, but also as both Abraham and Isaac. Jesus goes to the cross in obedience, although all he was sent to be and to do is at stake, although it makes no apparent sense, although he longs to have misunderstood what is required. However, because Jesus is also God, he is himself the sacrifice that God provides, he is both priest and victim, both the one who obeys and the one who commands. There is no gap between what the Son wills and what the Father wills here, no merciless Father and broken Son, only the costly and faithful action of God.

What of this episode's place in Abraham's own story? Does Abraham get ready to sacrifice Isaac, believing that, because of the way he has treated Hagar and Ishmael, he deserves to lose this son, too? If so, he meets what we meet when we approach the cross: the God who provides from his own mercy all that we need to be forgiven and restored.

COLLECT

Almighty God,
by whose grace alone we are accepted and called to your
    service:
strengthen us by your Holy Spirit
and make us worthy of our calling;
through Jesus Christ your Son our Lord,
who is alive and reigns with you,
in the unity of the Holy Spirit,
one God, now and for ever.

Psalms 20, 21, **23**
Genesis 23
Matthew 28.16-end

Genesis 23

'Give me property among you for a burying-place' (v.4)

Abraham does all that is proper at the death of Sarah, and it becomes an occasion for him to establish exactly how he is viewed by his neighbours. There is an elaborate exchange, in which Ephron and the other local landowners acknowledge Abraham as a 'mighty prince' among them (v.6), and Abraham demonstrates his wealth by refusing even to bargain over the price of the land he buys, which is to become first Sarah's burial ground and then the place of burial for Abraham and his descendants. Honour is satisfied all round. Does Abraham miss Sarah? We cannot tell, but it is interesting that it is only after her death that Abraham looks for a wife for Isaac, perhaps realizing that Sarah might not be ideal mother-in-law material.

The great irony of this chapter is that the land for Sarah's grave is the first land that Abraham actually owns of all the land that God has promised him. However, if there is an underlying lesson about the fact that death is the 'land' which we must all possess, there is also the reality of the God who went down into death to make it the Promised Land for all. God promises that, through the power of the cross and resurrection, generations past, present and yet unborn shall inherit the kingdom.

God of our salvation,
help us to turn away from those habits
which harm our bodies and poison our minds
and to choose again your gift of life,
revealed to us in Jesus Christ our Lord.

COLLECT

Monday 8 February

Galatians 1

'I am astonished ...' (v.6)

Sometimes Paul appears arrogant. So confident is he that he is right that he dismisses all other views out of hand. Galatians 1 is a good case in point. In this chapter Paul declares that the gospel he has proclaimed is the only possible gospel and that all others are misguided and wrong.

A little background, however, makes Paul's tone here easier to stomach. As we read on in Galatians, it becomes clear that the issue at stake is not an insubstantial, unimportant issue but one that strikes at the very heart of the gospel that Paul proclaims. The issue is circumcision and whether gentiles need to be circumcised – in other words become Jews – in order to follow Jesus.

The people against whom Paul is fighting here seem to be arguing that gentiles do need to become Jewish and follow the Jewish law in order to be 'in Christ'. This goes against the very essence of what Paul has proclaimed. This is why his language is so passionate. What Paul proclaims – that Jesus offers love and redemption to everyone no matter what their background, status or gender – lies at the very heart of his faith. His tone may be off-putting, but his message remains as relevant today as it was then.

COLLECT

Almighty Father,
whose Son was revealed in majesty
before he suffered death upon the cross:
give us grace to perceive his glory,
that we may be strengthened to suffer with him
and be changed into his likeness, from glory to glory;
who is alive and reigns with you,
in the unity of the Holy Spirit,
one God, now and for ever.

Psalms 32, **36**
Genesis 37.12-end
Galatians 2.1-10

Galatians 2.1-10

'... remember the poor' (v.10)

It is easy to imagine that the conflicts that our churches face today are the most difficult and least resolvable conflicts that the Church has ever faced. An exploration of Galatians reminds us that it was ever thus. As we noticed in the previous passage, the conflict between Paul and the rest was over whether followers of Jesus needed to be circumcised or not. Galatians 2.9 suggests that they agreed to part company as friends and to concentrate their energy on something that they all considered to be important.

James, Cephas (Peter) and John asked Paul to remember the poor. The implication of the Greek word used here is that Paul should keep them in mind, should think about them and, in doing so, act on their behalf. The solution to the conflict feels profoundly relevant today. Sometimes it feels as though our Christian communities simply roll from one conflict to another; barely have we resolved one disagreement than a new one rears its head and threatens to tear us apart.

Galatians 2.10 suggests that the solution to this cycle of disagreement remains the same as it was in the time of Paul – to focus our attention on something about which we all agree and which lies at the heart of Jesus' teaching: to remember the poor and to do everything in our power to ensure that they do not remain poor.

Holy God,
you know the disorder of our sinful lives:
set straight our crooked hearts,
and bend our wills to love your goodness
and your glory
in Jesus Christ our Lord.

COLLECT

Wednesday 10 February

Ash Wednesday

Psalm **38**
Daniel 9.3-6, 17-19
1 Timothy 6.6-19

1 Timothy 6.6-19

'... godliness combined with contentment' (v.6)

At first glance this passage appears to be one of those classic killjoy passages: don't enjoy yourself, avoid money or any other form of enjoyment. Coming as it does on Ash Wednesday, it would be all too easy to read this as the command to misery for the next six weeks.

On closer reading, however, it is clear that in fact the message of this passage is quite the opposite. This is a passage that urges us towards contentment but reminds us of where this contentment can truly be found. The problem of money is that it is never enough. Those who want to be rich can so easily be sucked into wanting more and more, and hence into destructive and ruinous behaviours.

It is not money itself that is the problem but the love of money: a love that calls to us seductively telling us that this item or that activity will make us truly happy. It is interesting, in fact, that this passage does not use the word happy, nor indeed any word that can be translated 'happy'. Instead it uses two striking words: 'godliness' and 'contentment'. In other words, our aim should not be the immediate high of happiness but the worship of God, the one in whom we will find true life and deep contentment.

COLLECT

Almighty and everlasting God,
you hate nothing that you have made
and forgive the sins of all those who are penitent:
create and make in us new and contrite hearts
that we, worthily lamenting our sins
and acknowledging our wretchedness,
may receive from you, the God of all mercy,
perfect remission and forgiveness;
through Jesus Christ your Son our Lord,
who is alive and reigns with you,
in the unity of the Holy Spirit,
one God, now and for ever.

Psalm **77** *or* **37***
Genesis 39
Galatians 2.11-end

Galatians 2.11-end

'... for fear of the circumcision faction' (v.12)

It is hard for us to appreciate the depth of feeling evoked by the debate about circumcision among the early Christians. Today, in our largely gentile Church, that Paul is right seems blatantly obvious, but to the early Christians this was very much not the case. At the time of Paul, *all* followers of Jesus were Jewish, as indeed was Jesus himself. It therefore seems obvious to them that everyone who followed Jesus would need to be Jewish. Paul's argument that they did not was bewildering and disorientating and had ramifications far beyond just 'ideas'.

One of the very practical ramifications of this was the whole question of who you could eat with. The problem was that if a Jew ate with gentiles, they became unclean and therefore could not go back to their normal life as a Jew without careful purification. It meant that Jews who followed Christ were cut off from their families and friendship groups. It is no wonder that Peter wobbled on this front – the implications of agreeing with Paul on the inclusion of gentiles went far beyond intellectual agreement. It was the emotional implications of his decision that seem to have caused Peter to come unstuck.

While we do not have exactly the same dilemma today, the issue of the emotional implications of our faith resonates in all sorts of ways and might make us feel a level of sympathy for Peter.

Holy God,
our lives are laid open before you:
rescue us from the chaos of sin
and through the death of your Son
bring us healing and make us whole
in Jesus Christ our Lord.

COLLECT

71

Friday 12 February

Psalms **3**, 7 *or* **31**
Genesis 40
Galatians 3.1-14

Galatians 3.1-14

'Who has bewitched you?' (v.1)

Paul's frustrations continue to boil away in this chapter. Here he is still talking about the issue of circumcision and whether gentiles need to be circumcised or not. Reading between the lines, what seems to have happened is that the gentiles who became Christians, while listening to the gospel that Paul proclaimed, have later been influenced by Jewish Christians who have persuaded them that it would be better to be circumcised. Paul's point here is that they had accepted the death of Jesus (v.1); they had already received the Spirit (v. 2) and they really did not need to do anything else in order to be a follower of Christ. Paul then goes on to use the example of Abraham whose faith established a true relationship with God without him following any of the Mosaic law; by extension the Galatians need do nothing more either.

Paul's frustration gets right to the heart of the Christian gospel. It is so easy to feel that there is always more to be done in order to be properly accepted as a Christian. It is not hard to imagine the Galatians almost sighing with relief in the knowledge that all they had to do was to be circumcised. The point is that they were wrong. They needed to do nothing more than accept God's gift and respond to him in faith. It really is that easy!

COLLECT

Almighty and everlasting God,
you hate nothing that you have made
and forgive the sins of all those who are penitent:
create and make in us new and contrite hearts
that we, worthily lamenting our sins
and acknowledging our wretchedness,
may receive from you, the God of all mercy,
perfect remission and forgiveness;
through Jesus Christ your Son our Lord,
who is alive and reigns with you,
in the unity of the Holy Spirit,
one God, now and for ever.

Galatians 3.15-22

'The promises were made' (v.16)

At this point in Galatians 3, Paul appears to be getting really rather convoluted. In order to make sense of what is going on, we need to recognize that Paul is using a very Jewish line of argument that pays close attention to the text and makes much of what he notices there.

His key argument is that God's fundamental covenant was with Abraham, a covenant that applied to him and to his 'offspring'. Paul understood 'offspring' to refer to a very particular offspring – Jesus. Therefore, while the Mosaic covenant was good, right and proper, it was superseded when Abraham's offspring – Jesus – arrived. His point, therefore, is that there is nothing, absolutely nothing, wrong with the law. It served its purpose and while it did, it was valuable. It just isn't needed now that Abraham's true offspring has arrived. Those who have faith in Jesus are incorporated into him and are automatically included in God's promise to Abraham.

This is one of those occasions where 'the workings' of Paul's argument are probably more confusing than the point he is trying to make, which is simply this: Abraham's faith was the foundation of his relationship with God; just like him we too can share in that relationship through our belief in Christ, and by doing so we inherit the promises of God's love and faithfulness first made to Abraham. Paul's argument may be complicated, but his point is simple.

Holy God,
our lives are laid open before you:
rescue us from the chaos of sin
and through the death of your Son
bring us healing and make us whole
in Jesus Christ our Lord.

COLLECT

Galatians 3.23 – 4.7

'... all of you are one in Christ Jesus' (3.28)

There are some verses that we are so used to reading on their own that it can seem odd to come across them in a passage. Galatians 3.28 is surely one of those verses. It is so often quoted alone that we forget the context in which it is found in Galatians. Despite the fact that it is most often quoted in the context of the relationship between men and women, Galatians 3.28 is not primarily about that. As you will gather after reading the sweep of Galatians to this point, Paul is primarily talking about the relationship between Jews and gentiles; his examples of slave or free, male and female are additional examples but not more than that.

Paul's point here, then, is that it doesn't matter who we were before baptism; now that we are clothed in Christ, we are all one. He goes on in chapter 4 to talk some more about what this means – it means that we should act (and by implication treat others) as full heirs of God. We are able now to call God 'father' and so should treat each other as sisters and brothers of the one father.

The really important verses are probably not so much Galatians 3.28 as Galatians 4.6-7. Our ability to call God 'father' with all that entails is what transforms us, shaping our relationship with God and with each other.

COLLECT

Almighty God,
whose Son Jesus Christ fasted forty days in the wilderness,
and was tempted as we are, yet without sin:
give us grace to discipline ourselves in obedience to your Spirit;
and, as you know our weakness,
so may we know your power to save;
through Jesus Christ your Son our Lord,
who is alive and reigns with you,
in the unity of the Holy Spirit,
one God, now and for ever.

Psalm **44** *or* **48**, 52
Genesis 41.46 – 42.5
Galatians 4.8-20

Galatians 4.8-20

'I wish I ... could change my tone' (v.20)

If you are still in any quandary about Paul's seeming arrogance towards the Galatians, this passage may (or may not!) assuage your fears. After the full frontal assault of his opening chapter, Paul now allows us to see into his emotion and anxiety.

As we all know, a discussion by email can go badly wrong simply because we cannot see the facial expressions of the person writing to us and so can misunderstand what they are saying. It may be reassuring to know that this is nothing new. Lying behind what Paul says in this passage is his recognition that face-to-face meetings are much more effective than communication by letter.

It is important to notice that Paul's relationship with the Galatians began in vulnerability. We do not know what was wrong with him, but Paul was clearly ill when he first met them, and it was his illness that allowed him to proclaim the gospel (v.13). Letters like the one to the Galatians, opening in the way it did, make it hard for us to imagine Paul vulnerable, but he clearly was on many occasions (see also 2 Corinthians), and it was his vulnerability that seems to have made his ministry so effective.

Paul recognizes here that good relationships can only begin – and then be mended – face to face, because it is only then that we can see people for who they really are.

Heavenly Father,
your Son battled with the powers of darkness,
and grew closer to you in the desert:
help us to use these days to grow in wisdom and prayer
that we may witness to your saving love
in Jesus Christ our Lord.

COLLECT

Wednesday 17 February

Psalms **6**, 17 *or* **119.57-80**
Genesis 42.6-17
Galatians 4.21 – 5.1

Galatians 4.21 – 5.1

'For freedom Christ has set us free' (5.1)

In verse 4.21 Paul returns to his theme again. Back in his discussion about whether gentiles really need to embrace the entirety of the Jewish law and be circumcised, Paul now gives the example of a rather elaborate allegory. He reflects in an imaginative way on the Hagar and Sarah story. Although, to our modern eyes, Paul's argument appears odd, it would have made excellent sense to that part of his audience that was Jewish.

There are many examples from this period of Jews reading Old Testament passages as though they were a direct commentary on the world around them. This is what Paul is doing here, though we need to be aware of how offensive his likening of the Jews to Hagar was. They, of course, saw Isaac as their ancestor not Ishmael. This is why Paul uses this example; he challenges his audience to think deeply about ancestry, arguing that what makes you a descendant of Isaac is not so much bloodline as attitude – and, in particular, being truly free.

Christians are called to deep, abiding freedom, but our human nature sucks us back time and time again into slavery. Somehow we allow ourselves to be enslaved by others, by circumstances or by mental attitude. Christ has set us free, but staying free and refusing to be enslaved again takes an act of will.

COLLECT

Almighty God,
whose Son Jesus Christ fasted forty days in the wilderness,
and was tempted as we are, yet without sin:
give us grace to discipline ourselves in obedience to your Spirit;
and, as you know our weakness,
so may we know your power to save;
through Jesus Christ your Son our Lord,
who is alive and reigns with you,
in the unity of the Holy Spirit,
one God, now and for ever.

Galatians 5.2-15

'... you were called to freedom' (v.13)

Real truth can often only be found in paradox. This part of Galatians serves up a great paradox, which requires profound reflection.

The Galatians are free. Christ has made them free. So they are now free to make any choice they want. The irony is that they have used their freedom to enslave themselves unnecessarily to the principles of some who argue that they 'must' do this, follow that and observe the other.

Real freedom, Paul maintains, can only be found in the choice to be slaves to one another, not because we should, but because we love. Love transforms everything, and if love is mutual, then there is nothing more freeing than acting as a slave out of love to someone who loves you. The vision of Christian community that Paul holds up here is a vision of a community whose members so love one another, so seek for the others' welfare, that it is the most freeing experience possible to be a slave within it.

The opposite vision that he introduces in verse 15 is spine-chilling – the vision of a community whose members so bite and devour one another with unloving demands and self-centred concern that it consumes itself. As Christians, we are not called to consume one another, instead we are called to the paradox that the greatest freedom can be found in choosing to act as slaves to one another in love.

Heavenly Father,
your Son battled with the powers of darkness,
and grew closer to you in the desert:
help us to use these days to grow in wisdom and prayer
that we may witness to your saving love
in Jesus Christ our Lord.

COLLECT

Friday 19 February

Psalm **22** *or* **51**, 54
Genesis 42.29-end
Galatians 5.16-end

Galatians 5.16-end

'... the fruit of the Spirit' (v.22)

This passage follows on from the rest of what Paul has been saying for the whole of the letter, and it is worth remembering this as we reflect on a passage that is easier to get our heads around and therefore much better known.

Paul's image here is worth pausing on, not least because it is reminiscent of Jesus' teaching in places like Matthew 7.15-20, where he talks about trees bearing fruit that reveals what kind of tree they are. Paul's image is similar here. We need to be very clear that Paul is talking here of the fruit of the Spirit, not gifts of the Spirit. Gifts of the Spirit are optional: we all have some, but we don't all have them all. The fruit of the Spirit is not optional: we do not get to choose to have love and joy, for example, but not faithfulness and self-control (v.22).

Paul's point is that our life in the Spirit reveals who we are, but it also requires a positive choice to live in that way. A life lived in the Spirit will bear the fruit of the Spirit, but at the same time we need to choose to be guided by the Spirit; otherwise the fruit will fade and drop. The process works outside in as well as inside out. If we bite and consume one another as the Galatians were doing (5.15), then the fruit will fade pretty quickly.

COLLECT

Almighty God,
whose Son Jesus Christ fasted forty days in the wilderness,
and was tempted as we are, yet without sin:
give us grace to discipline ourselves in obedience to your Spirit;
and, as you know our weakness,
so may we know your power to save;
through Jesus Christ your Son our Lord,
who is alive and reigns with you,
in the unity of the Holy Spirit,
one God, now and for ever.

Galatians 6

'... restore such a one in a spirit of gentleness' (v.1)

Paul's teaching is hard in two ways: sometimes it is hard to understand; at other times it is easy to understand but hard to do. Galatians 6 falls into the second category. In summary, Galatians 6 is about living in such a way that gives life and support for the good of all.

This chapter is a helpful corrective to the previous passage. It is easy to become so obsessed with our own spiritual life and well-being that we focus almost entirely on what fruits of the Spirit we have or do not have, and completely miss the welfare of those around us.

In this chapter, Paul points to the tightrope that we must walk in attempting to live a faithful Christian life. On the one hand, if we see people engaging in something that goes against the life of the Spirit, we should restore them with a spirit of gentleness (v.1). On the other hand, we need to keep a sharp eye on ourselves and ensure that what we are doing coheres with the life of the Spirit.

Paul's teaching is best summed up in verses 2 and 5: 'Bear one another's burdens' and 'all must carry their own loads'. Together these two give you the key to successful community living: compassionate care for those around us while at the same time taking responsibility for ourselves. If everyone in a community did that, it really would function for the good of all.

Heavenly Father,
your Son battled with the powers of darkness,
and grew closer to you in the desert:
help us to use these days to grow in wisdom and prayer
that we may witness to your saving love
in Jesus Christ our Lord.

Monday 22 February

Hebrews 1

'He is the reflection of God's glory and the exact imprint of God's very being' (v.3)

The opening of the Epistle to the Hebrews reads like a miniature creed, focused on the person of the Son. In four verses, it discusses revelation, the creation and preservation of the universe, the atonement and the ascension. At the heart lies a statement about both God and the incarnation. The Son, we read, is 'the reflection of God's glory and the exact imprint of God's very being' (v.3).

The Son redoubles the Father, as his exact reflection, and yet there is only one God, because that reflection is perfect. Only add the Holy Spirit, and we have the doctrine of the Trinity. With the incarnation, exactly the same principle applies: Jesus is the perfect image of the Father, made flesh. Jesus could therefore say of himself 'Whoever has seen me has seen the Father' (John 14.9).

If this seems rather abstract – although also important and true – then we might note that the word at the centre of these four verses has much to say about the Christian life. The Son is the 'exact imprint' of the Father. The Greek word is *charactēr*: the word for the stamp left in sealing wax. It is the origin of our English word 'character', meaning both our moral quality and the mark left by an inscription. The early Church linked these two meanings. Christians are to display the (moral) character of Christ and can do so because in baptism they are embossed with his life, as his brothers and sisters.

COLLECT

Almighty God,
you show to those who are in error the light of your truth,
that they may return to the way of righteousness:
grant to all those who are admitted
    into the fellowship of Christ's religion,
that they may reject those things
    that are contrary to their profession,
and follow all such things as are agreeable to the same;
through our Lord Jesus Christ,
who is alive and reigns with you,
in the unity of the Holy Spirit,
one God, now and for ever.

Tuesday 23 February

Hebrews 2.1-9

*'As it is, we do not yet see everything in subjection to them,
but we do see Jesus' (vv.8-9)*

This passage is very much addressed to the Church as it *now* exists, in between the triumph of Christ's resurrection and the final triumph of his return. It addresses a Church that has already been set on the right way, but which has not yet arrived, and which can therefore still wander. It addresses a Church that should, and does, contemplate the 'so great ... salvation' (v.3) that Christ has accomplished, but which still does not yet 'see everything in subjection to him': that is, with its proper order restored by being fully ordered to Christ. (The NRSV gives us 'in subjection to them', but the Greek is 'him'.)

Existing in this in-between state, the Christian receives at least three aids to a healthy perspective. The first is to acknowledge the real exaltation of Christ, and to be exultant in that: Christ *is* 'crowned with glory and honour' (v.9). The second is a due realism about what it means for the world still to be out of kilter, and especially to be out of kilter with Christ: for Christ it meant 'the suffering of death' (v.9), and for us, who are identified with him, it may also mean suffering. The third point picks up just that note of identification: whatever the Christian might go through, indeed whatever *anyone* might go through, we do so alongside Christ, who 'tasted death for everyone' (v.9). While Christ's death does not mean that no one else will die, it does change the character of death: we now have him alongside us, even there.

Almighty God,
by the prayer and discipline of Lent
may we enter into the mystery of Christ's sufferings,
and by following in his Way
come to share in his glory;
through Jesus Christ our Lord.

COLLECT

Wednesday 24 February

Hebrews 2.10-end

'Since, therefore, the children share flesh and blood,
he himself likewise shared the same things' (v.14)

Our reading today is full of the theme of sharing. Christ came to share sonship, for instance: the Son of God was incarnate in order to share with us what he has and is. He came so that he and we together might 'have one Father' (v.11). Sharing also runs in the other direction. Not only does God share what he is with us, but God also shares in what we are. Since those whom Christ came to redeem 'share' flesh and blood (it is what we have 'in common'), the Son shared this with us. Becoming flesh and blood, God now shares in what human beings share in common.

Theologians never tire of revisiting this dynamic of sharing, from God to us and from us to God. 'He became what we are, so that we might become what he is', wrote Athanasius (296–373 AD), among others. He took the *whole* of human nature upon himself, wrote Gregory Nazianzen (c.329–390 AD), since 'what he did not assume [or *share*], he did not heal'. Clement of Alexandria (150–215 AD) even went so far as to say that God created the human race 'for sharing' (*Paedagogus*, 'The Teacher', II.13). However, this emphasis on sharing at the centre of Christian thought, is not only, or necessarily, a comfortable idea; it also has ethical implications, as Clement recognized. If those who are wealthy should say 'I have more than I need, why not just enjoy it?' then, in Clement's estimation, they are neglecting sharing, and that is 'not properly human'.

COLLECT

Almighty God,
you show to those who are in error the light of your truth,
that they may return to the way of righteousness:
grant to all those who are admitted
    into the fellowship of Christ's religion,
that they may reject those things
    that are contrary to their profession,
and follow all such things as are agreeable to the same;
through our Lord Jesus Christ,
who is alive and reigns with you,
in the unity of the Holy Spirit,
one God, now and for ever.

Psalm **34** *or* **78.1-39***
Genesis 45.1-15
Hebrews 3.1-6

Hebrews 3.1-6

'... the builder of a house has more honour than the house itself' (v.3)

God's work as creator is given forceful expression in an extended metaphor that runs through our passage today: 'the builder of all things is God' (v.4). This allows for a clear ascription of divinity to Jesus, since this 'builder' is identified as Christ: he is the one, as John put it, *through whom* all things were made (John 1.3).

God is the builder of all things. That lends a beauty to the trade or occupation that Jesus – we have every reason to suppose – learned from Joseph, his guardian. A boy of Christ's time would be all-but-expected to learn the trade of the man of the house.

Jesus, we read in the Greek, was a tekton (Mark 6.3). We typically translate that word as 'carpenter', but this may be too limited. It can mean a worker in any kind of material, a builder as much as to a carpenter. In the ancient world, the distinction between them was not so sharp. Joseph might put a coat peg in a wall, and Jesus after him, but he might also build the wall of the house. Certainly, Christ's parables suggest a familiarity with building towers (Luke 14.28-30) and with what sort of foundations withstand floods, and which do not (Matthew 7.24-7).

Reading Hebrews today, we can both rejoice in the dignity that the incarnate Son gives to workers of all sorts, not least to those who build, and rejoice in the poetry of the connection between Jesus the builder of Galilee and Jesus 'the builder of all things'.

Almighty God,
by the prayer and discipline of Lent
may we enter into the mystery of Christ's sufferings,
and by following in his Way
come to share in his glory;
through Jesus Christ our Lord.

COLLECT

Friday 26 February

Psalms 40, **41** or **55**
Genesis 45.16-end
Hebrews 3.7-end

Hebrews 3.7-end

'But exhort one another every day, as long as it is called "today"'
(v. 13)

The opening quotation today comes from Psalm 95. Known as the *Venite*, after its opening word in Latin ('Come, let us sing to the Lord'), it was once just about the most frequently recited psalm, since it was how morning prayer began every day, not least in the Book of Common Prayer but also in other rites with mediaeval roots. It still performs that task in the Roman Catholic morning 'Office of Readings'.

Today, in many Churches, we often like our Psalms sanitized. So, when Psalm 95 shows up, as it does reasonably often, although not as often as before, the final section is made optional. As if to serve us right, that excised section is all that the Letter to the Hebrews quotes.

These lines serve as a warning in the psalm and they serve as a warning in our Epistle: 'Take care, brothers and sisters', we read (v.12). But as always with the Gospel, the warning comes with an invitation, just as the invitation comes with a warning. 'Say yes to Christ', we are exhorted, and let those who have said yes not throw the gift of God idly away. Preserve urgency in the present moment, we are told, neither resting on our past laurels, nor deferring anything to the future. Remain before God in the present moment, and both the past and the future will look after themselves.

COLLECT

Almighty God,
you show to those who are in error the light of your truth,
that they may return to the way of righteousness:
grant to all those who are admitted
    into the fellowship of Christ's religion,
that they may reject those things
    that are contrary to their profession,
and follow all such things as are agreeable to the same;
through our Lord Jesus Christ,
who is alive and reigns with you,
in the unity of the Holy Spirit,
one God, now and for ever.

Saturday 27 February

Hebrews 4.1-13

'... while the promise of entering his rest is still open, let us take care that none of you should seem to have failed to reach it' (v.1)

Today's passage is about rest. In a striking conjunction of images, we are told that we should *strive* to *rest*: 'Let us therefore make every effort to enter that [eternal sabbath] rest' (v.11). In our time, more than ever, honouring rest in this way is often countercultural. Many of us have forgotten how to rest. If so, we can take God as our example. He may be, as we saw yesterday, the most active builder, but he is also the one who rests: 'God rested on the seventh day from all his works' (v.4).

The persistent metaphor for rest, running throughout the passage today, is of the sabbath: 'the seventh day'. For the Christian, the sabbath has become Sunday: not the seventh (and last) day of the week, but on what is called the eighth day – the first day of the new creation. If rest is countercultural, and if it is difficult for us to achieve, then the weekly Sunday sabbath presents an opportunity. On this day, more than any other, we are urged by the Church to look ahead and anticipate the world that is to come. Observing the day of the resurrection as a particular day of rejoicing and rest (as far as we are able) means at least three things: it is a countercultural witness; it is a way to discipline workaholic tendencies; and it is a foretaste of the world to come, of that 'sabbath rest [which] still remains for the people of God' (v.9).

Almighty God,
by the prayer and discipline of Lent
may we enter into the mystery of Christ's sufferings,
and by following in his Way
come to share in his glory;
through Jesus Christ our Lord.

COLLECT

Monday 29 February

Psalms **5**, 7 *or* **80**, 82
Genesis 47.1-27
Hebrews 4.14 – 5.10

Hebrews 4.14 – 5.10

'Although he was a Son, he learned obedience through what he suffered' (v.8)

Two features of Israelite priesthood are mentioned in our passage: every priest was *called* and every priest must *sympathize*. Those two features are worked through, first in relation to the ancient Hebrew priesthood and then in relation to Christ. The Hebrew priest had to 'deal gently' (5.2) with the wayward, remembering that he himself is a sinner. The Greek here actually goes beyond externalities ('deal gently') to the priest's inner life: he is to 'feel for' the people. As for the second point, as we have seen, the priest is also *called*, since 'one does not presume to take this honour' (5.4) – even if that calling comes through family and birth.

What was said last about the ancient Hebrew priesthood is said first about Christ. He was called, or 'appointed' by God. Then, just like the priesthood of old, he is also full of sympathy. In his case, that follows not from being a sinner among sinners, but from having suffered every human woe as one of us. In a reference that reveals the author to be familiar with Gospel stories, he invokes the agony in the Garden of Gethsemane. Jesus, who was perfect as God, became also the perfect human being. He was 'made perfect' (5.9), not in the sense of having previously been lacking, but in the sense of having offered his life perfectly to God, right to the end. In this way, his divinely perfect humanity becomes what will perfect our errant humanity: 'having been made perfect, he became the source of eternal salvation for all who obey him' (5.9).

COLLECT

Almighty God,
whose most dear Son went not up to joy but first he suffered pain,
and entered not into glory before he was crucified:
merrcifully grant that we, walking in the way of the cross,
may find it none other than the way of life and peace;
through Jesus Christ your Son our Lord,
who is alive and reigns with you,
in the unity of the Holy Spirit,
one God, now and for ever.

Psalms 6, **9** *or* 87, **89**.1-18
Genesis 47.28 – end of 48
Hebrews 5.11 – 6.12

Hebrews 5.11 – 6.12

'... by this time you ought to be teachers' (5.12)

Yesterday we read about the perfection of Jesus. Today's passage is about the perfection of the Christian. The same Greek root underlies both the word for 'perfect' applied to Christ yesterday (5.9) and the word 'mature' today: 'solid food is for the mature' (5.14).

Progress in the Christian life is not always easy, and the part played by learning, thinking and the life of the mind was easily overlooked – it seems – in the first century, just as it is often overlooked now. Not that we are talking simply about abstract theological notions: the idea is of receiving a Christian understanding of the world; it is about habits of mind in those 'trained by practice' (5.14). In the Great Commission, Jesus told his followers to 'make disciples' (Matthew 28.19). We should not forget that the word means both 'one who has been disciplined' or 'one who has learned'. The letter tells us to 'leave behind' various basic teachings (6.1). That is not because they are unimportant or forgettable. It is simply that, although irreplaceable, the foundation is not the whole building.

If the passage about the impossibility of repentance in certain circumstances is alarming, that is its main purpose. It warns the reader not to give up or to take the faith lightly, rather than being primarily a description of what might or might not happen to other people. Happily, the author of the epistle is 'confident' that his readers will not fall into these traps.

Eternal God,
give us insight
to discern your will for us,
to give up what harms us,
and to seek the perfection we are promised
in Jesus Christ our Lord.

COLLECT

Psalm **38** or **119.105-128**
Genesis 49.1-32
Hebrews 6.13-end

Hebrews 6.13-end

*'When God made a promise to Abraham, because he had no one
greater by whom to swear, he swore by himself' (v.13)*

This is a passage about hope and why we have good grounds for hope.
It is also a discussion of a knotty theological topic, namely whether God
– who is free and sovereign – is under any obligations. We might say
that 'God owes us nothing', and in a sense that is right. Whether that
leaves you feeling a little uneasy depends on how you understand God.
How do we know that God will not simply blot us out, or change his
mind about loving us? Well, if God does not owe us anything
'absolutely' speaking, he does nonetheless owe it *to himself* to be true
to himself. As the Anglican theologian Richard Hooker put it in the
sixteenth century, in the opening of *The Laws of Ecclesiastical Polity*,
'the being of God is a kind of law to his working'.

That might satisfy the theologian, but God goes further. To make it all
clear, God *promises* to bless us, as embodied in his promise to Abraham.
What is more, God even swears 'by himself' since 'he had no one
greater by whom to swear'. God binds himself to his own word by
swearing upon himself, so that he would be bound to us and we to
him. This is the ground for our hope; this is where the Christian can
'take refuge'; these are the grounds for hope, upon which we can
'seize' (v.18). This is what makes our hope both 'sure' and 'steadfast'
(v.19), the first word meaning clearly and outwardly stable (like the
outward oath) and the second meaning internally secure (like the
character of God).

COLLECT

Almighty God,
whose most dear Son went not up to joy but first he suffered pain,
and entered not into glory before he was crucified:
mercifully grant that we, walking in the way of the cross,
may find it none other than the way of life and peace;
through Jesus Christ your Son our Lord,
who is alive and reigns with you,
in the unity of the Holy Spirit,
one God, now and for ever.

Psalms **56**, 57 *or* 90, **92**
Genesis 49.33 – end of 50
Hebrews 7.1-10

Hebrews 7.1-10

'... resembling the Son of God, he remains a priest for ever' (v.3)

The author of Hebrews was fascinated by the figure of Melchizedek, for all he appears only twice in the Old Testament: first in the story of Abraham, as the priest of 'God Most High', who offers a sacrifice for Abraham after a victory in battle (Genesis 14), and then in Psalm 110.4, a messianic poem that likens the Davidic lineage to this mysterious figure. We will encounter that psalm verse tomorrow: 'You are a priest for ever according to the order of Melchizedek' (v.11).

Almost nothing is known about Melchizedek, and the author of our epistle makes something of this ignorance, in an almost playful mood. Look, he writes, Melchizedek appears in the Bible 'without father, without mother, without genealogy' (v.3) (making up that word for 'without lineage' as he goes). Melchizedek is like a figure from beyond time, turning up within the world, just like the Son of God, our author points out.

Yet, we might add, that is only half the story. The other figure in the passage is Abraham, and here that includes all of his progeny; Abraham acts on behalf of all of his descendents down the ages, present in his 'loins'. One of those descendants, we might point out, was Jesus. So, in the reading today we have both Melchizedek, symbol of the eternal and somewhat timeless priest, and Abraham, the symbol of human lineage. In Christ, both are embodied: the eternal and the time-bound, the mysterious and the earthy, a divine nature and a human nature.

Eternal God,
give us insight
to discern your will for us,
to give up what harms us,
and to seek the perfection we are promised
in Jesus Christ our Lord.

COLLECT

Friday 4 March

Hebrews 7.11-end

'... a better hope, through which we approach God' (v. 19)

We have encountered the idea of perfection in Hebrews before, but even for a letter that makes much of this concept, perfection is particularly prominent in today's passage (vv. 11, 19, 28, and 'for all time' in v. 25 could mean 'perfectly'). In the contemporary Church, we are most likely to encounter the quest for perfection as part of the heritage of Methodism and in the Roman Catholic Church. The quest for perfect holiness was an important part of the teaching of the Wesleys, and the Roman Catholic Church's veneration of the saints (with its parallels in Anglican churches) holds up examples of 'the spirits of the righteous made perfect' (Hebrews 12.23).

These traditions remind us of something important, that God's purpose is for us to attain perfection (v.11). That is God's purpose just as much as it ever was (even if that was not ever attained before). The route to perfection, however, is radically changed compared to the old system of law and animal sacrifice. Something astonishing has happened with the birth, death and resurrection of Christ; something new has dawned ('arisen' in v. 15 has astronomical associations) – a priest has come from the tribe of Judah, rather than the tribe of Aaron, which is something archetypically unexpected for the letter's Hebrew readers. Through this unexpected priest, through this radical departure, the old goal of perfection is newly in view, and newly possible, maybe not in this life but certainly in the life to come.

COLLECT

Almighty God,
whose most dear Son went not up to joy but first he suffered pain,
and entered not into glory before he was crucified:
mercifully grant that we, walking in the way of the cross,
may find it none other than the way of life and peace;
through Jesus Christ your Son our Lord,
who is alive and reigns with you,
in the unity of the Holy Spirit,
one God, now and for ever.

Hebrews 8

'Now the main point in what we are saying is this ...' (v.1)

With chapter 8, we have arrived at the beginning of the extended, central passage of Hebrews, which deals with Christ as our high priest, interceding for us in heaven. It trades frequently on a contrast between the priesthood of the ascended Christ and the priesthood of the Old Testament, between the heavenly altar and the offering of Christ, and the human tent of temple and the sacrifice of animals.

The contrast certainly sets Christ in place as the new, perfect and eternal priest, but that but does not entirely demean the old priesthood in the process. The Old Testament priesthood had a value and a dignity, precisely because it was a likeness and foreshadowing of the eternal priesthood of Christ. It may have been only a 'sketch and shadow' (v.5), but that, again, is not to run something down, when the model is a 'pattern' based on the prayer of Jesus to his Father.

The Letter to the Hebrews is one of the most complicated books of the New Testament, so we can be grateful that the author provides us with a summary, here at the centre of the book, of what strikes him as its central message: we have a high priest, Jesus, who is right next to the Father, and who has the perfect offering to present, namely his own self – and what is more pleasing to God, who said of Jesus 'This is my Son, the Beloved, with whom I am well pleased' (Matthew 3.17)?

Eternal God,
give us insight
to discern your will for us,
to give up what harms us,
and to seek the perfection we are promised
in Jesus Christ our Lord.

COLLECT

Monday 7 March

Psalms 70, **77** or **98**, 99, 101
Exodus 2.11-22
Hebrews 9.1-14

Hebrews 9.1-14

'... through the greater and perfect tent' (v.11)

The Bible Museum in Amsterdam is well worth a visit. But if you are expecting to see lots of different kinds of bibles on display, you'll be disappointed. True, there are some important translations, including the first bible in Dutch. There is a garden of plants from Egypt and Palestine, and there are artifacts and archaeological objects from biblical times. But the centre-piece of the museum is the enormous scale model of the portable shrine erected by the Israelites after their exodus from Egypt and the model of the Temple Mount built in Jerusalem, a sacred place for the three religions: Judaism, Christianity and Islam.

What strikes many Christian visitors to the museum, looking at the models of the temple or Jewish shrines, is just how alien these constructions look today. Many synagogues can look quite like churches, but the Hebrew buildings for worship of the Old Testament were quite different. They had fire, animals, sacrifice, screened-off areas, inner sanctuaries, and some objects that were never to be looked upon by ordinary mortals.

The beginning of John's gospel (John 1.14) tells us that God became flesh and dwelt among us, but the more literal rendering of the verse is that God 'pitched his tent' among us. The writer of the book of Hebrews now claims that Jesus himself is 'the true tent that the Lord ... set up' (Hebrews 8.2). God, in Christ, has settled in the midst of the whole of humanity.

COLLECT

Merciful Lord,
absolve your people from their offences,
that through your bountiful goodness
we may all be delivered from the chains of those sins
which by our frailty we have committed;
grant this, heavenly Father,
for Jesus Christ's sake, our blessed Lord and Saviour,
who is alive and reigns with you,
in the unity of the Holy Spirit,
one God, now and for ever.

Hebrews 9.15-end

*'... he has appeared once for all ... to remove sin
by the sacrifice of himself' (v. 26)*

There are several ideas and images that the New Testament presents to us that attempt to convey the meaning and the depth of Christ's death. Some of those ideas and images (such as 'ransom' or 'sacrifice') are imaginative metaphors that seek to communicate a range of complex truths. Our scriptures don't give us one single notion of atonement to subscribe to, but rather several that are simultaneously competitive and complementary.

The ones offered in today's scripture are essentially contractual. Even though images of blood and purity flow through the reading, the central issue is value. What is our value to God, and what is the value of Christ's sacrifice for us? The English phrase 'paid on the nail' relates to the bronze pillars, also called nails, that have large flat tops – the size of large plates or serving dishes. These nails can still be seen outside the Corn Exchange in Bristol and the Stock Exchanges in Limerick and Liverpool. From late medieval times, business deals were often sealed by money being exchanged on these large flat-headed nails. The songwriter and worship leader, Graham Kendrick's folk song from 1974 ('How Much Do You Think You Are Worth?') takes this idea up, and says that our lives have been valued, and 'a price had been paid on the nail' for each of us. The great beauty of the Christian story is that we can't get to heaven and abide with God in our own strength. The good news is that it is God who reaches down, touches us, bleeds and dies for us, enabling the door of heaven to be opened to all. Christ's death is a one-off, single payment for entry.

Merciful Lord,
you know our struggle to serve you:
when sin spoils our lives
and overshadows our hearts,
come to our aid
and turn us back to you again;
through Jesus Christ our Lord.

COLLECT

Wednesday 9 March

Psalms 63, **90** *or* 110, **111**, 112
Exodus 4.1-23
Hebrews 10.1-18

Hebrews 10.1-18

'... through the offering of the body of Jesus Christ once for all' (v.10)

One of the very best modern representations of the sacrifice and death of Jesus comes in a short story by Walter Wangerin, the Canadian writer. Wangerin's tale 'Ragman', features an old-fashioned rag-and-bone man, who tours the city and its slums. However, he does not look for valuable scrap or cast-offs. His cry throughout the city is that he will give 'new for old'. And the tale has a twist. He does not take objects, but rather the infirmities that cripple people, or render them marginalized and cast-outs from society. So, from a young girl with a bandaged head, dirty and stained with old blood, he takes the bandage and gives her a new bonnet, but the bandage he takes from her he now wears, and his blood flows freely through it.

In each encounter, the Ragman – a Christ-like figure – takes on the infirmities of all those he touches in exchange for their healing. He sacrifices himself for those he encounters. This idea would not have been strange to the early Church. 'For that which he [i.e. Christ] has not taken upon himself, he has not healed; but that which is united to his Godhead is also saved', wrote Irenaeus in his *Against Heresies* (c. 180 AD). Irenaeus understood that unless God had come among us in true humanity, and experienced our sense of desolation, suffering and despair, then these could not be redeemed.

Jesus redeems us through becoming one with us, for us, and of us. The word made flesh takes and transforms our frail bodies through his suffering and ultimate sacrifice.

COLLECT

Merciful Lord,
absolve your people from their offences,
that through your bountiful goodness
we may all be delivered from the chains of those sins
which by our frailty we have committed;
grant this, heavenly Father,
for Jesus Christ's sake, our blessed Lord and Saviour,
who is alive and reigns with you,
in the unity of the Holy Spirit,
one God, now and for ever.

Psalms 53, **86** *or* 113, **115**
Exodus 4.27 – 6.1
Hebrews 10.19-25

Hebrews 10.19-25

'Therefore, my friends, since we have confidence ...' (v.19)

How can we possibly have confidence? The word means 'to trust boldly'. Can we trust God in this way? The writer of the Hebrews is in no doubt. All we need to do is turn to God, and then realize that having turned, it will turn out fine if we are turned over to God. All we need to do is give back some of the love that has already been shown to us. Love is the lesson – the lesson that God teaches us, and asks us to practise with our fellow believers and the whole of humanity. We are to 'provoke' (!) one another to love and good deeds. As William Langland puts it in *Piers Plowman* (c. 1370):

> 'Counseilleth me, Kynde', quod I, 'what craft be best to lerne?'
> 'Lerne to love,' quod Kynde, 'and leef alle othere.'

So, the writer of Hebrews encourages us: we need not waver, but rather can hold fast to the one who holds fast to us. The God who has promised is faithful. There is nothing we can do that will make God love us any less or any more. God's love for us is full and complete, abundant and overwhelming. The mystics say that even God has one flaw – a frailty from which grace flows, which will teach us all we need to know about power made perfect in weakness. God's heart: it is too soft. And it is from God's open heart that we learn about God's open hands and embrace. So let us love one another, as God loves us.

Merciful Lord,
you know our struggle to serve you:
when sin spoils our lives
and overshadows our hearts,
come to our aid
and turn us back to you again;
through Jesus Christ our Lord.

COLLECT

95

Friday 11 March

Hebrews 10.26-end

'For you need endurance ...' (v.36)

The Christian life is a marathon, not a sprint. Endurance is needed for the journey. Jesus, indeed, takes time to prepare his disciples with much advice on what to take for the road ahead. The rest of the New Testament testifies to the patience and endurance needed for the kingdom of God to be established. Like Rome, it won't be built in a day.

So we should not be surprised that passion and mercy meet in Jesus – because both are in the heart of God for humanity, and thus at the centre of our discipleship. The spiritual passion we are urged to embody is not just about the expulsion of energy.

The endurance we are asked to practise is not supposed to be about rationing our resources and energy: 'My soul takes no pleasure in anyone who shrinks back' (v. 38). So, we should not be allowed to blunt the energy and enthusiasm that flow from living the gospel. To be sure, orderliness and calculation have their place, but this should not be allowed to control and marginalize our passion for the gospel, because true religion, of course, is about extremes: extreme love, extreme sacrifice, and extreme selflessness that go beyond reason.

Religion in moderation is, arguably, a contradiction in terms. It should offend, cajole, probe and interrogate. One might say that a faith that does not get up your nose sometimes is hardly worth the candle. Endurance is crucial, but equally, don't hold back from proclaiming God's love.

Merciful Lord,
absolve your people from their offences,
that through your bountiful goodness
we may all be delivered from the chains of those sins
which by our frailty we have committed;
grant this, heavenly Father,
for Jesus Christ's sake, our blessed Lord and Saviour,
who is alive and reigns with you,
in the unity of the Holy Spirit,
one God, now and for ever.

Psalm **32** *or* 120, **121**, 122
Exodus 7.8-end
Hebrews 11.1-16

Hebrews 11.1-16

'If they had been thinking of the land that they had left behind ...'
(v.15)

As Søren Kierkegaard, the Danish theologian, said: 'Life can only be understood backwards; but it must be lived forwards.' In today's reading, we are given example after example of people who have lived forwards. They did not yearn for a return to where they had come from, but rather walked – by faith – into a new and uncertain future.

Often, this is the vocation of every Christian. But if this true, what are the next steps? How would you know you were called? How could you be sure? You can't of course, but there are two simple things to bear in mind.

First, have courage. Many journeys of faith and adventure with God never begin – because of fear. Fear of failure, or perhaps just of getting it wrong – suppose someone rumbles that I am just ordinary? Suppose I really make a mess of it? But failure is not the worst thing; letting it defeat you is. It takes a special kind of wisdom and courage to face failure and defeat, and then to try and move on from this.

Second, have patience. The Christian life is often lived more in waiting and hope than in results. Our journey of discipleship is weighed and measured over the entire course of a life. It takes a long time to appreciate just how much God has called us to. It takes daily devotion to see that our calling is not about affirmation or success at all, but rather faithfulness. Sometimes we are called not to win – even for God – but merely, by faith to walk with Christ.

Merciful Lord,
you know our struggle to serve you:
when sin spoils our lives
and overshadows our hearts,
come to our aid
and turn us back to you again;
through Jesus Christ our Lord.

COLLECT

Monday 14 March

Psalms **73**, 121
or 123, 124, 125, **126**
Exodus 8.1-19
Hebrews 11.17-31

Hebrews 11.17-31

'By faith Abraham ...' (v.17)

It's strange, isn't it, how our heroes of the faith also have feet of clay. Even in this impressive list – Abraham, Isaac, Jacob, Moses – the Bible does not spare us their fallibility and failure, as much as the Scriptures also applaud their faith. The key to this list is simple enough. God works through our strengths *and* weaknesses. This is part of what it means to try and cope with his grace. He can even use our imperfections for his glory.

This is clever stuff, to be sure. One of the artful things asked of us in discipleship is to check not only on what is going well – and what God is doing in that – but on what is not going so well – and what God might be doing in that too. This, indeed, is how God uses Abraham's foolishness. At the point where Abraham almost slays his son, God still speaks through this situation and fundamentally shifts Abraham's perceptions on worship and sacrifice.

This is why the Apostle Paul's well-known phrase is so vital to remember: 'power is made perfect in weakness' (2 Corinthians 12.9). God uses our weaknesses – even the foolish and base things of the world – to bring about change. He does not use Abraham, Isaac, Jacob and Moses because they are perfect. They are not. He uses them because they are willing, and will place their trust and future in God's hands. The list, then, is never quite complete. You can add your own name to this list too. By faith ...

COLLECT

Most merciful God,
who by the death and resurrection of your Son Jesus Christ
delivered and saved the world:
grant that by faith in him who suffered on the cross
we may triumph in the power of his victory;
through Jesus Christ your Son our Lord,
who is alive and reigns with you,
in the unity of the Holy Spirit,
one God, now and for ever.

Psalms **35**, 123 *or* **132**, 133
Exodus 8.20-end
Hebrews 11.32 – 12.2

Hebrews 11.32 – 12.2

'… let us run with perseverance the race that is set before us' (v.1)

Douglas Adams, in *The Hitchhiker's Guide to the Galaxy*, says that there is an art to flying. The knack lies in 'learning how to throw yourself at the ground and miss'. When we speak of falling, we can barely conceive of it in positive terms. To fall is dangerous … I have had a fall and broken a bone. We speak of fallen leaders, fallen men or women. The Fall ends the creation story in Genesis, and a fall begins the final chapters of our salvation story – Jesus falls on the Via Dolorosa.

The list of heroes of the faith today is a mixed bag. Some have succeeded outright, but others have failed – and conspicuously too. Yet God can even do great things with failure, because what matters to God is not success or failure, but faithfulness. The race that God asks us to run is like no other. It is more of a marathon than a sprint, and with few laurels at the end. Points don't mean prizes, alas.

Christians are called to follow a servant, not a winner – the one who led not by dominating, but by serving; the one who led not by triumphing, but by sacrificing; the one who led not by being first on the podium, but by falling to the ground and dying. It is from here we rise. For all discipleship requires us to give ourselves fully to God: to fall to and for him; to die with him, so that we might not only be raised, but also see the fruit grow from the many seeds that God is, even now, seeking to sow in his world.

Gracious Father,
you gave up your Son
out of love for the world:
lead us to ponder the mysteries of his passion,
that we may know eternal peace
through the shedding of our Saviour's blood,
Jesus Christ our Lord.

COLLECT

Wednesday 16 March

Psalms **55**, 124 *or* **119.153-end**
Exodus 9.1-12
Hebrews 12.3-13

Hebrews 12.3-13

'Now, discipline always seems painful rather than pleasant at the time ...' (v.11)

When Jesus speaks of himself as the true vine and of his father as the gardener (John 15.1) , he might have had in mind the same connections between discipline and discipleship that we find in today's reading. Jesus speaks of pruning (John 15.2), and Paul speaks of grace being poured out in Jesus (Titus 3.6). The bearing of fruit requires the gardener to be loving, encouraging – but also a pruner too. There is discipline in discipleship. Fruit takes time to grow.

Leslie Hunter (Bishop of Sheffield 1939–62), writing in *The Seed and the Fruit*, tells a parable about the world as it nears the end through war, famine and disaster. People, he tells us, begin to dream of a time when they can enter into a spacious store or shop in which the gifts of God to humanity are all kept. There is an angel behind the counter. The people cry out they have run out of the fruits of the Spirit and plead with the angel: 'Can you restock us?' The angel at first appears to refuse the request, prompting the people to complain bitterly that in place of war, afflictions, injustice, lying and lust, humanity now needs love, joy, peace, integrity, discipline – 'without these, we shall all be lost'. But the angel behind the counter can only reply: 'We do not stock fruits here ... only seeds'.

The reading today is about seeds growing fruit, the careful and disciplining husbandry that produces mature spirituality. There is no 'instant discipleship' – only one that is born out of a life of discipline, endurance and patience.

COLLECT

Most merciful God,
who by the death and resurrection of your Son Jesus Christ
delivered and saved the world:
grant that by faith in him who suffered on the cross
we may triumph in the power of his victory;
through Jesus Christ your Son our Lord,
who is alive and reigns with you,
in the unity of the Holy Spirit,
one God, now and for ever.

Hebrews 12.14-end

'... our God is a consuming fire' (v.29)

Christians, we are told, are to pursue peace with everyone, and attain a holiness without which no one can see God. It seems a tall order, especially when we are told that God is a consuming fire.

According to one Jewish tradition, we are all in the hands of God, but it is the souls of the righteous that 'will shine forth, and will run like sparks through the stubble' (Wisdom 3). So how shall we be? How shall we live? To answer this, you have to look into your heart and ask some searching questions. What random and costly acts of kindness and generosity will you perform today? Can you love and serve others – putting all before your self – and yet not count the cost? Can you, at the same time, radiate warmth, peace, openness and hospitality? Can you be a beam of God's light and warmth in a world that is sometimes dark and cold? Can your friends and colleagues say, hand on heart, that to know you is somehow to have been touched by the presence of God?

Christians, of course, know that they are not the fire; that is God. But Christians might know that they are the fuel for that fire. As one Eastern Orthodox prayer puts it: 'Set our hearts on fire with love for thee, O Christ, that in that flame we may love thee ... and our neighbours as ourselves.' Yes, our portion may be heaven, but we are here to glow, to light up the earth. May we, therefore, be a foretaste for others of the heaven prepared for us all.

Gracious Father,
you gave up your Son
out of love for the world:
lead us to ponder the mysteries of his passion,
that we may know eternal peace
through the shedding of our Saviour's blood,
Jesus Christ our Lord.

COLLECT

Psalms **22**, 126 *or* 142, **144**
Exodus 10
Hebrews 13.1-16

Hebrews 13.1-16

'Do not neglect to show hospitality to strangers ...' (v.2)

The theologian Mark Oakley says that 'Jesus is the body language of God'. The life Jesus leads expresses the wisdom of God. It is not just what he says; it is also what he doesn't say. It is not just what he does, but what doesn't do. His silence speaks as much as his words. His wisdom is embodied. And that is our calling: to let the Spirit of God dwell in us – to become a people where God is truly at home. The houses and homes that Jesus lived and stayed in tended to be pretty busy places – ones that practised God's hospitality. But with Jesus present, these were no longer ordinary homes. Many people came into these spaces and places for Jesus' teaching and healing ministry. The conversations and encounters that ensued were utterly transformative; both individuals and societies were changed. There is a sense in which our churches can also follow this – through gathering, convening and drawing all in, becoming an agent of God's gracious, proactive hospitality.

True Christian hospitality ought to make us a little uncomfortable; otherwise the dinner or lunch we offer is just like having friends over. The hospitality that Jesus exhorted his disciples to practise was one that broke down tribal barriers. It overcame divisions of race and gender, of age and class. Jesus welcomed all. That's why churches need to remember that it's not 'our altar' or 'our communion service'. It is Jesus' table; it is his meal. He desires to share with sinners. With the widow too, and the orphans, the prisoners, the lame, the leprous and the Samaritans. Jesus lives the hospitality of God. He now invites us to live and practise God's hospitable heart.

COLLECT

Most merciful God,
who by the death and resurrection of your Son Jesus Christ
delivered and saved the world:
grant that by faith in him who suffered on the cross
we may triumph in the power of his victory;
through Jesus Christ your Son our Lord,
who is alive and reigns with you,
in the unity of the Holy Spirit,
one God, now and for ever.

Psalms 25, 147.1-12
Isaiah 11.1-10
Matthew 13.54-end

Saturday 19 March
Joseph of Nazareth

Matthew 13.54-end

'Is not this the carpenter's son?' (v.55)

It must have come as a shock to the friends, neighbours and family of Jesus. To discover that your son, cousin, brother or neighbour is gifted might not be such a surprise. The emerging revelation that Jesus is 'special' – and in what might be a unique way – would have caused many people to doubt their sense of discernment, and their intelligence. Their first reaction would be to try and contain and rationalize the perception. To admit otherwise would be to concede that, despite seeing plainly, they had in fact been blind all along. Few of us would rest easy with that sense of self-judgment.

So, what of this 'carpenter's son'? We know that by working in Joseph's trade – carpentry and building – he had, by living in Nazareth, been exposed to the nearby Roman town of Sepphoris, a Hellenized community of almost 30,000. So Nazareth, home to a mere 300, was a dormitory village supplying labour to a much larger cosmopolitan community nearby. It would have been full of gentiles of every kind.

This is significant. Jesus' kingdom of God project, from the outset, reached out beyond Judaism to the gentiles. Indeed, he often praised gentiles for their faith and often scolded the apparently 'orthodox' religion of his kith and kin for their insularity. Jesus saw that God was for everyone; he lived, practised and preached this. All this, arguably, made Jesus a great teacher for those beyond his neighbourhood, but not one that his own family and friends could easily take pride in. So the carpenter–prophet was honoured by many – but not in his own hometown.

God our Father,
who from the family of your servant David
raised up Joseph the carpenter
to be the guardian of your incarnate Son
and husband of the Blessed Virgin Mary:
give us grace to follow him
in faithful obedience to your commands;
through Jesus Christ your Son our Lord,
who is alive and reigns with you,
in the unity of the Holy Spirit,
one God, now and for ever.

COLLECT

Monday 21 March

Monday of Holy Week

Lamentations 1.1-12a

'Is it nothing to you, all you who pass by?' (v.12)

The first challenge of Holy Week is overcoming indifference. I'm not talking here about other people's indifference but our own. It is a hard thing to walk through the events the Church remembers in the next five days, even though we know that the cross leads to resurrection on Easter Day. It is a hard thing to follow the journey of the Lord we love through the pain and abandonment of his trial to his long and difficult death.

Reading Lamentations helps us prepare for that journey (and every other journey where we watch with compassion those who suffer). We are invited to lament, to attend to the suffering of the Holy City, personified, as she looks back on the day of her abandonment and chronicles her loss.

There are many emotions mingled together: regret, sorrow, repentance and shame. But the harshest pain (I think) is caused by the indifference of others to her suffering.

In the coming days there will be many distractions and many calls on our time. Is it possible to find time to sit and to be, and to overcome our indifference and our unwillingness to enter into this part of the story? As we enter into the suffering of Christ, so our hearts are softened in compassion towards others who suffer.

COLLECT

Almighty and everlasting God,
who in your tender love towards the human race
    sent your Son our Saviour Jesus Christ
to take upon him our flesh
and to suffer death upon the cross:
grant that we may follow the example of his patience and humility,
and also be made partakers of his resurrection;
through Jesus Christ your Son our Lord,
who is alive and reigns with you,
in the unity of the Holy Spirit,
one God, now and for ever.

Psalm 27
Lamentations 3.1-18
Luke 22.[24-38] 39-53

Lamentations 3.1-18

'He has made my teeth grind on gravel ...' (v.16)

These verses are a profound, anguished meditation on suffering. Once again the city 's pain is personified, its effects described in acute detail. All of this suffering is attributed to God, who is the subject of a series of verbs ('he besieged me ... he walled me about ... he shot into my vitals', vv.5,7,13).

These verses are agony to read and are still more painful to find yourself in when life is at its most difficult. However, I think the Lectionary makes a serious mistake in cutting off the reading at verse 18. Today we need to read on at least to verse 24 and possibly to verse 33.

Lamentations is not simply a raw cry of pain. Lamentations is poetry – a considered, albeit anguished, reflection on particular events in history. The poets have deliberately placed in counterpoint one of the starkest and most personal descriptions of pain and one of the most profound and rich affirmations of God's love.

Neither must be separated from the other in our reflection on the original context, nor in using these verses as a lens on Holy Week, nor in reflection on our own response to pain and suffering. The pain and difficulty in each may be more than we think we can bear. Yet there is a deeper truth still to be found in the midst of that valley.

True and humble king,
hailed by the crowd as Messiah:
grant us the faith to know you and love you,
that we may be found beside you
on the way of the cross,
which is the path of glory.

COLLECT

Wednesday 23 March

Wednesday of Holy Week

Psalm 102 [or 102.1-18]
Wisdom 1.16 – 2.1; 2.12–22
or Jeremiah 11.18-20
Luke 22.54-end

Jeremiah 11.18-20

'I was like a gentle lamb led to the slaughter ...' (v.19)

To the eye of faith, the Old Testament is full of images of the cross and kaleidoscopic patterns foreshadowing the life of Jesus. Some of these are in the great narrative of the story of Israel and of Jerusalem, as we have seen in Lamentations. Some are in the great institutions of Israel, such as the sacrificial system, as we will see tomorrow.

And some, as in today's reading, are in the lives of individuals. The reference here to the gentle lamb led to the slaughter is echoed in the great Servant Song of Isaiah 53 and again in John the Baptist's cry: 'Here is the Lamb of God who takes away the sin of the world!' (John 1.29). Although in Jeremiah 11 the image is one of innocent suffering, Isaiah 53 and John 1 go much further and connect the picture to the idea of a sacrifice offered on behalf of others.

However, the allusion to Jeremiah, the man of sorrows, takes us still deeper. Jeremiah more than any other prophet suffers for his message. Jeremiah more than any other prophet exposes his heart both to God in his prayers and to his readers in the oracles he leaves us. Seeing Jesus in his passion through the lens of Jeremiah gives new dimensions in our view of what is happening to the Man of Sorrows in this Holy Week.

COLLECT

Almighty and everlasting God,
who in your tender love towards the human race
    sent your Son our Saviour Jesus Christ
to take upon him our flesh
and to suffer death upon the cross:
grant that we may follow the example of his patience and humility,
and also be made partakers of his resurrection;
through Jesus Christ your Son our Lord,
who is alive and reigns with you,
in the unity of the Holy Spirit,
one God, now and for ever.

Thursday 24 March

Maundy Thursday

Leviticus 16.2-24

'Thus shall Aaron come into the holy place ...' (v.3)

Under the Old Covenant, the High Priest entered the Holy of Holies, the inner shrine of the tabernacle and the temple, on just one day of the year. The High Priest came into the holiest place only after the most elaborate ritual: an outer cleansing in water and dressing in special garments and then a spiritual cleansing through the sacrifice of a bull and, finally, the sending of the scapegoat into the wilderness, bearing the iniquities of the nation to a barren region.

On this day we celebrate the beginning of the New Covenant. On this day, in the course of the Last Supper, Christ gave meaning to the death he was about to suffer. In the words of Hebrews: 'he entered once for all into the Holy Place, not with the blood of goats and calves, but with his own blood, thus obtaining eternal redemption' (Hebrews 9.12). 'This is my blood which is shed for you...'

Christ made this offering so that you and I and all of humankind might ourselves come into the most holy place, the presence of the living God, cleansed and delivered from all sin and that we might enjoy friendship with God for ever.

Once again, the Old Testament image gives us both a foreshadowing of the greater salvation that is to come and a lens through which to view the cross of Christ: the inexhaustible well of our salvation.

True and humble king,
hailed by the crowd as Messiah:
grant us the faith to know you and love you,
that we may be found beside you
on the way of the cross,
which is the path of glory.

COLLECT

Friday 25 March
Good Friday

Psalm 69
Genesis 22.1-18
John 19.38-end *or* Hebrews 10.1-10

Genesis 22.1-18

'... but where is the lamb for a burnt-offering?' (v.7)

There is a peerless sentence in the Prayer Book service of Holy Communion: 'who made there (by his one oblation of himself once offered) a full, perfect and sufficient sacrifice, oblation and satisfaction for the sins of the whole world'.

The six central words are arranged in an ABCCBA pattern: sufficient sacrifice, perfect oblation, full satisfaction. However, it is the final part of the phrasing that always strikes me deeply when I say the prayer aloud: 'for the sins of the whole world'. The event we celebrate today must be a very great event indeed, larger than we can ever comprehend, however beautiful the language.

The story of Abraham and Isaac contains many resonances with the drama of Good Friday. The location (Mount Moriah, traditionally the temple mount); the father and the son; the wood that is first carried and then becomes an instrument of death; the love of the father for his son and yet a willingness to offer him, whatever the cost.

Yet, of course, there is a much greater drama before us today. For our Father in heaven does not hold back from the sacrifice of his Son. The Son goes willingly to his death out of love for his Father and for the world: a full, perfect and sufficient sacrifice, oblation and satisfaction for the sins of the whole world.

COLLECT

Almighty Father,
look with mercy on this your family
for which our Lord Jesus Christ was content to be betrayed
and given up into the hands of sinners
and to suffer death upon the cross;
who is alive and glorified with you and the Holy Spirit,
one God, now and for ever.

Psalm 142
Hosea 6.1-6
John 2.18-22

Saturday 26 March

Easter Eve

Hosea 6.1-6

'Come, let us return to the Lord' (v.1)

Repentance has many meanings. Here (as in the story of the prodigal son and the Emmaus Road), it means, quite literally 'to turn around'. The Hebrew word means 'to return'. We have been travelling in one direction, away from God, and now we deliberately change that direction and begin to come home. In other places, repentance is about renewal. The Greek word normally used in the New Testament means 'a change of mind and heart'.

In this sacred space between Good Friday and Easter Day, our goal should be repentance in both of these senses. As we contemplate the cross and the reality and cost of forgiveness offered to us, we set our minds and hearts to turn again back towards the Lord in all those areas where we have walked away or become indifferent.

As we look ahead to the cries of joy on Easter Day, to the reality of resurrection, we pray for our own renewal and transformation through the days of Easter, that we might become more like Christ, more ready to receive the Spirit.

Hosea reminds us that repentance in both kinds must be more than ritual, deeper than outward observance. What we offer to God must be the best fruit of our inner lives, longer lasting than the dew and the morning cloud: love that is steadfast, knowledge of God that is real.

COLLECT

Grant, Lord,
that we who are baptized into the death
of your Son our Saviour Jesus Christ
may continually put to death our evil desires
and be buried with him;
and that through the grave and gate of death
we may pass to our joyful resurrection;
through his merits,
who died and was buried and rose again for us,
your Son Jesus Christ our Lord.

Monday 28 March

Monday of Easter Week

1 Corinthians 15.1-11

'Last of all ... he appeared also to me' (v.8)

Easter is not a feast but a season. The Church takes the 40 days of Lent to prepare to remember the passion of Christ. We then take 40 days to sound the depths of meaning in the glorious truth that Christ is risen. There is no better way to begin this 40 days of joy than by reading slowly and carefully Paul's 58 verses on the theme of resurrection in 1 Corinthians 15.

We begin today with the glorious assertion of the good news that is at the heart of everything ('which you received ... in which you stand ... through which you are being saved', vv.1-2). Paul offers a concise summary of that gospel as the foundation for all that is to come: 'Christ died ... was buried ... and was raised' (vv.3-4). Our faith is rooted in a series of historical events that are themselves the fulfilment of scripture and have a profound meaning.

The historical fact of the resurrection is established in an impressive list of witnesses. Our faith is grounded in real events. But faith in the resurrection is also lived experience. Paul's experience of the risen Christ is both a last and a first. He is the last of the apostles to experience a vision of the risen Lord. Yet he is the first of countless millions of Christians to encounter the risen Christ and hear his call.

COLLECT

Lord of all life and power,
who through the mighty resurrection of your Son
overcame the old order of sin and death
to make all things new in him:
grant that we, being dead to sin
and alive to you in Jesus Christ,
may reign with him in glory;
to whom with you and the Holy Spirit
be praise and honour, glory and might,
now and in all eternity.

Psalms **112**, 147.1-12
Exodus 12.14-36
1 Corinthians 15.12-19

1 Corinthians 15.12-19

'If there is no resurrection of the dead ...' (v.13)

It's hard for most of us to imagine what the Church was like before the Gospels were written down, before the creeds were agreed, before the faith settled into the shape by which we know it today. Everything could be contested.

Clearly some in Corinth, like the Sadducees in Acts, did not believe in the resurrection of the dead. Paul establishes in these verses, for all of Christian history, an unmistakable connection between the resurrection of Christ and the promise of the general resurrection of the dead. The theme recurs in every verse. One resurrection depends on the other. Because we know that Christ has been raised (because of the witnesses), then we can be sure and confident that there will be a resurrection from the dead.

Sometimes, as Christians, we become so heavenly minded that we are no earthly use. However, there is also an opposite danger: our thinking is so grounded in the earth that we forget to nurture our vision of heaven. There is a proper tension between the two.

We are called as Christians to invest in heaven, where our greater treasure is and where our heart should lie. But we are called to invest in heaven primarily by investing in the kingdom of God on earth.

COLLECT

God of glory,
by the raising of your Son
you have broken the chains of death and hell:
fill your Church with faith and hope;
for a new day has dawned
and the way to life stands open
in our Saviour Jesus Christ.

Wednesday 30 March

Wednesday of Easter Week

Psalms 113, 147.13-end
Exodus 12.37-end
1 Corinthians 15.20-28

1 Corinthians 15.20-28

'The last enemy to be destroyed is death' (v.26)

Understanding the resurrection means having some understanding of the end times. If the dead are to rise, when will that be? How is their resurrection related to the resurrection of Christ, which has already happened? And how can the resurrection of one man affect all people everywhere?

Paul answers these questions first with the image of first fruits (vv.20,23). Christ's resurrection is the guarantee of the general resurrection of the dead, but it is in advance of that resurrection. It is a powerful and effective sign, received by faith, of all that is to come.

Second, Christ is no ordinary person, but he is, like Adam, a representative person in God's economy. As death came into the world to all through the first man, Adam, so resurrection will flow from one man, Christ. However, that resurrection will come only at the end of time, whenever that may be. The dead will rise at the end of all things, when the kingdom comes in all its fullness. Death is the last enemy to be destroyed, though death's power has been broken for ever in the resurrection of Christ.

We live then in the times between the resurrection of Christ, which begins a new age, and the general resurrection of the dead when the kingdom comes in all its fullness.

COLLECT

Lord of all life and power,
who through the mighty resurrection of your Son
overcame the old order of sin and death
to make all things new in him:
grant that we, being dead to sin
and alive to you in Jesus Christ,
may reign with him in glory;
to whom with you and the Holy Spirit
be praise and honour, glory and might,
now and in all eternity.

Psalms 114, 148
Exodus 13.1-16
1 Corinthians 15.29-34

Thursday of Easter Week

1 Corinthians 15.29-34

'I die every day!' (v.31)

Christian discipleship demands great courage. To be a disciple is to be prepared to live against the grain of our culture. For many in the world still, there is a risk of persecution and death for the sake of the faith they hold. To choose the Christian way is to choose the more demanding road in each and every situation.

Where do we find the resources to live courageous lives? Paul is clear that for him, this courage comes from the knowledge of the resurrection of Christ. It is the hope of the resurrection that sustains him in seeking to live a life for others and not for himself. If there is no resurrection, then the logical outworking is to live our lives only for ourselves, to eat and drink and enjoy the present with no thought for others or for the future.

The irony is that in Paul's day and in ours, many do live in that way, inside the Church as well as outside it. The resurrection is not given to lull us into a sleepy life, simply waiting for the gift of heaven.

Paul's appeal is a powerful one: to cleave to the truth of the resurrection once again as a life-giving truth and a strong source of courage and radical, risky Christian discipleship.

God of glory,
by the raising of your Son
you have broken the chains of death and hell:
fill your Church with faith and hope;
for a new day has dawned
and the way to life stands open
in our Saviour Jesus Christ.

COLLECT

113

1 Corinthians 15.35-50

'So it is with the resurrection of the dead' (v.42)

It's not a bad reading for April Fools' day. The hypothetical question sounds reasonable enough. If we are indeed to be raised from the dead, what kind of body will we have. But the question provokes a strong retort: 'Fool!' (v.36).

The difficulty lies in understanding the radical difference between this life and the resurrection life. The latter is not simply a longer or more intense version of the former. There are differences as well as similarities.

The illustration Paul uses here is both homely and immensely powerful: it is the analogy of seed. He continues the agricultural metaphor of 'first fruits' but with a very different meaning. As everyone knows, a seed is as different as can be from the plant it will become. Different seeds may look alike, but the plants themselves can be different from one another and from the seed that gives them life.

So it is with the resurrection body. Our resurrection life will not simply be a continuation of this life. It will be radically different in its nature and in its glory. The seed picture continues into one of the rhetorical high points of the chapter (vv.42-44): a series of sharp contrasts between this mortal body and the resurrection life. A foolish question leads Paul to unpack indescribable mysteries.

COLLECT

Lord of all life and power,
who through the mighty resurrection of your Son
overcame the old order of sin and death
to make all things new in him:
grant that we, being dead to sin
and alive to you in Jesus Christ,
may reign with him in glory;
to whom with you and the Holy Spirit
be praise and honour, glory and might,
now and in all eternity.

Psalms **116**, 150
Exodus 14.15-end
1 Corinthians 15.51-end

Saturday of Easter Week

1 Corinthians 15.51-end

'... in the Lord your labour is not in vain' (v.58)

One question remains before Paul brings us back to the lessons of these great truths. If there is such a radical difference between this life and resurrection life, what about those who are alive still when Christ returns? They will not pass through death. However, they (or we) will all be changed. At the consummation of all things there will be those who do not pass through death to come to life. Still, they will be transformed, in the twinkling of an eye, to be like those who have died and have been raised.

The end result of all of this is to return to where we began: to celebrate that in the resurrection of Jesus Christ, death has indeed been defeated once and for all.

What is the consequence of all of this for our daily living, our ordinary struggles, our perspective on illness, on difficulty, on temptation, on discernment?

The consequence is to build strength, courage, endurance, joy and fruitfulness 'in the work of the Lord' (v.58). Paul returns to the theme of futility and emptiness (echoing vv.14 and 17). The resurrection of Jesus demonstrates that our faith and our works are not 'in vain'. There is point and substance to them. That substance has been realized in the resurrection of Christ and will be realized in the resurrection of the dead. 'Where, O death, is your victory?' (v.55)

God of glory,
by the raising of your Son
you have broken the chains of death and hell:
fill your Church with faith and hope;
for a new day has dawned
and the way to life stands open
in our Saviour Jesus Christ.

COLLECT

Monday 4 April

Annunciation of Our Lord to the Blessed Virgin Mary

Romans 5.12-end

'... by the one man's obedience the many will be made righteous'
(v.19)

This is a dense and difficult passage, an excerpt from a longer argument that begins at 3.21, where Paul declares that, 'irrespective of law, the righteousness of God has been disclosed'. His concern in this earlier chapter, further explored in today's text, is to demonstrate that the saving righteousness of God has been accomplished and made available through the life, death and resurrection of Jesus Christ. The structure of Chapter 5 is shaped round three 'therefores' that introduce arguments of contrast; the second and third of these are included here, at verses 12 and 18.

As the American scholar Dwight M. Lundgren has commented, behind all the complex talk of sin and judgement, righteousness and justification, lies a message of love that makes clear that 'beyond empathy, beyond sympathy, there is identification' (*Feasting on the Word*). Jesus Christ lives his life within the nitty-gritty of the human story; his identification with us is total, so that, as Lundgren says, 'we may identify our true selves in him'.

And Jesus' entry into the human story was made possible through one very particular expression of obedience. Today we celebrate the feast of the Annunciation: the angel Gabriel's visit to Mary and her willing consent to be the bearer of God's son (Luke 1.26-38). It was a staggering leap of faith, and her willingness to bear the Christ-child made possible Jesus' subsequent fulfilment of his Father's will.

COLLECT

We beseech you, O Lord,
pour your grace into our hearts,
that as we have known the incarnation of your Son Jesus Christ
    by the message of an angel,
so by his cross and passion
we may be brought to the glory of his resurrection;
through Jesus Christ your Son our Lord,
who is alive and reigns with you,
in the unity of the Holy Spirit,
one God, now and for ever.

Psalms **8**, 20, 21 *or* **5**, 6 (8)
Exodus 15.22 – 16.10
Colossians 1.15-end

Colossians 1.15-end

'... in him all the fullness of God was pleased to dwell' (v.19)

Today's text is a wonderfully rich passage generally known as the Colossian hymn. It follows the book's introduction, in which the author has assured his readers of his continuing prayers, commended them for their love, and urged them to continue to grow in faith and to 'lead lives worthy of the Lord, fully pleasing to him' (Colossians 1.10).

The writer then encourages the Colossians to allow their faith to develop on a level deeper than that of simple day-to-day living. For believers both then and now, this is easier said than done. Most of us have little difficulty in expressing gratitude to God when things are going well. But how do we fare when tragedy strikes, or with the ordinary routine of everyday life when, perhaps, nothing much seems to be happening at all?

Whatever our present experience, this passage from Colossians encourages us to widen and deepen our vision: to reach out and trust in the one in whom 'all things hold together' (v.17). Like the early believers, many Christians today struggle to connect their experience of Jesus of Nazareth with Christ the agent of creation. Both poles are needed. Our immersion in the life and teachings of Jesus help us to model our own lives ever more closely on him, while an openness to the cosmic Christ exposes us ever more deeply to the divine mystery, which we can never fully articulate.

Almighty Father,
you have given your only Son to die for our sins
and to rise again for our justification:
grant us so to put away the leaven of malice and wickedness
that we may always serve you
in pureness of living and truth;
through the merits of your Son Jesus Christ our Lord,
who is alive and reigns with you,
in the unity of the Holy Spirit,
one God, now and for ever.

COLLECT

117

Wednesday 6 April

Psalms 16, **30** *or* **119.1-32**
Exodus 16.11-end
Colossians 2.1-15

Colossians 2.1-15

'Christ ... in whom are hidden all the treasures of wisdom and knowledge' (vv.2-3)

It soon becomes clear that Paul's urging of the Colossians to a fuller appreciation of Christ is not simply for the sake of deepening their spiritual growth. Yes, he very much desires their encouragement and common unity in Christ (v.2), but he is also concerned with their spiritual protection: 'I am saying this so that no one may deceive you with plausible arguments' (v.4). Paul doesn't at this stage elaborate further, but in his insistence that in Christ the Colossians had been circumcised 'with a spiritual circumcision' (v.11), it may be that some people were insisting that non-Jews still needed to submit themselves to physical circumcision. This is no longer necessary, insists Paul, because Christ's victory on the cross has superseded any need for this distinguishing mark of membership. Stand firm, he says, in the Christ you have received, and 'continue to live your lives in him' (v.6).

We are encouraged to hold fast to what we know and have experienced of Christ, but we are also urged to exercise discernment. Now, as then, many things are said of Christ and taught in his name, and not all will necessarily ring true with the understanding of Christ growing within us. A similar sentiment expressed in the first epistle of John encourages us to 'test the spirits to see whether they are from God; for many false prophets have gone out into the world' (1 John 4.1).

COLLECT
Almighty Father,
you have given your only Son to die for our sins
and to rise again for our justification:
grant us so to put away the leaven of malice and wickedness
that we may always serve you
in pureness of living and truth;
through the merits of your Son Jesus Christ our Lord,
who is alive and reigns with you,
in the unity of the Holy Spirit,
one God, now and for ever.

Colossians 2.16 – 3.11

'... you have died, and your life is hidden with Christ in God' (v.3)

The author begins by warning his readers not to be distracted by externals in their worship (2.16). These are only the shadow and shouldn't be confused with the substance, which is the fullness of Christ himself (2.17). Those who urge the Colossians to abase themselves, worship angels or resort to intellectual showing-off should likewise be resisted. The body already contains enough nourishment to sustain it, and should hold fast to the head, who is Christ (2.18-19).

Paul's message to the Colossians is universal, and equally applicable today. In the practice of our faith, how easily are we distracted by non-essentials? Are we able to distinguish the essential from the peripheral? We will naturally have our own preferences concerning styles of worship, but our main concentration should be focused on those things that *really* wreak havoc: sexual immorality, greed, evil desire, anger, malice (3.5,8) – human traits that we so easily allow into our lives without any hint of self-critique or judgement.

The remedy for Paul's readers applies also to us: to realize, and fully enter into, our divine birthright, for '[we] have died, and [our] life is hidden with Christ in God' (3.3). As the fourteenth-century mystic and spiritual writer Julian of Norwich wrote in her book *Revelations of Divine Love*: 'He is our clothing. In his love he wraps and holds us. He enfolds us for love and will never let us go'.

Risen Christ,
for whom no door is locked, no entrance barred:
open the doors of our hearts,
that we may seek the good of others
and walk the joyful road of sacrifice and peace,
to the praise of God the Father.

COLLECT

Colossians 3.12 – 4.1

'... let the peace of Christ rule in your hearts' (3.15)

Yesterday's concluding image of 'clothing' continues today, as Paul urges the Colossians to clothe themselves with 'compassion, kindness, humility, meekness and patience' (3.12). Such clothing is possible because of God's first love for them: they are his 'chosen ones' and, as such, must forgive one another just as they have been forgiven. The ultimate 'garment' is love (3.14), which works in people's lives to bring healing and balance to relationships, in both family and the wider society, and enables the peace of Christ to rule their hearts (3.15).

How easy do we find it to let the peace of Christ rule in our hearts? For most of the time, I suspect, we're too full of wayward desires and contrary motives to get anything but fleeting glimpses of the wonderful reality Paul was writing about. During a conversation between Thich Nhat Hanh and Thomas Merton in 1966, the Buddhist monk said, 'We don't teach meditation to the young monks. They are not ready for it until they stop slamming doors.'

In what ways do we 'slam doors', and what might be the motives that drive us to do so? A starting point, perhaps, would be to acknowledge that we do experience flashpoints of ego-centred anger, and then to offer that acknowledgement to God. This then opens us up to receive the precious gift of Christ's peace, with its potential to bring healing within ourselves, our families and communities.

COLLECT

Almighty Father,
you have given your only Son to die for our sins
and to rise again for our justification:
grant us so to put away the leaven of malice and wickedness
that we may always serve you
in pureness of living and truth;
through the merits of your Son Jesus Christ our Lord,
who is alive and reigns with you,
in the unity of the Holy Spirit,
one God, now and for ever.

Psalms 63, **84** *or* 20, 21, **23**
Exodus 18.13-end
Colossians 4.2-end

Colossians 4.2-end

'Devote yourselves to prayer...' (v.2)

As Paul brings his letter to a close, he urges his readers to devote themselves to prayer. Three aspects are emphasized: the need to remain alert in prayer; the importance of praying always with a thankful heart; and the vital place that prayer holds in Christian mission (vv.2-4).

Much of our prayer, whether alone or in community, is likely to take the form of petition or intercession; we verbally express to God what we perceive of our own needs, the needs of those we love, and those of the wider community. When we pray in this manner, the pattern is likely to be volatile; it will shift and change as it reflects the changing needs and circumstances of our lives as time passes.

But behind this vital petition and intercession there needs to be another form of prayer: the prayer of silent waiting upon God. The anonymous fourteenth-century author of *The Cloud of Unknowing* taught his readers: 'Lift up your heart to God with a humble impulse of love; and have himself as your aim, not any of his goods' (Chapter 3). We find this simple, silent impulse of love far from easy, perhaps fearing that God won't understand us unless we explain ourselves adequately. And yet it is in this silent communion with God that we feel the subtle stirrings of his love within us, and begin to learn intuitively the direction our verbal prayer should take.

Risen Christ,
for whom no door is locked, no entrance barred:
open the doors of our hearts,
that we may seek the good of others
and walk the joyful road of sacrifice and peace,
to the praise of God the Father.

COLLECT

Luke 1.1-25

'How will I know that this is so?' (v.18)

It's been said that if we don't move forward in our spiritual growth, we don't stay in the same place – we move backwards. Might this account for what happened to Zechariah, when the angel Gabriel visited him to announce the forthcoming birth of John the Baptist?

'How will I know that this is so?' asks Zechariah, 'For I am an old man, and my wife is getting on in years' (v.18). For this question, Gabriel tells Zechariah he will be struck dumb until the child's birth, because 'you did not believe my words' (v.20). When Mary asks an almost identically framed question (as we shall read tomorrow), there is no punishment, and she does receive an explanation, however mysterious.

Why the difference? Perhaps Zechariah, with his priestly background, ought to have known better. He and his wife Elizabeth had lived their long lives in accordance with God's commandments (v.6). But there's also a suggestion in verse 13 that Gabriel's visit was in response to an earlier prayer of Zechariah's concerning Elizabeth's barrenness; and the rebuke is on account of his reluctance to accept God's response.

God's guidance may present as a brightly lit path, or a subtle inner nudge. There may be times when the way forward isn't clear, and we are asked to step out in faith, trusting to the experience God has already given us.

COLLECT

Almighty Father,
who in your great mercy gladdened the disciples
   with the sight of the risen Lord:
give us such knowledge of his presence with us,
that we may be strengthened and sustained by his risen life
and serve you continually in righteousness and truth;
through Jesus Christ your Son our Lord,
who is alive and reigns with you,
in the unity of the Holy Spirit,
one God, now and for ever.

Psalms **98**, 99, 100 *or* 32, **36**
Exodus 20.1-21
Luke 1.26-38

Luke 1.26-38

'How can this be?' (v.34)

God's ways are not our ways, nor are his thoughts our thoughts (Isaiah 55.8). We see the truth of this when we consider the people God calls to serve him in specific ways throughout scripture. From David, the youngest (and therefore, humanly, the least considered) son of Jesse (1 Samuel 16), to Saul, the persecutor of Christians (Acts 9), God's choice of those he calls to serve so often challenges our human judgements.

Mary was a young girl betrothed to a carpenter, living in an insignificant backwater of the Roman Empire. There was nothing in her past that could have prepared her for what Gabriel told her was to happen. She has been specially chosen – favoured – by God (v.30), but she appears to share nothing of those features that many today associate with that favour: good health, wealth or high social status. Mary's 'blessing' was to bear a child out of wedlock (which could have seen her stoned to death) – a child who would later be executed as a criminal. The experience of Mary should remind us that God's blessing has no connection with human standards of acceptability, wealth or comfort, and offers no easy reassurances.

In opening ourselves to receive God's blessings, we, like Mary, are encouraged to step out in trust. Like her, we too are challenged to 'go out into the darkness and put [our] hand into the Hand of God' (Minnie Louise Haskins, *The Gate of the Year*).

Risen Christ,
you filled your disciples with boldness and fresh hope:
strengthen us to proclaim your risen life
and fill us with your peace,
to the glory of God the Father.

COLLECT

123

Wednesday 13 April

Luke 1.39-56

'Blessed is she who believed ...' (v.45)

Today's passage relates the joyful meeting between Mary and her older relative Elizabeth, as together they give thanks for their pregnancies and the divine significance of the children they will bear. Luke describes a very specific timescale: Mary's pregnancy is in its earliest stages, while Elizabeth's is five months advanced. Mary stays with Elizabeth for three months, and returns home a short time before Elizabeth gives birth.

There is huge divine importance in this meeting, but by being so specific about the time, Luke also conveys its practical significance. Mary must surely have valued the reassurance and wisdom of the older woman, and Mary's company must have been a welcome relief to Elizabeth, who to this point had endured her pregnancy in seclusion (v.24) and with a mute husband! This practical reality makes Elizabeth's words especially heartfelt: '... blessed is she who believed that there would be a fulfilment of what was spoken to her by the Lord' (v.45).

What does belief mean for us? We sometimes think doubt is a betrayal of faith, but this has never been the case. Even Jesus had moments of struggle – 'My God, my God, why have you forsaken me?' (Matthew 27.46). Faith without doubt is not faith, but a kind of certainty we can't have this side of heaven. As Paul famously stated, 'Now I know only in part; then I will know fully, even as I have been fully known' (1 Corinthians 13.12).

COLLECT

Almighty Father,
who in your great mercy gladdened the disciples
    with the sight of the risen Lord:
give us such knowledge of his presence with us,
that we may be strengthened and sustained by his risen life
and serve you continually in righteousness and truth;
through Jesus Christ your Son our Lord,
who is alive and reigns with you,
in the unity of the Holy Spirit,
one God, now and for ever.

Psalm **136** *or* **37***
Exodus 25.1-22
Luke 1.57-end

Luke 1.57-end

'Immediately his mouth was opened ... and he began to speak' (v.64)

Last Monday, we saw how Luke described Zechariah's being struck dumb as a punishment for having questioned the possibility of his wife's pregnancy. But I wonder if Zechariah's period of enforced silence may not also have served a more positive purpose? Jesus retreated to the wilderness alone for 40 days before the beginning of his public ministry (Luke 4.1-13). He would also at times withdraw at night between one busy day's end and the beginning of the next (Matthew 14.23), and especially before important decisions were to be made (Luke 6.12). Saul, 'breathing threats and murder against the disciples of the Lord' (Acts 9.1), was on his way to Damascus before his dramatic meeting with the risen Christ. He was literally stopped in his tracks, his world-view upended, and he became for three days, not mute like Zechariah, but blind. He was so helpless that his companions 'led him by the hand and brought him into Damascus' (9.8).

These biblical periods of withdrawal, whether freely chosen or enforced, seem to allow space for the transformation, or sharpening, of the person's spiritual focus. Zechariah found himself more confident as the father of the Baptist (1.67-79); Jesus' closeness to his Father enabled him to sustain his ministry up to and beyond the cross; and Saul/Paul became the apostle of Christianity to the Gentile world.

How easy do you find it to build times of retreat, and quiet periods of withdrawal, into your life?

Risen Christ,
you filled your disciples with boldness and fresh hope:
strengthen us to proclaim your risen life
and fill us with your peace,
to the glory of God the Father.

COLLECT

Friday 15 April

Psalm **107** *or* **31**
Exodus 28.1-4a, 29-38
Luke 2.1-20

Luke 2.1-20

'Mary treasured all these words and pondered them in her heart'
(v.19)

Luke's nativity narrative is familiar and well loved. However, this very familiarity tends to blunt its shock value, as we hear it related again year after year. But shocking it was, and its impact on Mary and Joseph must have been disorienting and full of mystery. This account brings to a conclusion what was promised to Mary by the angel Gabriel, but it does more than this: it also gives us a real insight into Mary's character. When the shepherds came, she listened to their experience, treasured their words 'and pondered them in her heart' (v 19).

Not content to be simply a passive vessel, Mary engages deeply with her experience, meditating on the meaning of the wonderful thing that has happened. As Jesus' life continues to gather momentum, we will learn that understanding, for Mary, does not come easily. When she and Joseph take Jesus to the temple at eight days old, they were 'amazed' at what was said about their son (as we shall read about tomorrow), and there were to be later incidents in Jesus' life when Mary's bafflement was equally apparent (Luke 2.48).

Today, the pressure is for everything to be done instantly, with no real time for thought or reflection. God's ways are mysterious (Isaiah 55.8), but if we are willing to 'ponder' our life-experiences in his presence, we will discover that we are somehow 'plugged in' to the flow of his life and work in our world.

COLLECT

Almighty Father,
who in your great mercy gladdened the disciples
    with the sight of the risen Lord:
give us such knowledge of his presence with us,
that we may be strengthened and sustained by his risen life
and serve you continually in righteousness and truth;
through Jesus Christ your Son our Lord,
who is alive and reigns with you,
in the unity of the Holy Spirit,
one God, now and for ever.

Psalms 108, **110**, 111 *or* 41, **42**, 43
Exodus 29.1-9
Luke 2.21-40

Luke 2.21-40

'Guided by the Spirit, Simeon came into the temple' (v.27)

Yesterday, we were thinking about the pressure on us in today's world to respond to situations and demands instantly, with no time allowed for thought or reflection. Such reflection, as we have seen, was a feature of Mary's life and character, and we see that feature also at work in the two people Mary and Joseph meet when they take the baby Jesus to the temple: Simeon and Anna.

Closely akin to this quality in both was another: the willingness to wait on God patiently, day after day, in hope and expectation. Simeon had been promised that he would not die 'before he had seen the Lord's Messiah' (v.26). He could not have known precisely what that meant, but his long, patient time of obedient waiting on God meant that he was instantly able to see in the baby Jesus the Messiah he had been waiting for (vv.29-32). And the aged Anna, who never left the temple 'but worshipped there with fasting and prayer night and day' (v.37) also recognized the Christ, and immediately began to speak of him 'to all who were looking for the redemption of Jerusalem' (v.38).

The encouragement to wait on God was already centuries old (Psalm 27.14), and remains equally valid for us today. It is not usually a way of instant understanding, but of a slow, imperceptible growth in spiritual insight.

In hope and trust, how much time are you prepared to give today to waiting on God?

Risen Christ,
you filled your disciples with boldness and fresh hope:
strengthen us to proclaim your risen life
and fill us with your peace,
to the glory of God the Father.

COLLECT

Monday 18 April

Psalm **103** *or* **44**
Exodus 32.1-14
Luke 2.41-end

Luke 2.41-end

'Why were you searching for me?' (v.49)

This is the only story of Jesus' youth that we have, and it includes Luke's reporting of the first words of Jesus: 'Why were you searching for me? Did you not know that I must be in my Father's house?' (v.49). Mary has had an awful time – losing her son in the travellers' caravan – and now she is spoken to as if she is not wanted. Simeon's prophecy is already coming true: 'a sword will pierce your own soul' (Luke 2.35).

Luke, however, is revealing the lessons being learned by Mary and Joseph, because they are truths he wants us to understand too. First, Jesus has a natural authority, found in his questioning as much as in any easy answers. We shall see later in the Gospel that this boy who scrutinized the religious authorities begins to teach with a persistently figurative style, where the meaning of his stories tends to hover poetically rather than come in easily to land. Such a conversational exploration of the soul was first learned in his Father's house.

The second truth is that Jesus is *at home* in the temple. Later in the Gospel, Jesus will return there to throw out those who had forgotten it was a place of prayer (Luke 19.45-46). In Luke's Gospel, Jesus prays often. It is the source of his insight. When he tackles the temple traders, he does it out of obedience and love for the one he knows most intimately through this relationship, his Father, and it reflects that early close, but sometimes painful, relationship with those who loved him most in Nazareth (v.51).

COLLECT

Almighty God,
whose Son Jesus Christ is the resurrection and the life:
raise us, who trust in him,
from the death of sin to the life of righteousness,
that we may seek those things which are above,
where he reigns with you
in the unity of the Holy Spirit,
one God, now and for ever.

Psalms **139** *or* **48**, 52
Exodus 32.15-34
Luke 3.1-14

Luke 3.1-14

'... the axe is lying at the root of the trees' (v.9)

I once saw a preacher ask the congregation to move seats. Slowly, and resentfully, they did so, but it took a long and sluggish time. The preacher continued, 'If it's taken so much effort just to change seats, imagine what it's going to take to change your life'.

I suspect John the Baptist would have approved. He preached in the wilderness, and people had to make the effort to go out of their way to hear him. That was the first step. The second, he said, was to repent. This does not mean simply apologizing. It means making a U-turn in life, showing in practic ways that you mean what you say about regrets and the need for amendments. Only in the space that opens up in such recognition can God's forgiveness change the full-stops of your life into commas.

Only Luke spells out John's ethical teaching. John focuses on those who are in positions where exploitation can be too easy or can go unchallenged – those with wealth, authority and power. John is preaching the uncomfortable truth that the social form of love is justice, and that we all need judgement – a reality-check on ourselves – in order to be liberated into lives of integrity. Only by understanding love better will we be prepared for the Lord. John is fulfilling Zechariah's hope that he would 'turn the hearts of ... the disobedient to the wisdom of the righteous' (Luke 1.17).

Risen Christ,
faithful shepherd of your Father's sheep:
teach us to hear your voice
and to follow your command,
that all your people may be gathered into one flock,
to the glory of God the Father.

COLLECT

Wednesday 20 April

Psalm **135** or **119.57-80**
Exodus 33
Luke 3.15-22

Luke 3.15-22

'... a voice came from heaven' (v.22)

Martin Luther King Jr once said that his greatest enemies in the fight for civil rights were not the extremists but the moderates who are always devoted to order more than justice, preferring the absence of tension to the positive peace of justice's presence. It should not surprise us that John, for similar reasons, was locked away by Herod. Bright lights are unwelcome if we are living largely concealed and with secretive motivations. We often remove inconvenient people with the excuse that we are protecting others.

As John's freedom is taken away, so Jesus' comes into its own and his ministry begins. Jesus slips under the water. All the voices from the riverbank are drowned out. He can hear his heart, his existence. He comes up, takes a new breath and then hears the one voice that matters, that of his Father from heaven. It is to this voice that he continues to listen in the years ahead, even when others are louder and more threatening. Our lives take shape around the voices we dance to.

A dove appears, as one once did to Noah (Genesis 8.11) confirming a covenant of love into the future. It is an embodiment of the Holy Spirit, the divine energy driving all the events of Jesus' life described in Luke's Gospel. Luke makes it clear that Jesus is baptized 'when all the people were baptized' (v.21). From the very beginning, Jesus associates himself with ordinary folk by the river and not with the studious religious bureaucrats at headquarters. Through this association baptism becomes the sacrament in which, through Christ, we also belong to one another. For the Christian, water is thicker than blood.

COLLECT

Almighty God,
whose Son Jesus Christ is the resurrection and the life:
raise us, who trust in him,
from the death of sin to the life of righteousness,
that we may seek those things which are above,
where he reigns with you
in the unity of the Holy Spirit,
one God, now and for ever.

Psalms **118** *or* 56, **57** (63*)
Exodus 34.1-10, 27-end
Luke 4.1-13

Luke 4.1-13

'... serve only him' (v.8)

Almost still wet from his baptism, Jesus goes into the wilderness. At his baptism Jesus had heard the one voice that matters, but now other voices come in and seek to tempt him away from this orientation of spirit that gives truth to his ministry. He has been claimed as God's beloved Son but now has to practise what has been proclaimed.

Quite often in the Gospels, it is when people are praising Jesus that he quickly finds the need to go away alone. Flattery can curdle our integrity. We can too easily begin to believe the false things said about us and even try to live up to them. So, here, the devil tries to seduce Jesus by reminding him who he is and what he is capable of. Temptations to misuse power, to follow the way of the world and to seek dramatic status rather than humble service of God and neighbour – these are all close to the bone for those who have an authority that appears unique. The devil knows what he is doing. He also quotes Scripture a lot – showing that mere quotation of the Bible is never enough to get near God's truth. We must always read the love between its lines too.

The devil fails in his attempt to get Jesus to surrender to self-assertion. His last suggestion is that Jesus go up to the pinnacle of the temple and throw himself off to show how the angels will protect him. Not succeeding, the devil departs 'until an opportune time' (v.13). This will be Gethsemane and will result in Jesus being on a cross, not a temple, and deserted, not upheld, by his followers. Even at the end he refuses to sacrifice humility and its demands.

Risen Christ,
faithful shepherd of your Father's sheep:
teach us to hear your voice
and to follow your command,
that all your people may be gathered into one flock,
to the glory of God the Father.

COLLECT

131

Friday 22 April

Luke 4.14-30

'... he has anointed me to bring good news to the poor' (v.18)

Twice in this section of the Gospel we are told that Jesus was going down well with the crowds (v.15 and v.22). It all goes wrong though. By verse 28 they are all in a rage and trying to throw him off a cliff. Why? What is it that Jesus does to our expectations that makes him such a threat?

We read here Jesus' first sermon. Using words from Isaiah 61.1, Jesus spells out God's priorities and how his own ministry is to embody these. He isn't doing this as an egomaniac but as one 'filled with the power of the Spirit' (v.14). Jesus defines the mission of God as speaking good things to the poor and marginalized, releasing the imprisoned, letting blindness give way to sight and, in the translation of the King James Bible, 'to set at liberty them that are bruised' (v.18). The truth may set us free, but before this it tends to really annoy us. The people wonder what's going on, but when Jesus tells them, his own neighbours, that their faith in this God is so lacking, so full of low expectation, that goodness cannot come of it, they turn on him. We often blame those who make us feel guilty.

What is clear from this passage is that, at the heart of Jesus' belief, God desires his people to be free from all the chains – mental, physical, past or future – that hold us down. His heart is with the oppressed, the vulnerable and those whose needs are too easily overlooked. Any group of Christians today need only read this passage to see whether they are really following the man from Nazareth or managers of a self-regarding institution. However, lest we get too hard on ourselves, Luke leaves out half a sentence in his Isaiah quotation – the reference to the 'day of vengeance of our God' (Isaiah 61.2).

COLLECT

Almighty God,
whose Son Jesus Christ is the resurrection and the life:
raise us, who trust in him,
from the death of sin to the life of righteousness,
that we may seek those things which are above,
where he reigns with you
in the unity of the Holy Spirit,
one God, now and for ever.

Psalms 5, 146
Joshua 1.1-9
Ephesians 6.10-20

George, martyr, patron of England

Ephesians 6.10-20

'... be strong in the Lord' (v.10)

The legend that St George was a soldier leads us to this exhortation by the author of the letter to the Ephesians to be resilient in the spiritual adventure we call life. Although some of the cosmology here is not ours today, we are urgently reminded that human beings do actually have a will and that they can engage it, or not, in ways that give shape to their own existence and those of others. The writer is very aware that forces are at work in our world that are destructive and evil – sometimes these are obvious, but sometimes they are very subtle: 'the wiles of the devil' (v.11). How awake is our discernment?

We are urged to find a spiritual strength that will match a spiritual crisis. This is done with the strong metaphor of putting on armour (vv.13-17). The belt of truth stops us tripping up over our loose-hanging deceits, and a breastplate of righteousness protects the heart. Shoes keep us on the move, and the shield of faith stops us from getting a battering when things get tough. The helmet of salvation protects the mind, and the sword of the Spirit slices through falsity and pretence.

It is tempting to see all this as relating only to an individual's life of faith. The implications are, however, that the Christian must develop a spirituality of speaking up for others, while the armour of God keeps us protected. The last verses (vv.18-20) bring us back to the source of Christian life itself – prayer. Without this relationship in place, all our armour would be creaky, heavy or just polished for show.

COLLECT

God of hosts,
who so kindled the flame of love
in the heart of your servant George
that he bore witness to the risen Lord
by his life and by his death:
give us the same faith and power of love
that we who rejoice in his triumphs
may come to share with him the fullness of the resurrection;
through Jesus Christ your Son our Lord,
who is alive and reigns with you,
in the unity of the Holy Spirit,
one God, now and for ever.

133

Monday 25 April

Mark the Evangelist

Psalms 37.23-end, 148
Isaiah 62.6-10
or Ecclesiasticus 51.13-end
Acts 12.25 – 13.13

Acts 12.25 – 13.13

'... they laid their hands on them and sent them off' (13.3)

The church in Antioch was a young church founded by refugees from persecution (Acts 11.20-26). After prayer and commissioning, it now becomes an active missionary church as it sends Paul and Barnabas on a journey. They have an assistant with them, John Mark, whose feast day is celebrated today, and these ambassadors for Christ begin their work of making the Christian faith contagious.

Paul is not mealy-mouthed on his first mission. He tells Elymas exactly what he thinks of him. Elymas is described as being a 'magus', like the 'magi' that visited the child Jesus in Matthew's Gospel. Placing down their gold and smoke may have been them discarding their superstitious show and beginning a new life. So here Paul makes Elymas blind so that his eyes are washed out to see truth afresh. One is struck at how Paul makes Elymas go through the same experience of conversion that he himself underwent (Acts 9.1-20). Luke is keen to show how Christian faith is not so much about opinions and information, and the blather of arguments, as about human formation and lives changed so radically that talk of blindness and regained sight is the only way it can be begun to be expressed.

We don't hear much about John Mark, nor about why he left Paul and Barnabas and got on a ship travelling eastwards to Jerusalem. If this is the same man who wrote the Gospel of Mark, it is humbling to think that this incidental figure shaped the first narrative of the life of Jesus that still resonates and intrigues us today, just as the faith he was learning more about in his heart and in his friends did then.

COLLECT

Almighty God,
who enlightened your holy Church
through the inspired witness of your evangelist Saint Mark:
grant that we, being firmly grounded in the truth of the gospel,
may be faithful to its teaching both in word and deed;
through Jesus Christ your Son our Lord,
who is alive and reigns with you,
in the unity of the Holy Spirit,
one God, now and for ever.

Psalms **19**, 147.1-12 *or* **73**
Numbers 11.1-33
Luke 5.1-11

Luke 5.1-11

'... they left everything and followed him' (v.11)

Only Luke and John tell the story of the miraculous catch of fish, but they tell the story in very different contexts. Whereas John makes it a post-resurrection episode, Luke makes it part of the story of Jesus calling his disciples. Either way what is clear is that the miracle is a dramatic enactment of Jesus' promise that 'from now on you will be catching people' (v.10).

In Luke's version of the story, it is Peter who has the spotlight on him. Throughout Luke's Gospel it is very clear that it is the sinful not the righteous whom Jesus has come to call, but that there must be a recognition of who we have become before beginning the new journey with God. Spiritually, we see by first being seen. We love by being loved first.

So Peter sees himself and repents before being the first disciple to be called. He becomes us, as it were, not least in his later betrayal of Jesus too. Though the beginnings of our faith feel like a honeymoon and can be miraculous, we learn over time with Peter that conversion is a lifelong project. It has all the fulfilments and frustrations of a relationship, not a romance, with God.

Only in this knowledge and stability can Peter later be given the primary pastoral charge.

COLLECT

Almighty God,
who through your only-begotten Son Jesus Christ
have overcome death and opened to us the gate of everlasting life:
grant that, as by your grace going before us
you put into our minds good desires,
so by your continual help
we may bring them to good effect;
through Jesus Christ our risen Lord,
who is alive and reigns with you,
in the unity of the Holy Spirit,
one God, now and for ever.

Wednesday 27 April

Luke 5.12-26

'Jesus stretched out his hand' (v.13)

'Leprosy' in the Gospels refers to a number of skin diseases that were physically and spiritually feared; they made a person ritually unclean and so excluded from worship and social engagement. By being 'unclean' and untouchable, a person with such a disease was isolated into his or her own marginalized and vulnerable existence.

Christian religion has often focused on guilt – on what we feel when we have done something wrong. Many of those Jesus encounters, however, are not guilty; instead they live with shame. Shame is the feeling that *we* are somehow wrong. It comes when people tell us that it is *who we are*, not what we have done, that is offensive. To those burdened with such shame, Jesus gives back their dignity; he invites them to live up to what God says to them and not live down to what people say about them. He does the same with the paralyzed man, getting him to rise off his bed and rise in spirit at the same time.

In order for the leper to reclaim his God-given identity, Jesus must touch him – what everyone else refused to do – and connect humanly with him as a friend and equal. Then the authorities of the day had to certify he was indeed clean for the man to hold his head high again. God's image in everyone must be seen within ourselves, but also recognized in the way society operates and prioritizes. It is incredible, sometimes, what one human reaching out to another can do for them both – and for all of us.

COLLECT

Almighty God,
who through your only-begotten Son Jesus Christ
have overcome death and opened to us the gate of everlasting life:
grant that, as by your grace going before us
    you put into our minds good desires,
so by your continual help
we may bring them to good effect;
through Jesus Christ our risen Lord,
who is alive and reigns with you,
in the unity of the Holy Spirit,
one God, now and for ever.

Psalms **57**, 148 *or* **78.1-39***
Numbers 13.1-3, 17-end
Luke 5.27-end

Luke 5.27-end

'... your disciples eat and drink' (v.33)

In yesterday's reading we saw how Jesus treated a marginalized man, a leper, at some cost presumably to what people thought about him. We may not think tax-collectors are similar to lepers, but in Jesus' day they were equally shunned because they worked for the occupying power and often took money for themselves unjustly in the process. When Levi 'left everything', we may be being told that he left behind former behaviours rather than just belongings (v.28). The grace shown to him, and which transforms him, is worthy of a big blow-out meal.

The radical generosity of Jesus towards those who are disliked or ostracized, whether with money or not, is what any follower of his is called to reflect. Jesus argued that there will always be something surprising and dislocating about such living, like something new and fresh that won't quite fit onto what we already have, and that this is how faith must dare to translate itself.

Like the character in the *Goon Show* sketch who always knew what time it was because someone had written it down for him on a piece of paper, we are easily seduced by our own habits of thought and prejudice, and cannot see where God is most at work. Sin can be a surprisingly conservative thing sometimes.

Risen Christ,
your wounds declare your love for the world
and the wonder of your risen life:
give us compassion and courage
to risk ourselves for those we serve,
to the glory of God the Father.

COLLECT

Friday 29 April

Luke 6.1-11

'... they discussed with one another what they might do to Jesus'
(v.11)

In one of his speeches, the civil rights leader Martin Luther King Jr reminded people that cowardice will always ask the question 'Is it safe?'; expediency will ask 'Is it politic?'; and vanity will ask 'Is it popular?' Only conscience will ask 'Is it right?' When Jesus is approached about what he and his friends think they are doing, behaving as they are on the sabbath, Jesus appeals to their deeper sense of what matters: 'Is it lawful to do good or to do harm on the sabbath?' (v.9).

What strikes us here – and what gets the scribes and Pharisees pretty mad with Jesus – is that this question of what matters trumps any question of what is religiously correct or traditionally expected. Jesus, not the self-appointed guardians of God, is 'lord of the sabbath' and so, therefore, is compassion.

We are told that Jesus looks around at them all before asking the man to stretch out his withered hand. Jesus can see that their hearts are just as withered and unfit for purpose, and that they needed to be outstretched towards human need just as he is doing – regardless of what day it is, what people will say or how angry it will make them. This is not Jesus 'meek and mild'. This is Jesus the *agent provocateur* for mercy and the universal, graceful love of God.

COLLECT

Almighty God,
who through your only-begotten Son Jesus Christ
have overcome death and opened to us the gate of everlasting life:
grant that, as by your grace going before us
    you put into our minds good desires,
so by your continual help
we may bring them to good effect;
through Jesus Christ our risen Lord,
who is alive and reigns with you,
in the unity of the Holy Spirit,
one God, now and for ever.

Luke 6.12-26

'Woe to you when all speak well of you' (v.26)

In Luke's Gospel, it is just as Jesus is winding the authorities up that, after a night of prayer, he decides who to ask to join him. By then his followers will have got something of the flavour of the man and the sort of opposition they might attract. The disciples join the journey with their eyes opened a little to what might come. Courage is the same thing as being afraid, but doing it anyway. We must not forget the courage of those early followers of Jesus.

It is Matthew's version of the 'sermon on the mount' that is readily quoted and more known than the sermon that Luke recounts. Matthew shows the ethical righteousness demanded of us beyond the confines of the law. Luke's version is more radical still. Jesus here calls on everyone to recognize the nature of the community he is bringing about in the name of God. This community is made up of the poor, the hungry, the crying and the excluded. What the world misses and works against, God sees most and blesses more extravagantly. This community of God is a vulnerable, injured and misunderstood group of men and women who have found their home in a love that makes hope resilient and faith possible.

It begs the question of what radical things we must do in our discipleship that will make us poorer, less satisfied, more exposed and laughed at. Jesus preaches that it is the things that make us most vulnerable that bring us closer to the God who shakes the foundations of lazy, fearful and selfish lives.

Risen Christ,
your wounds declare your love for the world
and the wonder of your risen life:
give us compassion and courage
to risk ourselves for those we serve,
to the glory of God the Father.

COLLECT

Monday 2 May

Philip and James, Apostles

Psalms 139, 146
Proverbs 4.10-18
James 1.1-12

James 1.1-12

'whenever you face trials … consider it nothing but joy' (v.2)

One of the many cartoon characters created by 'Mr Men' children's author Roger Hargreaves is the orange, bean-shaped Mr Topsy-Turvy, who sees and does everything back-to-front and upside-down, thereby confounding the right-way-up, straightforward world through which he passes from time to time. Wearing socks on his hands and going down the up escalator, Mr Topsy-Turvy challenges the status quo; he disturbs the equilibrium.

In the opening verses of his letter, James turns his readers' perception of the world on its head by presenting an altogether different way of understanding experience, by setting the here and now in the perspective of the ever after. In James' topsy-turvy world, trials are a joy (v.2), the lowly are raised up, the rich are brought low (vv.9-10), and those who are tested are blessed (v.12).

This is the world of the *Magnificat* where the hungry are fed and the rich sent away empty (Luke 1.53); of the workers in the vineyard where 'the last will be first and the first will be last' (Matthew 20.16); of the cross where foolishness is wisdom and weakness strength (1 Corinthians 1.25).

How difficult it is to understand suffering as blessing, to trust in the justice of eternity when dismayed by contemporary wrongs. Such countercultural insight is a gift of God, and so we pray for wisdom (v.5) that we may be given the understanding that will enable us to endure even the fiercest trial – to travel up the down escalator and find nothing strange in this at all.

COLLECT

Almighty Father,
whom truly to know is eternal life:
teach us to know your Son Jesus Christ
as the way, the truth, and the life;
that we may follow the steps of your holy apostles
    Philip and James,
and walk steadfastly in the way that leads to your glory;
through Jesus Christ your Son our Lord,
who is alive and reigns with you,
in the unity of the Holy Spirit,
one God, now and for ever.

Psalms 124, 125, **126**, 127
or 87, **89.1-18**
Numbers 16.36-end
Luke 6.39-end

Luke 6.39-end

'Why do you call me "Lord, Lord" and do not do what I tell you?'
(v.46)

One of a priest's great privileges is to stand behind the table at Holy Communion and lead the people in the words of the Lord's Prayer. It is often a deeply poignant moment. 'Forgive us our sins', priest and people say, 'as we forgive those who sin against us', and in silent prayers the priest gives thanks for those who are known to have forgiven others, often at great cost. Yet such thanksgiving can be shadowed with lament, as shards of conversations the priest has shared pierce the heart: 'I just can't forgive him'; 'I know I'm supposed to forgive, but...' For priests at such times, the brokenness is not only in the bread but also in themselves and in the people they serve.

Jesus said: 'Why do you call me "Lord, Lord" and do not do what I tell you?' (v.46). What a sharp, real question this is. We pray, sing and speak of forgiveness, for example, but fail to release our friends into its liberty, holding them captive instead in the chains of our resentment. We call Jesus Lord, but we do not always do what he tells us.

The work of doing what Jesus tells us is demanding, back-breaking. It is to dig deep (v.48), to dig far beneath our human impulses, with all their faultlines and fragilities, to the strong, rich seam of God's wisdom. This bedrock is hard won, but it is unshakeable. Dig deep.

God our redeemer,
you have delivered us from the power of darkness
and brought us into the kingdom of your Son:
grant, that as by his death he has recalled us to life,
so by his continual presence in us he may raise us to eternal joy;
through Jesus Christ your Son our Lord,
who is alive and reigns with you,
in the unity of the Holy Spirit,
one God, now and for ever.

Wednesday 4 May

Psalms **132**, 133 *or* **119.105-128**
Numbers 17.1-11
Luke 7.1-10

Luke 7.1-10

'... only speak the word' (v.7)

Although we call Jesus 'Lord', we do not always do what he asks of us (Luke 6.46). Although we call Jesus 'Lord' – the one, that is, with power and authority – we often do not expect him to do what *we* ask of *him*.

The low expectations of the faithful account for Jesus' astonishment when the centurion shows he believes, without reservation, that his slave will be healed if Jesus only commands it (v.7). 'Not even in Israel have I found such faith,' Jesus says (v.9).

How do our prayers compare with the centurion's? Are they, like his, straightforward, faith-fuelled – 'only speak the word'? Or are they tentative, equivocal, calling into question our belief in Jesus' authority even as we name him 'Lord'? The episode's outcome commends the centurion's view of Jesus to us. Through the healing of the centurion's slave, Luke demonstrates what John states explicitly: that Jesus is the effective Word of God (John 1.1); he speaks, and through him resurrection and life are born (John 11.25).

Jesus has been given authority by his Father (Matthew 28.18), and so we can address our prayers 'with boldness' (Hebrews 4.16), confident not of the precise outcome necessarily, but of Jesus' ability to respond in ways that are consistent with God's rule. This is to pray, as he taught us, 'your kingdom come, your will be done', acknowledging both his power and his sovereignty in determining how that power is exercised.

COLLECT

God our redeemer,
you have delivered us from the power of darkness
and brought us into the kingdom of your Son:
grant, that as by his death he has recalled us to life,
so by his continual presence in us he may raise us to eternal joy;
through Jesus Christ your Son our Lord,
who is alive and reigns with you,
in the unity of the Holy Spirit,
one God, now and for ever.

Hebrews 7.[11-25] 26-end

'... he always lives to make intercession for them' (v.25)

During their ordination service, those to be ordained priest listen to the Bishop reading a description of priestly ministry. Amongst the stirring, poetic phrases that describe all that a priest is to be and do, comes this simple injunction: that they are to 'intercede for all in need'.

The priest's prayer is patterned on that of Jesus, the high priest, who 'always lives to make intercession' (v.25) for those who approach God through him. But what is this prayer of Jesus like?

First, Jesus' prayer is unceasing: he prays 'for all time' (v.25). There is no endpoint to Jesus' prayer, no pause in the prayerful communication of Son to Father on behalf of his people.

Second, Jesus' prayer is deeply insightful, shot through with priceless empathy, for while he is now 'separated from sinners, and exalted above the heavens' (v.26), he bears upon his ascended body the marks of human suffering. We see this in a final, post-resurrection appearance to his disciples when Jesus shows them his wounds and, as he ascends, raises his nail-scarred hands in blessing (Luke 24.36-51). These 'rich wounds, yet visible above' (in the words of they hymn 'Crown him with many crowns') act as guarantors that the one who prays for us understands us, bearing our experience on his body and in his heart.

Jesus prays for us unceasingly, with heart-felt, hard-won compassion.

COLLECT

Grant, we pray, almighty God,
that as we believe your only-begotten Son
our Lord Jesus Christ
to have ascended into the heavens,
so we in heart and mind may also ascend
and with him continually dwell;
who is alive and reigns with you,
in the unity of the Holy Spirit,
one God, now and for ever.

Friday 6 May

Psalms 20, **81** or **88** (95)
Exodus 35.30 – 36.1
Galatians 5.13-end

Exodus 35.30 – 36.1

'... the Lord ... has filled him with divine spirit' (35.30-31)

God said, 'Let there be' and there was: a polka-dotted ladybird; a big-dipper dolphin; a chiselled mountain-range; a rainbow painted with watercolour brushstrokes; and a diverse and beautiful humanity moulded, breathed, to reflect God's own image.

As the biblical narrative unfolds, God's hands, which 'flung stars into space' in the playful, extravagant act of giving birth to creation, work more minutely on the sustaining of life, sewing adequate clothing for Adam and Eve (Genesis 3.21), baking cakes for Elijah (1 Kings 19.6) and knitting each one of us together in our mother's womb (Psalm 139.13).

The 'divine spirit' that God gives Bezalel and Oholiab is, then, the spirit of the Creator, which endows them 'with skill, intelligence, and knowledge in every kind of craft' (35.31). These men might be particularly gifted but, made in the image of God, we each have this creative spark within us.

Exercising our God-given creativity is important. Creativity gives life: through our writing, words are rearranged into unique patterns; through our drawing, familiar scenes are transfigured; through our baking, taste-buds are reawakened; through what we sing or dance or landscape we are intimately reconnected to the world around us. And creativity is worship: through it we honour the one who has so gifted us.

Make space for creativity. Take a photograph. Write a haiku. Try a new recipe. Give birth to what is within you in imitation and praise of your Creator.

COLLECT

Grant, we pray, almighty God,
that as we believe your only-begotten Son our Lord Jesus Christ
to have ascended into the heavens,
so we in heart and mind may also ascend
and with him continually dwell;
who is alive and reigns with you,
in the unity of the Holy Spirit,
one God, now and for ever.

Psalms 21, **47** *or* 96, **97**, 100
Numbers 11.16-17, 24-29
1 Corinthians 2

Saturday 7 May

Numbers 11.16-17, 24-29

'Would that all the Lord's people were prophets' (v.29)

If you were choosing the leader for a new, radical movement, you would not choose Moses. Such a leader, you consider, must be unimpeachable, decisive, articulate and resilient, and Moses simply does not meet the criteria. He is a killer. He is beset by self-doubt. He is horrified at the thought of public speaking. He gets so worn out that he fantasizes about the deep sleep of death.

Moses might never be your choice of leader, but he is God's. Untrammelled by a human understanding of meritocracy, God calls whomsoever he will, equipping them through his Spirit, who is like the wind that 'blows where it chooses' (John 3.8).

The scandal of God's approach is felt by Joshua who, dismayed by Eldad and Medad's sudden ability to prophesy, implores Moses to stop them. They are not amongst the 70 elders, Joshua implies, nor are they in the inner sanctum of the Tent of Meeting and yet the Spirit has rested on them. This is not how things should be done! Who do they think they are? Or, rather, who does God think they are?

By way of contrast, Moses welcomes the unbounded dance of the Spirit who shares his burdens with others. Like Moses, can you celebrate God's radical, gracious gift of the Spirit to others, however undeserving they seem? And are you open to the surprising possibility that God may have so blessed you, however unworthy you feel?

Risen Christ,
you have raised our human nature to the throne of heaven:
help us to seek and serve you,
that we may join you at the Father's side,
where you reign with the Spirit in glory,
now and for ever.

COLLECT

145

Monday 9 May

Numbers 27.15-end

'... that [they] may not be like sheep without a shepherd' (v.17)

For 40 wearisome years, Moses has led God's recalcitrant people around the wilderness that lies between slavery and freedom. Now, from a mountain top, God shows Moses the land he has promised his people and tells Moses again that, because of his rebellion, he will never enter this land himself (Numbers 27.12-13).

Moses' response is uncomplaining, compassionate and deeply poignant. He pleads not for himself but for the people who have worn him out, that they should 'not be like sheep without a shepherd' (v.17) but should have someone else to lead them.

God's appointment of Joshua seems a straightforward response to Moses' prayer. The deeper reality, of course, is that God himself has been, is, and always will be his people's shepherd. No matter how great their rejection of him, he remains faithful to them. No matter how far they stray, still he will seek them out, still he will lead them on. So it is that Joshua will be the shepherd of God's people only in imitation of the God who shepherds him. So it is that Joshua will lead God's people, only by following God's guidance as it is revealed to Eleazar the priest (vv.18-21).

Whatever ministry we exercise, it is not, first and foremost, 'ours' but God's, initiated and sustained by him. Human agents may come and go. It is the God of resurrection who works decisively, irresistibly, to fulfil his promises.

COLLECT

O God the King of glory,
you have exalted your only Son Jesus Christ
with great triumph to your kingdom in heaven:
we beseech you, leave us not comfortless,
but send your Holy Spirit to strengthen us
and exalt us to the place where our Saviour Christ is gone before,
who is alive and reigns with you,
in the unity of the Holy Spirit,
one God, now and for ever.

Psalms 98, **99**, 100 or **106*** (or 103)
1 Samuel 10.1-10
1 Corinthians 12.1-13

1 Samuel 10.1-10

'God gave him another heart' (v.9)

Reading a novel for a second time can be an unsettling business. Knowing the ending colours how you understand the beginning, and you fail to be charmed by the handsome stranger, for example, because you know all that lurks beneath his breathtaking exterior. Similarly, our reading of today's passage is in danger of being distorted by our knowledge of the man Saul becomes. Seeing this episode through the lens of Saul's later disintegration into superstition and murderous rage, we can be blind to the tentative young man who is actually before us and the transformation that God brings about within him.

Consulting Samuel on the whereabouts of his father's errant donkeys, Saul gets far more than he bargained for: not cattle, but the promise of a crown, a kingdom. Immediately, Saul objects that Samuel has the wrong man, that his humble origins disqualify him from such high office (1 Samuel 9.21).

Saul is bewildered, full of doubt. Lacking in self-confidence, how will he inspire confidence in others? How will he make an army follow him, a nation obey him? These things are possible only through God who gives Saul 'another heart' (v.9) – an altogether braver, more passionate heart – which makes him, for a time at least, an effective ruler.

God's work of resurrection begins in us long before we die; he gives us new hearts, new spirit, to enable us to fulfil our vocation. The God who calls us also equips us.

Risen, ascended Lord,
as we rejoice at your triumph,
fill your Church on earth with power and compassion,
that all who are estranged by sin
may find forgiveness and know your peace,
to the glory of God the Father.

COLLECT

Wednesday 11 May

Psalms 2, **29** or 110, **111**, 112
1 Kings 19.1-18
Matthew 3.13-end

1 Kings 19.1-18

'... after the fire a sound of sheer silence' (v.12)

'What is God like?' This is faith's most fundamental question. It is one to which we return repeatedly, continually re-shaping our response as we catch further glimpses of the God who comes near to us and yet remains beyond our imagining. Each fresh revelation of his complexity deepens rather than clarifies the mystery of God.

Elijah has been contending alongside an elemental, rain-withholding, fire-breathing God who commands and directs his faithful lieutenant and battles against the powers of darkness. Yet in his exhaustion and brokenness, Elijah encounters not this relentlessness of God, but the tenderness of God who, like a mother, wisely ignores the petulant request of his over-wrought child and, instead, tucks him up in bed, cooks him his favourite dinner, wakens him to feed him and soothes him back to sleep again. And when, finally, God speaks with Elijah, it is not with the irresistible command of a sergeant major but in the silent dialogue of the soul with its Creator, where understanding is felt as much as it is articulated.

Elijah wants to die (v.4) because he envisages only an implacable God with whom he can no longer keep pace. Instead Elijah encounters a deeply compassionate God who enables him to go on living.

Settling for what we have already seen of God can obscure rather than reveal him. Instead, we are to continue to seek him and, when we think we have seen him, to go on looking.

COLLECT

O God the King of glory,
you have exalted your only Son Jesus Christ
with great triumph to your kingdom in heaven:
we beseech you, leave us not comfortless,
but send your Holy Spirit to strengthen us
and exalt us to the place where our Saviour Christ is gone before,
who is alive and reigns with you,
in the unity of the Holy Spirit,
one God, now and for ever.

Psalms **24**, 72 *or* 113, **115**
Ezekiel 11.14-20
Matthew 9.35 – 10.20

Ezekiel 11.14-20

'I have been a sanctuary to them' (v.16)

In Psalm 137, worshippers recall one of the most poignant questions of their exile in Babylon: 'How shall we sing the Lord's song in a strange land?' (Psalm 137.4). Wrested from the temple where God had promised he would always reside (1 Kings 9.3), how are they to connect with God, to call upon his name? This is a searing question that is left hanging as if to confirm the worshippers' fear that, in exile, prayers will go unheard.

Through Ezekiel, however, God responds to such suggestions that the exiled Israelites are far from him: 'I have been a sanctuary to them', he says (v.16). Dislocated, rootless, broken-down, nonetheless the Israelites are not abandoned. The God who scattered them has also travelled with them and has become their safe haven, their soul's home from home, the place where even their unarticulated prayers are held.

At any one time, tens of thousands of people across the globe are forced from home, fleeing famine, disease or warfare. From time to time, even those of us who live in more stable countries, who stay at home, find ourselves in an exile of a different sort – the exile of bereavement or illness or the loss of a long-cherished hope – where singing the Lord's song seems impossible for us, too.

In those exiles God is, for us, a sanctuary within whom we are sheltered even when we feel far from him – within whom we are held until he brings us home.

Risen, ascended Lord,
as we rejoice at your triumph,
fill your Church on earth with power and compassion,
that all who are estranged by sin
may find forgiveness and know your peace,
to the glory of God the Father.

COLLECT

Friday 13 May

Ezekiel 36.22-28

'... a new spirit I will put within you' (v.26)

The 40th day of Lent is now over 50 days ago.

Do the reflections of Lent remain in sharp focus? Are its resolutions enshrined in daily practice or has the old life resurrected? Is chocolate once again in the ascendancy?

Considering these questions, we might feel as frustrated as Paul: 'I do not do the good I want, but the evil I do not want is what I do' (Romans 7.19). Like him, we might feel that we cannot quite subdue our more flamboyant appetites, that our end-of-term report is destined always to read 'must try harder'.

We are called to try harder, to return to this cycle of self-examination and self-discipline, not just in Lent but Sunday by Sunday, day by day, as we aim to shape our lives after the pattern of Jesus Christ. We are not left to do this work alone, however. In fact, holiness is not mainly the fruit of our own efforts but is a gift of God who sprinkles us with clean water (v.25), gives us a new heart and puts a new spirit within us (v.26). Our own dogged pursuit of the way of holiness is in thankful response to God who has already set us on this path and counted us as holy.

In Southwark Cathedral, a plaque to William Winkworth, 'late chaplain of this parish' concludes that 'he fell asleep in Jesus, a debtor to grace'. We are all 'debtors to grace'.

COLLECT

O God the King of glory,
you have exalted your only Son Jesus Christ
with great triumph to your kingdom in heaven:
we beseech you, leave us not comfortless,
but send your Holy Spirit to strengthen us
and exalt us to the place where our Saviour Christ is gone before,
who is alive and reigns with you,
in the unity of the Holy Spirit,
one God, now and for ever.

Psalms 16, 147.1-12
1 Samuel 2.27-35
Acts 2.37-end

Saturday 14 May

Matthias the Apostle

1 Samuel 2.27-35

'... those who honour me I will honour' (v.30)

Are you sitting comfortably? Perhaps you shouldn't be, for today is a day to reflect upon the consequences of a breakdown of relationship with God: Judas betrays Jesus and is replaced by Matthias; Eli, Hophni and Phineas dishonour God and are replaced by a 'faithful priest' (v.35). Each of them dies suddenly, horribly.

When God establishes his covenant with Israel, he sets before them 'life and death, blessings and curses' (Deuteronomy 30.19): life and blessings for those who enter whole-heartedly into relationship with him; death and curses for those who reject him. These are not the dispensations of a vengeful God, rather they are the consequences of choosing whether or not to live in the presence of the One from whom all good things come. 'Choose life!' God urges (Deuteronomy 30.19).

Hophni and Phineas' predicted deaths are, then, the consequence of their choice to have 'no regard for the Lord' (2.12). Turning their back on the Author of Life, they reject life itself and must, inevitably, die.

Almighty God seeks a relationship with us and graciously responds to our lead by honouring those who honour him (v.30). We must also confront the sobering corollary of this responsive goodness: that where, explicitly, we reject him, he will not impose himself upon us, but will pay us the respect of allowing us to live the life – or, rather, die the death – that we have elected.

We have been given a choice. Choose life.

Almighty God,
who in the place of the traitor Judas
chose your faithful servant Matthias
to be of the number of the Twelve:
preserve your Church from false apostles
and, by the ministry of faithful pastors and teachers,
keep us steadfast in your truth;
through Jesus Christ your Son our Lord,
who is alive and reigns with you,
in the unity of the Holy Spirit,
one God, now and for ever.

COLLECT

Psalms 123, 124, 125, **126**
Joshua 1
Luke 9.18-27

Joshua 1

'... be strong and courageous' (vv.6,7,9,18)

The hard part is over, one might think. The years of wilderness wandering are behind them. Moses is dead, taking with him the memories of thirst and starvation. A land now awaits the people of God, a land God is giving them, a land flowing with milk and honey. They have their God with them. They have God's law to guide them. They have a new leader in Joshua. What can possibly go wrong?

This story is written by people who know precisely what could and did go wrong. They know the land will be only partly won – and almost wholly lost again. They are not going to tell us a triumphant tale of glory and conquest. They are going to tell us the cold hard truth of what it means to be God's people in God's land.

But for the moment, there is Joshua. He has potential, but he is not Moses. Four times he needs to be told to be brave. Being the successor of a towering spiritual genius is not easy. He has the promise of God's presence and guidance, but we wonder whether that will be enough to make him the leader Israel needs.

However, the bags are packed and they are ready to go. Well, perhaps not quite ready, and Joshua is not perhaps as strong and courageous yet as he needs to be, as we will discover tomorrow.

COLLECT

O Lord, from whom all good things come:
grant to us your humble servants,
that by your holy inspiration
we may think those things that are good,
and by your merciful guiding may perform the same;
through our Lord Jesus Christ,
who is alive and reigns with you,
in the unity of the Holy Spirit,
one God, now and for ever.

Joshua 2

*'The Lord your God is indeed God in heaven above
and on earth below' (v.11)*

Before we reach the substance of the entry into the land of Israel, we are treated to a comic interlude. It has, of course, a serious point, but surely we do not expect the people's first foray into the land to take the form of a night in a brothel.

Joshua's leadership is still in question. Before he leads the people across the Jordan and into the land, he sends another scouting party to assess the potential opposition. The two spies do not exactly cover themselves in glory; they go straight to the Jericho brothel, have to be hidden by the lady of the house, are lowered to safety on a rope, and spend several days on the run before returning with a positive report that seems to be based on the flimsiest of evidence.

This story does have a hero, however. Joshua's wavering and the stupidity of his spies contrasts sharply with the courage and conviction of Rahab, the Canaanite prostitute. Look at Matthew 1.5 and there you will find her, tucked in among the great ancestors of Jesus, the woman of ill repute, the foreigner who knows the true God when she sees him, who risks her life to help his messengers, and saves her family from death. The potential for Israelites to be corrupted by Canaanites will be an ongoing concern for our authors, but here a Canaanite teaches Israelites a lesson in faith and courage.

O Lord, from whom all good things come:
grant to us your humble servants,
that by your holy inspiration
we may think those things that are good,
and by your merciful guiding may perform the same;
through our Lord Jesus Christ,
who is alive and reigns with you,
in the unity of the Holy Spirit,
one God, now and for ever.

COLLECT

Wednesday 18 May

Joshua 3

'... the Lord of all the earth' (v.11)

'The Lord your God' becomes 'the Lord of all the earth' in Joshua's speech to the people. The Lord, Yahweh, their God, has brought them through the wilderness, but this is a new phase of their adventure, and it is dangerous. On the other side of the Jordan lie fortified cities with determined and well-organized residents, who can be expected to resist any takeover attempt. Before the people can cross the Jordan, they need to know that the God who goes with them, whose presence is represented for them by the ark of the covenant, is not just the God of the desert and the Sinai volcano. They need to know that his power will work in Canaan too, that he can finally deliver on his promise to give them a land.

The path across the Jordan mirrors the crossing of the Red Sea, and delivers the miracle the people need to convince them of God's presence and commitment. 'The Lord of all the earth' has authority over the forces of nature, so how will Canaanites be able to resist him? Only divine power can stop a river in its flow, or indeed, centuries later, still a storm on a lake. Thus is demonstrated the power that divided the waters of chaos at the beginning of time. The Israelites are assured that they are in safe hands.

COLLECT

O Lord, from whom all good things come:
grant to us your humble servants,
that by your holy inspiration
we may think those things that are good,
and by your merciful guiding may perform the same;
through our Lord Jesus Christ,
who is alive and reigns with you,
in the unity of the Holy Spirit,
one God, now and for ever.

Joshua 4.1 – 5.1

'... a memorial for ever' (v.7)

The writers responsible for telling us the story of Israel in the books Joshua to 2 Kings understand the importance of remembering. Or rather, they know the danger of forgetting. A miraculous river crossing is easily forgotten by succeeding generations established as agricultural communities. They will forget that they came from outside, that they are not Canaanites, that the gods of the Canaanites are not their gods. They will forget their true allegiance, and the results will be catastrophic. And they have no excuse, the writers tell us. There is a memorial, created on the day. The Jordan stones prompt children's questions, so that the next generation, and the next, learn that Israel owes its very existence to its God alone.

Although we are told that the Israelites are a fighting force, their actions remind us of a liturgy more than of preparations for armed invasion. This is not a regular invasion. It is a theological step, a significant act of salvation, a time for priests and rituals, to be remembered with words and stones just as we remember with words and bread and wine. It is also an act of witness, a demonstration of the presence and power of the God of Israel.

It is this, we assume, that scares the Canaanite kings. It is not an army on the way, but a crusade, led by the God who can stop nature in its tracks.

O Lord, from whom all good things come:
grant to us your humble servants,
that by your holy inspiration
we may think those things that are good,
and by your merciful guiding may perform the same;
through our Lord Jesus Christ,
who is alive and reigns with you,
in the unity of the Holy Spirit,
one God, now and for ever.

COLLECT

Friday 20 May

Joshua 5.2-end

'Today I have rolled away from you the disgrace of Egypt' (v.9)

So what do you do when you have just crossed over into hostile territory as an invasion force? Temporarily disable every male, is Joshua's answer! If the last chapter hinted that this is no ordinary invasion, now we are quite clear. Scholars attempt to reconstruct the history of how Israel came to be in Palestine, and it is fascinating to try to match the biblical account to the evidence from archaeology. However, we suspect that the biblical authors would not have much patience with the task. They would tell us we were missing the point.

There will be fighting and killing. There will be destruction and building. There will be negotiations and treaties. But first and foremost, there is salvation. There is repentance and forgiveness, expressed in the ritual of circumcision. The Israelite men must be marked as God's. They are not Canaanites, and they must never be allowed to forget it. Past disobedience is dealt with and forgotten; it is God's salvation that is remembered, through the first Passover celebration in their land. These are preparations for no ordinary invasion. They establish the taking of the land as a theological task.

Joshua's encounter with the commander of the army of the Lord is mysterious. It reminds us of Moses at the burning bush, but stops before anything important is said. Joshua is clearly not quite a new Moses, for all we are told elsewhere.

COLLECT

O Lord, from whom all good things come:
grant to us your humble servants,
that by your holy inspiration
we may think those things that are good,
and by your merciful guiding may perform the same;
through our Lord Jesus Christ,
who is alive and reigns with you,
in the unity of the Holy Spirit,
one God, now and for ever.

Joshua 6.1-20

'See, I have handed Jericho over to you' (v.2)

Joshua fought the battle of Jericho, the song tells us, but a very strange battle it is. There is no fighting. Rather there are processions and trumpets. There are symbolic numbers – seven priests, seven circuits of the walls on the seventh day. The walls do not have to be scaled or attacked with battering rams, they simply fall down. Not a battle then.

Jericho is a deeply significant place. It is the first hurdle to be overcome. It is known for its size and grandeur. So around this place our storytellers weave an account not of a battle but of a gift accepted. Archaeologists tell us that at any plausible date for the Israelites' arrival, Jericho was far from grand, and certainly had no high walls to fall down – but that is not the point. The destruction of Jericho sets the tone for all that follows. It tells us that the land is God's gift, to be celebrated with trumpets and processions.

The lectionary does not want us to read the rest of the chapter, but we must. The celebration must not stay in our minds untainted. We move quickly from gift to conquest, and conquest is ugly and brutal. Using religious language to describe the slaughter of children does not help. We must read verse 21, and make our judgement on the behaviour of the warring parties in the land of Palestine, then as now.

O Lord, from whom all good things come:
grant to us your humble servants,
that by your holy inspiration
we may think those things that are good,
and by your merciful guiding may perform the same;
through our Lord Jesus Christ,
who is alive and reigns with you,
in the unity of the Holy Spirit,
one God, now and for ever.

COLLECT

Monday 23 May

Psalms 1, 2, 3
Joshua 7.1-15
Luke 10.25-37

Joshua 7.1-15

'The hearts of the people failed and turned to water' (v.5)

So soon! What has happened to the Jericho celebrations? Surely God has not let them down already. That is apparently what Joshua thinks, this shadow of Moses who does not understand that God must have his reasons.

The biblical historians want us to know about sin and consequences. At the end of their story they are going to have to explain the loss of this hard won land. Now is the moment to begin to teach their readers. If things go wrong, it is not God who is to blame. When disaster strikes, they should look first at themselves.

We cannot help feeling that God behaves a little unreasonably here. Thirty-six deaths in return for one man helping himself to some treasure seems excessive, but the point is made. This is not an ordinary conquest. Everything in the land has religious significance. The spoils of war are God's spoils, and stealing from God is a serious crime. To use this book's distinctive language, it transgresses God's covenant. God has kept his side of the deal by delivering Jericho, but the agreement will not hold unless Israel plays its part too. The proposed solution seems brutal, but it provides a way of getting rid of the offence and starting afresh.

These chapters are not easy to read. They challenge us to ask profound questions about the relationship between this God, who is also our God, and his people.

COLLECT

Almighty and everlasting God,
you have given us your servants grace,
by the confession of a true faith,
to acknowledge the glory of the eternal Trinity
and in the power of the divine majesty to worship the Unity:
keep us steadfast in this faith,
that we may evermore be defended from all adversities;
through Jesus Christ your Son our Lord,
who is alive and reigns with you,
in the unity of the Holy Spirit,
one God, now and for ever.

Tuesday 24 May

Joshua 7.16-end

'Why did you bring trouble on us?' (v.25)

Achan's children have done nothing wrong. Nor, for that matter, have his animals, but they are all killed and burned. However hard we try, we cannot approve. Nor can we escape the narrator's insistence that this course of action is commanded by God. Do we tell ourselves that Joshua has misunderstood? Or that what we have here is something peculiar to the Old Testament that we Christians can ignore? Perhaps better to look for the principle underlying this story.

Sometimes repentance is not enough. Sometimes sin infects a whole community, and has to be removed. We know in our own time how this works. We see, for example, how abused children become abusing adults, and how whole communities can be affected by abuse. In those circumstances punishing individuals is not enough. There must be inquiries. People must resign. Corporate responsibility must be acknowledged. There must be clear signs that the sin has been rooted out and dealt with, the community cleansed of it.

That is what happens here, if we look beyond the brutality. One person's sin has infected the whole community. Someone has transgressed what is sacred and done damage that is hard to heal. The destruction that follows cleanses the community, and a memorial is left, not as a warning but as a reassurance. It reminds the people that God provides a way to ensure that his project is not derailed.

Holy God,
faithful and unchanging:
enlarge our minds with the knowledge of your truth,
and draw us more deeply into the mystery of your love,
that we may truly worship you,
Father, Son and Holy Spirit,
one God, now and for ever.

COLLECT

159

Wednesday 25 May	Psalm 119.1-32
	Joshua 8.1-29
	Luke 11.1-13

Joshua 8.1-29

'... the smoke of the city was rising to the sky' (v.20)

This time there is a battle, and Joshua seems to have developed an unexpected talent for military strategy, unlike the unfortunate king of Ai. Because this account is less obviously theological and ritualistic than the capture of Jericho, it draws our attention even more to the aspects of it that challenge our ethical sensibilities.

War is ugly, then as now. People die. We regret it, but recognize it as part of our human reality. The difficulty here is that Joshua's war crimes are sanctioned, even commanded, by God. We can tell ourselves that the Old Testament writers sometimes misunderstand the nature of God as we know it in Christ, or that Canaanites were wicked pagans and deserved to die, but none of that seems satisfactory. So perhaps we need to consider the possible intentions of the writers of this story. What if they were telling the story for the benefit of the generation that had lost the land and were in danger of losing their faith in the God who seemed to have deserted them?

The Canaanites represent for these authors the temptation that ultimately destroys Israel. Of course God wants the Canaanites killed. It is not the death of individual people that is commanded, but the removal of danger. We are right to judge the actions described in the story as morally wrong, but we can perhaps understand why this particular story is told.

COLLECT

Almighty and everlasting God,
you have given us your servants grace,
by the confession of a true faith,
to acknowledge the glory of the eternal Trinity
and in the power of the divine majesty to worship the Unity:
keep us steadfast in this faith,
that we may evermore be defended from all adversities;
through Jesus Christ your Son our Lord,
who is alive and reigns with you,
in the unity of the Holy Spirit,
one God, now and for ever.

Psalm 147
Deuteronomy 8.2-16
1 Corinthians 10.1-17

Day of Thanksgiving for the Institution of the Holy Communion (Corpus Christi)

1 Corinthians 10.1-17

'God is faithful' (v.13)

Today we take a break from considering the activities of the Israelites as we celebrate the feast of Corpus Christi. We are not, however, allowed an escape from thoughts of violent death. The sharing of the body and blood of Christ are tied to events including an execution just as cruel as that meted out on the inhabitants of Ai, and St Paul picks up some of the themes we have been considering.

Paul draws attention to the Israelites in the wilderness, who despite miraculous food, and water gushing from dry rocks, complained about their lot and generally behaved badly. The Canaanites do not make an appearance in Paul's analysis, but perhaps they are implied. Those who share the body and blood of Christ form a single unit, Paul argues. They become one, and they become distinct, just as the Israelites who had shared manna in the desert should have been a community distinct from the Canaanites.

Death, food and life: these are connected in the story of Israel in the wilderness and their new land, and in the story of the birth of the Church united around a table where the body of Christ is broken and shared. Israel had trouble trusting that God was enough, and so do we. There are always alternative attractions and philosophies tempting us away, but Paul urges commitment: one bread, one body, one Church, one God.

COLLECT

Lord Jesus Christ,
we thank you that in this wonderful sacrament
you have given us the memorial of your passion:
grant us so to reverence the sacred mysteries
of your body and blood
that we may know within ourselves
and show forth in our lives
the fruits of your redemption;
for you are alive and reign with the Father
in the unity of the Holy Spirit,
one God, now and for ever.

Friday 27 May

Psalms 17, **19**
Joshua 9.3-26
Luke 11.29-36

Joshua 9.3-26

'... the leaders ... did not ask direction from the Lord' (v.14)

The Israelites have so far been successful at getting rid of the current inhabitants of their land. With God's help, their winning streak looks set to continue, but our writers know that there were always Canaanites living alongside and among the people of Israel. So they tell us how some clever Canaanites ensure their ongoing existence, albeit with an inferior status. Once again, Joshua is no Moses. He does, however, perhaps to our surprise and relief at this stage, understand how to keep a promise.

The evidence suggests that Canaanite culture was sophisticated, and Canaanite city states an effective form of government. The Old Testament writers knew this. Indeed, they knew that Canaanite and Israelite culture mingled. Jerusalem itself was run as a Canaanite city, and its temple worship modelled on Canaanite practices. The distinction between an Israelite and a Canaanite was not very pronounced.

The key element in this story is that 'the leaders ... did not ask direction from the Lord' (v.14). These writers believe that Joshua was wrong to allow Canaanites to live. Here, for them, the rot begins to set in. Other Old Testament writers disagree; they are happy to borrow from Canaanite thinking in order to speak more richly of God as creator and redeemer. Their differences challenge us to consider our own situation: how might we live alongside and interact with those with beliefs and cultures that differ from our own?

COLLECT

Almighty and everlasting God,
you have given us your servants grace,
by the confession of a true faith,
to acknowledge the glory of the eternal Trinity
and in the power of the divine majesty to worship the Unity:
keep us steadfast in this faith,
that we may evermore be defended from all adversities;
through Jesus Christ your Son our Lord,
who is alive and reigns with you,
in the unity of the Holy Spirit,
one God, now and for ever.

Joshua 10.1-15

'... the Lord fought for Israel' (v.14)

On one level, this is one more story of the inevitably chaotic entry of the Israelites into Canaan. An alliance of kings attacks the Israelites' new allies, and Israel goes to their defence. However, God is now even more involved in the action. Once more readers are reminded that Israel does not owe its military success to its own prowess. The memory is of a day of miracles, when nature itself fights on Israel's side, and the victory is God's alone.

In all our reading of the book of Joshua, we cannot help thinking about the land that is at issue. Palestine has been fought over, infiltrated and invaded throughout its history, and a belief in divinely authorized entitlement to the land has played a key role in that story. Thus the account of Joshua's invasion causes us some discomfort. Although the Canaanites clearly were not destroyed or displaced, the narrative suggests that was God's aim, and we cannot ignore the damage the biblical writings have done in fuelling Palestine's more recent troubles.

At the end of the story that begins with Joshua, Israel loses its land. It does so, the biblical writers tell us, because it has not learned how to be the people of God. The bigger picture is important. Israel exists to be God's servant in the world. Perhaps we now understand that God's people do not need a land in order to fulfil that purpose.

Holy God,
faithful and unchanging:
enlarge our minds with the knowledge of your truth,
and draw us more deeply into the mystery of your love,
that we may truly worship you,
Father, Son and Holy Spirit,
one God, now and for ever.

COLLECT

Monday 30 May

Joshua 14

'And the land had rest from war' (v.15)

Today's reading – and others like it from the Old Testament – might be said to be part of the problem in contributing to the ongoing conflict in Israel–Palestine, and certainly not the solution. For the 'name it and claim it' mentality abounds in this passage. This is our land, not yours. Other, older claimants, can scram.

But read the passage with care, and the themes of blessing and gift emerge that should cause us to ponder more deeply. Everything God gives us and blesses us with is for sharing. A wedding blesses a couple, but is also for the good of society and the nourishment of our shared life in community. A eucharist, communion or mass is a blessing for those who receive, but also radiates out into wider society through the members who are fed and nourished by the bread and wine. Land, when given by God, and blessed, is for sharing. God's gifts and blessings are not for keeping to ourselves. They are not our private property. If we try to possess God's gifts for ourselves, we ignore God's hospitable heart. The gifts of God are always to be passed on. If we become possessive of our blessings, they quickly turn into burdens.

We are merely custodians of the treasures, gifts and resources God blesses us with. All is for sharing, for a greater good. So I pray for peace in Palestine. I pray for the peace of Jerusalem. I pray that any land God gives to anybody will be a blessing to many more than the chosen few who receive it, because like everything God blesses, it was always entrusted for sharing.

COLLECT

O God,
the strength of all those who put their trust in you,
mercifully accept our prayers
and, because through the weakness of our mortal nature
we can do no good thing without you,
grant us the help of your grace,
that in the keeping of your commandments
we may please you both in will and deed;
through Jesus Christ your Son our Lord,
who is alive and reigns with you,
in the unity of the Holy Spirit,
one God, now and for ever.

Tuesday 31 May

Visit of the Blessed Virgin Mary to Elizabeth

1 Samuel 2.1-10

'... those who were hungry are fat with spoil' (v.5)

The Song of Hannah is a dress rehearsal for Mary's Magnificat (Luke 1.46-55). There are very few passages in the Old Testament so directly mirrored in the New Testament. So the relationship between Hannah and Mary's song is crucial, even core, to our discipleship. The message is uncompromising. Scripture can be like that.

What it says is this: the kingdom that is to come, from God, in its establishment, threatens all existing forms of establishment. The old order will be swept away; the new is to come. There will not be a cosy relationship between God's blueprint for humanity and the prevailing powers.

It comes as a bit of a spiritual shock to discover that God *prefers* the company of the despised, poor and the powerless. His love is biased – towards the poor. The message of Scripture is not one in which those who already have get a bit more. God has an eye on the have-nots. Jesus, we should remember, does not have much to say about money, but he does have quite a bit to say about wealth. So, the world is to be turned upside down: rulers toppled, and the rich actually *deprived of* what they have, the hungry fed with 'good things', the lowly raised up and the powerful *dispossessed*. How is one to respond to this? Surely this gospel is too demanding? Brother Roger of Taizé used to reply to just that question with these words: *'Il ne demande pas trop – mais il demande tout'* ('He doesn't ask too much – but he asks for everything').

Mighty God,
by whose grace Elizabeth rejoiced with Mary
and greeted her as the mother of the Lord:
look with favour on your lowly servants
that, with Mary, we may magnify your holy name
and rejoice to acclaim her Son our Saviour,
who is alive and reigns with you,
in the unity of the Holy Spirit,
one God, now and for ever.

COLLECT

Wednesday 1 June

Joshua 22.9-end

'... the whole assembly of the Israelites gathered at Shiloh' (v.12)

There is trouble brewing. The Israelites gather at Shiloh because they suspect they Reubenites and Gadites of idolatry. The Israelites prepare for war, but conflict is averted through meeting, conversation and listening. Peace breaks out; resolution comes; the matter is settled.

Sometimes, we do well to remember that Christian history is essentially about making progress through tense meetings. The great councils of Nicaea and Chalcedon, right the way through to the First and Second Vatican Councils, and to Lambeth Conferences, are gatherings of differences and diversity. These are places where ideas clash, are discerned and distilled, before slowly forming into a rich harmony that is infused with both diversity and agreement. As any parish priest knows, it is no different in the local church. Christians work through differences to find common ground.

Tense meetings can be rather uncomfortable – especially when disunity threatens, as it does in today's reading. But unity is not to be confused with uniformity. Conflict is not a bad thing in itself; it can be creative and lead to greater, shared clarity.

Our churches are essentially long-term projects composed out of committed relationships. 'Church' is not a short-term relationship that depends on full agreement in the present. In communion between tribes or between Christians – and rather like a good marriage – we work *through* conflict and difficulty. Our faithfulness to God, and to one another, sees to it that we eventually find enrichment rather than weakness in our apparent arguments. If you don't believe me, just ask the Reubenites and Gadites.

COLLECT

O God,
the strength of all those who put their trust in you,
mercifully accept our prayers
and, because through the weakness of our mortal nature
we can do no good thing without you,
grant us the help of your grace,
that in the keeping of your commandments
we may please you both in will and deed;
through Jesus Christ your Son our Lord,
who is alive and reigns with you,
in the unity of the Holy Spirit,
one God, now and for ever.

Psalm **37***
Joshua 23
Luke 12.32-40

Joshua 23

'... all that is written in the book of the law of Moses' (v.6)

The Ten Commandments – it would be hard, even in a secular culture, not to find some acknowledgement of their ongoing influence. Even when translated into film and art, the abiding image of Moses-from-the-mountain, tablets in hand and revealing the will of God to the Israelites, remains utterly iconic. Even in cartoons and comedy, there is the sense that these words from God, mediated through Moses, are to be obeyed. How else does one explain comedic quips such as 'the good news is, I beat him down to ten … the bad news is, adultery is still in' (Dave Allen).

The Commandments are part of the rich and direct way in which God's will and purpose for humanity are revealed. What they represent is a distillation of how God expects us to relate to him, and to one another. These are the rules of life so far as God is concerned, the core curriculum for human flourishing. That these Commandments can be numbered on the fingers of our hands gives some indication of God's sense of proportion.

There are many summaries of religious life that are sound. All faiths eat, pray and love. These things are at the heart of all our major religions. When I was Principal of Ripon College, Cuddesdon, a seminary for training clergy, I sometimes talked about the three core activities common to all theological and bible colleges: worshipping, eating and learning together.

The Commandments Joshua hands on from Moses are God's biddings. They are not guidelines, advice or handy hints for better living. These Commandments are simply to be obeyed as God's distilled wisdom for ordering human life and society.

God of truth,
help us to keep your law of love
and to walk in ways of wisdom,
that we may find true life
in Jesus Christ your Son.

COLLECT

Friday 3 June

Psalm **31**
Joshua 24.1-28
Luke 12.41-48

Joshua 24.1-28

'He is a jealous God' (v.19)

We sometimes forget that God seeks our undivided attention. We get distracted easily. And just occasionally, we seek to reshape God's plans – pragmatically, and even prayerfully – if we feel things are not going as well as they should be. We forget, perhaps, that God might have other plans. We come face to face with this in today's reading. The Israelites have become unfaithful to God. Instead of worshipping God, and God alone, they have gone for the mixed economy, the proverbial 'pick-and-mix' that was as available then as it is now.

Joshua calls for order, and for stern reflection. He knows very well that some Israelites still carry a candle for the old gods of the past. But Joshua reminds the Israelites that God is jealous. Like the Old Testament prophets hundreds of years later, Joshua will have nothing to do with the Israelites' ill-founded attempt to reconstruct religion as a buffet menu of options from which to browse, taste and eat. God has given us a set menu. It is more than enough for humanity. It is abundant and ever-replenished manna.

God's message to us is simple and uncompromising. In many ways, that message can be summed up in one word, and indeed it also sums up the Old Testament: wait. Yes, wait. Wait for God's good time. Learn the lessons from the past. Try and see history and destiny through God's eyes, not ours. And stick to what God has provided. Don't try and cook up a religion – and a god – of your own.

COLLECT

O God,
the strength of all those who put their trust in you,
mercifully accept our prayers
and, because through the weakness of our mortal nature
we can do no good thing without you,
grant us the help of your grace,
that in the keeping of your commandments
we may please you both in will and deed;
through Jesus Christ your Son our Lord,
who is alive and reigns with you,
in the unity of the Holy Spirit,
one God, now and for ever.

Psalms 41, **42**, 43
Joshua 24.29-end
Luke 12.49-end

Joshua 24.29-end

'Joshua son of Nun, the servant of the Lord, died ...' (v.29)

Death is just nature's way of slowing you down. Joshua has had a full and active life. Now he takes his rest amongst his forebears. There is something deeply touching about the death of Joshua: the tenderness with which it is recorded, and his extraordinary legacy – all of it beautifully remembered. Thanks and gratitude permeate the grief. But there is perspective too. This is a good death. Joshua makes way for a new future.

When the Israelites come to recollect Joshua, and commend him to God, they remember with gratitude. Just as we might remember those who have kept and held us together when we felt we might fall apart. We do this in remembrance – we recall with gratitude, as much as this might be tinged with regret. But God remembers differently. For when God recalls us, he re-members us in a whole new way. Remembrance is not just recollection. It is also about putting things together again: re-membering. He cherishes all that he knows of us – his creatures and his creation. Nothing is lost to him.

In the presence of death we are turned over to God. And in our loss and grief, we can also sometimes allow ourselves to dwell on the goodness of God – that we are loved by the God who remembers each and every one of us, and can even number all the hairs of our head. But there is more. God gazes upon us with gratitude for the love and service we render to one another. And this invites a simple question. If Joshua was so remembered with such love, and cherished for his service to God, how shall we be remembered?

God of truth,
help us to keep your law of love
and to walk in ways of wisdom,
that we may find true life
in Jesus Christ your Son.

COLLECT

Monday 6 June

Judges 2

*'But whenever the judge died, they would relapse
and behave worse' (v.19)*

The ancient Christian literature on repentance is really quite beautiful –
full of simplicity, humility, and spreading peace. There is nothing in it of
masochism or despair. Those who know themselves to be greatly forgiven
are far from gloomy, but are flooded with joy and deep tranquillity. Those
who are forgiven much, love much. They find it hard to hold grudges
against others; they find it hard to hold anything in this life very tightly. For
the Christian, two things seem to be ever linked: sorrow over sin, and
gratitude for forgiveness. Repentance is the source of life and joy.

Terms from the ancient languages cast further light. The Greek word
for repentance, *metanoia*, means a transformation of the mind,
whereby greater clarity and insight are obtained. It doesn't refer to
emotion. St Paul says, 'be transformed by the renewing of your
mind' (Romans 12.2). We may lapse. Everyone does. But when
relapse becomes a habit, try repentance.

I once heard an enthusiastic preacher say, 'Repentance means turning
yourself completely around. It means turning around 360 degrees'. I could
only agree that, too often, that's exactly what it means (namely, relapse).
This is the invitation set before the Israelites: to turn around 180 degrees,
away from what distracts us from God – to repent. To do so is not to
deprive yourself of something better. Repentance is not some nasty
medicine God makes us take before the sweet milk of the gospel.
Repentance saves us from ourselves and from those things that lead not to
light, but to darkness. Turning to God is always life, not death. And so, we
turn.

COLLECT

Lord, you have taught us
that all our doings without love are nothing worth:
send your Holy Spirit
and pour into our hearts that most excellent gift of love,
the true bond of peace and of all virtues,
without which whoever lives is counted dead before you.
Grant this for your only Son Jesus Christ's sake,
who is alive and reigns with you,
in the unity of the Holy Spirit,
one God, now and for ever.

Judges 4.1-23

'The Israelites again did what was evil in the sight of the Lord' (v.1)

Leaving aside the gruesome death that befalls Sisera – camping can be quite dangerous, it seems – we are once again given an account of a rescue package for the Israelites. As before, they have gone astray. As before, they cry out for deliverance. As before, God sends them a deliverer. This time it is the remarkable and doughty Deborah – a prophetess, judge and warrior. Not a woman to be messed with. She stands in for God here, who is not to be messed with either. Both the Canaanites and the Israelites will now be dealt with, and the normal order of things restored. But here again, there is a need to repent.

Fr Alexander Men was an outspoken Russian priest who was assassinated in 1990 at the end of Perestroika. In his way, he was a Deborah – a judge and prophet, who spoke out for God. He proclaimed to his people that the good news of Christ was preceded by a call to repentance; the very first word of Jesus' teaching was 'Repent'. In Hebrew this word means 'turn around' or 'turn away from the wrong road.' It requires us to *rethink* our lives. This is the beginning of our healing. Repentance is not delving around in the depths of our soul; nor is it about humiliating ourselves. Humility and humiliation are different, and we easily confuse them. But repentance cuts through all this and leads to action – and to new life.

Faithful Creator,
whose mercy never fails:
deepen our faithfulness to you
and to your living Word,
Jesus Christ our Lord.

COLLECT

Wednesday 8 June

Psalm **119.57-80**
Judges 5
Luke 13.22-end

Judges 5

'Deborah, arose as a mother in Israel' (v.7)

This song of praise for the feats of Deborah is a remarkable testament to a woman of might, valour and integrity. Although modern readers might squirm at the details towards the end of this passage, we are simply dealing here with the consequences of ancient warfare. There are winners and losers. Here, the Israelites have had a stunning victory, with a woman at the head of the army. The expected spoils of victory – girls treated as plunder (one or two given to every victorious man), and fine cloth and treasures shared (v.30) – are just part of the economy of war.

The writer even takes time out to indulge in some goading. The mother of Sisera, we are told, was curtain twitching through the window, watching and waiting for her son to come home in his top-of-the-range chariot after a hard day's battle. But he'll never return; the hoofbeats of the horses are not heard. He's been unavoidably detained – permanently pegged down, so to speak.

Yet to dwell on the darker texts of the Old Testament that indulge in war and blood lust is sometimes to miss the point. Context is all. This story belongs to a longer, bigger narrative. It is this: if, like the Israelites, we are resolved to move daily further into union with God, we must be ready for a journey – to face our sins, the things that hold us back, and to let God begin to heal them. Repentance is the way back to God. It is both the door and the path to a new life.

COLLECT

Lord, you have taught us
that all our doings without love are nothing worth:
send your Holy Spirit
and pour into our hearts that most excellent gift of love,
the true bond of peace and of all virtues,
without which whoever lives is counted dead before you.
Grant this for your only Son Jesus Christ's sake,
who is alive and reigns with you,
in the unity of the Holy Spirit,
one God, now and for ever.

Judges 6.1-24

'The Lord is with you, you mighty warrior' (v.12)

Gideon belongs to the tribe of Israel, but to one of the weakest clans. Moreover, for the last seven years, the Israelites have been oppressed by the Midianites and economically ravaged. The Midianites take everything – crops, livestock and all the food the Israelites grow. The Israelites are reduced to growing crops in secret. The Midianites feed off the Israelites like locusts.

The book of Judges goes out of its way to stress Gideon's insignificance; he's threshing wheat in a winepress – hard, secretive work that he has to do for his people, as well as serving his oppressors. Gideon is the least of his clan, and his clan, the least of clans. So Gideon is the least of the least. So small and insignificant, in fact, that he can sneak away and hide his work. No one notices him; he's not worth bothering with.

So it is a surprise that the angel addresses him as 'mighty warrior'. When the angel tells Gideon that they are going to fight the Midianites and win, Gideon is understandably sceptical. The angel knows that the scepticism of Gideon would be deep and rational. We should not underestimate the absurdity of the promise to Gideon. So, not unreasonably, he asks for signs from God, the reason being, I think, that he does not want to raise false hopes. The signs he asks for are not about his lack of faith, but rather his responsibility and fidelity to his desperate people. God can do something with Gideon's faithful care for his people – and so it begins. Gideon does not want to let his people down, and God isn't about to let this happen either.

Faithful Creator,
whose mercy never fails:
deepen our faithfulness to you
and to your living Word,
Jesus Christ our Lord.

COLLECT

Friday 10 June

Psalms **51**, 54
Judges 6.25-end
Luke 14.12-24

Judges 6.25-end

'... let me, please, make trial with the fleece just once more' (v.39)

Gideon wants to be sure that the mission he is being asked to embark upon might have a sliver of a chance of succeeding. Gideon is being invited to pitch his pathetic compatriots against the combined forces of the Amorites, Midianites and Amelakites. He wants to be sure that the angel is truly a messenger from God, and not simply a hopeless optimist. So he sets some tests.

The angel obliges Gideon on each of his tests, but Gideon is still hesitant. He has to commit his puny forces against the might of his enemies. The risks are enormous; the chances, slim. But at the risk of a cliché, he must now set aside his fear and step out in faith.

American pastor and author Larry Keefauver suggests that this story can be neatly summarized: God sent an angel to tell a nobody that he was indeed somebody in God's sight. God does that. God uses those who are small in their own eyes to do great things. The story encourages us to derive our confidence from choosing to see ourselves as God sees us. Gideon saw himself as weak and helpless. But God's perspective on Gideon is different: he is a 'mighty man of valour'. So, we are challenged to see ourselves as God sees us. The invitation is simply to let go of those insecurities that often keep us from enjoying the fullness of God's hopes for our lives. God sometimes commands his angels to lift us up: to propel us above poor self-imagery or those other circumstances that might conspire to grip and shape our minds.

COLLECT

Lord, you have taught us
that all our doings without love are nothing worth:
send your Holy Spirit
and pour into our hearts that most excellent gift of love,
the true bond of peace and of all virtues,
without which whoever lives is counted dead before you.
Grant this for your only Son Jesus Christ's sake,
who is alive and reigns with you,
in the unity of the Holy Spirit,
one God, now and for ever.

Psalms 100, 101, 117
Jeremiah 9.23-24
Acts 4.32-end

Saturday 11 June

Barnabas the Apostle

Jeremiah 9.23-24

'Do not let the wise boast in their wisdom' (v.23)

We often think that wisdom comes with age. Jeremiah, with his calling, feared that he might be too young. But God often uses the weak and foolish things of the world to shame the wise. God likes to surprise us. He starts with young, apparently unpromising material.

True wisdom is not just about great learning, peerless intellect or abstract knowledge. True wisdom is also about character and its formation; it is about virtue. A wisdom that does not lead us into being better people – kinder, more compassionate, just, merciful, loving and generous – is a wisdom of dubious provenance. Wisdom is both spiritual and social, both heart and mind. Wisdom calls us to herself (Proverbs 8.1) and bids us engage in that perpetual process and vocation of loving and relearning.

Jesus is the embodied wisdom of God. God's wisdom is not like ours; it is in a most unexpected incarnation that the wisdom of God is revealed. Indeed to many, this must have seemed such an unpromising and unwise beginning – a cradle in a tiny village within occupied territory, in a distant part of the Roman Empire. God came among us as a defenceless child. That is the invitation. If we can delight in and welcome a newborn babe in a backstreet of Bethlehem, can we not also delight in steadfast love, justice, and righteousness? For in these things God delights. But it doesn't stop there. We are not asked simply to dwell in God's house staring at an image of the Christ-child, but rather to become a dwelling place for God's true wisdom. Let God's wisdom be at home in you.

Bountiful God, giver of all gifts,
who poured your Spirit upon your servant Barnabas
and gave him grace to encourage others:
help us, by his example,
to be generous in our judgements
and unselfish in our service;
through Jesus Christ your Son our Lord,
who is alive and reigns with you,
in the unity of the Holy Spirit,
one God, now and for ever.

COLLECT

Monday 13 June

Judges 8.22-end

'I will not rule over you' (v.23)

Gideon is a complex character. Like all of us, his motives are mixed, and the truth that he knows in his head has not yet fully penetrated his heart.

With the previous judges, after God has delivered the people from oppression, the only further detail we are given is the length of time they all enjoyed peace. With Gideon, it is not so straightforward. The people want Gideon to be their king, but he stridently rejects their request and proclaims the truth that 'the Lord will rule over you' (v.23). And yet, no sooner does he say this than he starts acting like their king. He even calls one son Abimelech (which means 'My father is king'!).

We know that the gap between head and heart can be vast. In Christian ministry this often manifests itself in the need to be needed. We want people to look to us for guidance and leadership, even while telling them that God is king. Gideon reminds us that this is the way of ruin since 'as soon as Gideon died, the Israelites relapsed' (v.33).

Paul says to the Ephesian elders: 'keep watch over yourselves and over all the flock' (Acts 20.28). The order is important – we cannot watch over others if we're not regularly examining our own lives to be sure that the truth we know in our mind is penetrating our hearts.

COLLECT

Almighty God,
you have broken the tyranny of sin
and have sent the Spirit of your Son into our hearts
     whereby we call you Father:
give us grace to dedicate our freedom to your service,
that we and all creation may be brought
     to the glorious liberty of the children of God;
through Jesus Christ your Son our Lord,
who is alive and reigns with you,
in the unity of the Holy Spirit,
one God, now and for ever.

Judges 9.1-21

'... their hearts inclined to follow Abimelech' (v.3)

We get the leaders we deserve. The story of Abimelech would appear to support this aphorism. Having grasped power, Abimelech finds himself leader of a divided people who eventually mete out to him the violence he has used to rule. As his brother predicts (v.20), he burns the people and the people burn him.

Every other leader in Judges is called by God without seeking the role, but Abimelech has always been an outsider. As the son of Gideon's concubine, he has no inheritance rights and 70 half-brothers to keep him in his place. No doubt this planted within him a formidable desire to take what he could from life, by force if necessary. So his rise to power is facilitated not by obedience to God but by ruthless violence.

It is worth reflecting on how we choose our leaders, both political and religious. There is a strong pull towards pragmatism, popularity and outward brilliance. For leaders themselves, there is a strong temptation to plan their rise to status, influence and authority. Yet here, as elsewhere in the Bible, we are reminded that character comes first, and the way we treat family, friends and neighbours will determine the sort of leader we will be and the sort of people who will lead us. We can't compartmentalize our lives into public and private. Character governs both.

COLLECT

God our saviour,
look on this wounded world
in pity and in power;
hold us fast to your promises of peace
won for us by your Son,
our Saviour Jesus Christ.

Wednesday 15 June

Judges 9.22-end

'Thus God repaid Abimelech ...' (v.56)

More blood than a Hollywood blockbuster, more treachery than a British soap, this passage is a sordid mess. Yet in verse 23 ('God sent an evil spirit') and verse 56 ('Thus God repaid Abimelech ...') the narrator lifts the curtain on human affairs to give us a glimpse of what God was doing. Sadly, we are still left with many questions.

We sometimes use the expression 'living hell' to describe situations of extreme suffering when God appears to be absent. To the people of Shechem and the people of Thebez, this time must surely have felt like a living hell. Thankfully, Abimilech's 'reign' lasted only three years and in the opening verses of the next chapter we see God's grace displayed once more as two new judges are raised up to bring peace.

However, it is too easy to rush on to the next chapter. Sometimes we have to live with the questions. Where is God when so many people are suffering? Can we really attribute such suffering to the outworking of God's judgement? Does God judge whole nations for the sins of individuals? Why is God's judgement sometimes delayed and other times swift? We have no divinely inspired narrator to lift the curtain on current events and tell us what God is doing, so sometimes it's best to be honest, admit we have no answers, cry out for mercy and get on with working for justice and peace.

COLLECT

Almighty God,
you have broken the tyranny of sin
and have sent the Spirit of your Son into our hearts
    whereby we call you Father:
give us grace to dedicate our freedom to your service,
that we and all creation may be brought
    to the glorious liberty of the children of God;
through Jesus Christ your Son our Lord,
who is alive and reigns with you,
in the unity of the Holy Spirit,
one God, now and for ever.

Psalm **78.1-39***
Judges 11.1-11
Luke 16.19-end

Judges 11.1-11

'Nevertheless, we have now turned back to you ...' (v.8)

'Sorry seems to be the hardest word' sang Elton John. My children regularly prove his point – and when they do say sorry, it is often with decidedly mixed motives, but does this matter?

The Gilead's dialogue with Jephthah in verses 7-10 is very similar to the Israelites' dialogue with God in the last chapter (Judges 10.10-16). They both presume that they will immediately get what they want, and when they don't, they try negotiation. It could be argued that the people of Gilead never truly apologize for their woeful mistreatment of Jephthah as a young man. As a result, their 'turning back' to Jephthah is more about expediency rather than true sorrow for sin. However Jephthah accepts their request, just as God does in 10.15-16.

Repentance is about turning back to God and turning around our lives. John the Baptist spoke of the 'fruit of repentance' (Luke 3.8), and the gospels tell stories of tax collectors repaying what they have taken. This would suggest that we should worry less about the words and the mixed motives behind them, and more about the turning back and the turning around evidenced by our actions. Next time we find ourselves having to say sorry, it would be worth thinking about how we show this in our actions.

God our saviour,
look on this wounded world
in pity and in power;
hold us fast to your promises of peace
won for us by your Son,
our Saviour Jesus Christ.

COLLECT

Friday 17 June

Psalm **55**
Judges 11.29-end
Luke 17.1-10

Judges 11.29-end

*'When he saw her, he tore his clothes, and said,
"Alas, my daughter!"' (v.35)*

It is sometimes observed that winning the peace is harder than winning the war. This is true of Christian ministry, particularly as it relates to family life.

Jephthah was at heart a warrior. He thrived in battle and he was clearly good at it. Like many Christian ministers, he was highly committed, single-minded in his pursuit of the goal and willing to give his all to winning. This is good, but where does it leave our families? Jephthah's vow speaks not only of a warped view of God's character (did God really require such a sacrifice?), but also a terribly distorted view of his family (surely he didn't regard his daughter as no different from an animal?).

The simple application of this passage is that we should be careful what we promise. Our words reveal what is in our heart – as do our diaries. Yes, God asks us to give our all and make God king over the whole of our lives (the peace as well as the war). However, there is always the danger that we become so absorbed in the battle, so desensitized to the needs of people around us and so accustomed to thinking that 'it all depends on me', that without us noticing, our daughters and sons and spouses go out every year 'to lament the daughter of Jephthah the Gileadite' (v.40).

COLLECT

Almighty God,
you have broken the tyranny of sin
and have sent the Spirit of your Son into our hearts
    whereby we call you Father:
give us grace to dedicate our freedom to your service,
that we and all creation may be brought
    to the glorious liberty of the children of God;
through Jesus Christ your Son our Lord,
who is alive and reigns with you,
in the unity of the Holy Spirit,
one God, now and for ever.

Judges 12.1-7

'Then Jephthah ... fought with Ephraim' (v.4)

How do we view conflict? Most of us want to avoid it, but increasingly in the Church we are learning that there will always be conflict of one sort or another and the decision we have to make is about which of the many conflicts will occupy our attention and how we will respond.

No sooner does Jephthah's war with external enemies come to an end than internal warfare breaks out. Once again we see that his default response to conflict is to fight. No running way, negotiation or compromise for him. However, this internal strife is nothing new. Other judges had serious quarrels with other tribes, but the downward spiral of the book is highlighted as the narrator states that 42,000 Ephraimites were killed at that time (v.6).

In our own time, Churches divide over issues that to the outsider appear trivial and irrelevant. Church leaders write newspaper articles denouncing brothers and sisters in Christ over their 'errors'. We console ourselves that no one gets killed because of such attacks, but we don't always stop to think about how this affects the reputation of God's Church and how it occupies our attention. Perhaps if we were more ready to overlook insults and learn skills of reconciliation, we would have more time to pay attention to the serious conflicts of our world today, where many thousands are being killed in the name of religion, tribalism and nationalism.

God our saviour,
look on this wounded world
in pity and in power;
hold us fast to your promises of peace
won for us by your Son,
our Saviour Jesus Christ.

COLLECT

Monday 20 June

Psalms **80**, 82
Judges 13.1-24
Luke 17.20-end

Judges 13.1-24

'... to him who works wonders' (v.19)

Do you dare to believe in grace? In a book that recounts the downward spiral of sin and idolatry, we are suddenly presented with a chapter that speaks beautifully of grace. However, to readers who know the rest of the story (with all Samson's contradictions), it can be hard to hold on to grace.

The people 'did what was evil in the sight of the Lord' (v.1). There is no hint that they recognized their actions as evil and no suggestion that they cried out to the Lord for help. Yet verse 2 begins the account of how God raised up a saviour.

Much has been written on the subject of grace, but it is still hard for many people to believe that God relentlessly pours out love and mercy on those who don't deserve it or seek it or even appreciate it. The book of Judges invites us, even in the face of atrocities and great evil, to keep our eyes fixed on 'him who works wonders' (v.19). Ultimately, it is not the judges who are the heroes of this book. It is God. When we focus on God, remembering the ways God has shown grace in the past, so we are filled with expectation, anticipation and hope for the future. This enables us to hold on even in times of darkness and struggle.

COLLECT

O God, the protector of all who trust in you,
without whom nothing is strong, nothing is holy:
increase and multiply upon us your mercy;
that with you as our ruler and guide
we may so pass through things temporal
that we lose not our hold on things eternal;
grant this, heavenly Father,
for our Lord Jesus Christ's sake,
who is alive and reigns with you,
in the unity of the Holy Spirit,
one God, now and for ever.

Judges 14

'... for [the Lord] was seeking a pretext to act against the Philistines' (v.4)

The term 'philistine' has come to be used of someone who undervalues or despises culture (in the sense of art, beauty and intellect). However, in this narrative it is Samson who is in danger of losing his culture (in the sense of the distinct identity of his people). He apparently saw no issue with accepting the customs and values of the Philistines. This is cultural accommodation bordering on assimilation, which could easily have signalled the end of Israel as a distinct people. So the Lord acts.

This raises the fascinating (and dangerous) question of how God continues to stir up cultural conflict to ensure God's people retain their distinctiveness. This is not the same as saying that it is our task to stir up conflict, but it does invite us to reflect on our own cultural accommodation. On the one hand, if we are known only for our historic buildings or our annual fetes, then there is something seriously wrong. However, it is no different if we are known only as those who judge others and talk only of sexual ethics. The core distinction for God's people (according to the law) was the concept of holiness and a community life that put the needs of the vulnerable and the stranger at the centre.

Gracious Father,
by the obedience of Jesus
you brought salvation to our wayward world:
draw us into harmony with your will,
that we may find all things restored in him,
our Saviour Jesus Christ.

COLLECT

Wednesday 22 June

Judges 15.1 – 16.3

'... the spirit of the Lord rushed on him' (v.14)

How should we view Samson? Is he a terrorist or a hero, a mass murderer or a servant of God? The question is made more complex by the narrator's intervention. Three times in chapters 14 and 15 we are told 'the spirit of the Lord rushed on him'. Does this mean that the mass slaughters and acts of revenge were carried out with God's prompting, power and blessing?

There is an important if subtle distinction to be made here. Samson's great strength and fighting skill is a gift from God – a gift of the Spirit – but this doesn't mean that the way he uses this gift is right. The New Testament makes it clear that it is possible to be tremendously gifted and yet not show the fruit of the Spirit (1 Corinthians 13.1-3) or use these gifts in accord with God's will (Luke 9.49-50). We may still wonder why God appears to bless Samson when he commits such atrocities, but this is more of a reminder that we cannot put God in a box. God's grace is displayed in the way he showers even sinners with good gifts. How we use those gifts is up to us.

This, then, is a good moment to reflect on the gifts God has given us and how we are using them to display his love and extend his kingdom.

COLLECT

O God, the protector of all who trust in you,
without whom nothing is strong, nothing is holy:
increase and multiply upon us your mercy;
that with you as our ruler and guide
we may so pass through things temporal
that we lose not our hold on things eternal;
grant this, heavenly Father,
for our Lord Jesus Christ's sake,
who is alive and reigns with you,
in the unity of the Holy Spirit,
one God, now and for ever.

Judges 16.4-end

'But he did not know that the Lord had left him' (v20)

The poet and author Lewis Hyde, in his classic work *The Gift*, says that any object can be either a gift or a commodity. The one engenders feelings of gratitude and appreciation and an obligation to reciprocate; the other engenders lust, desire and a sense that we have earned the right to use the object how we will.

In this famous story, Samson lets slip the secret of his nazirite vow and, even though his hair is cut, he still goes out to face the Philistines 'as at other times' (v.20). Up to this point, no matter how often Samson has been violent, selfish and vengeful, God has continued to give him strength. However, it would appear that the point has now been reached when Samson no longer sees his strength as a gift but rather as a commodity. He assumes it is his to use and is surprised to find that 'the Lord had left him' (v.20).

The danger of forgetting that 'all things come from you and of your own have we given you' (1 Chronicles 29.14) is that we wake up one morning to find that, not only is the gift no longer there, but we have lost our relationship with the giver. Gifts are intended to create relationship and grow community. How tragic if we are so taken up with commodities that we lose our relationship with the giver of 'every perfect gift' (James 1.17).

Gracious Father,
by the obedience of Jesus
you brought salvation to our wayward world:
draw us into harmony with your will,
that we may find all things restored in him,
our Saviour Jesus Christ.

COLLECT

Friday 24 June

Birth of John the Baptist

Psalms 50, 149
Ecclesiasticus 48.1-10
or Malachi 3.1-6
Luke 3.1-17

Malachi 3.1-6

'I am sending my messenger to prepare the way before me' (v.1)

They say that there are two ways to try to remove a dragon from its lair so you can steel its treasure. Some knights take the direct approach and try to slay the dragon; others use cunning and coax the dragon out. The same can be true of any problem, including warning people of coming judgement.

The messenger is to prepare the way. Exactly what this involves we are not told, but we can guess, given that the Lord will come suddenly to the temple (v.1); the Lord will be like a refiner's fire and fuller's soap (v.2); and the Lord will judge and bear witness against those who have broken the commandments (v.5). The messenger's task then is to warn people. But there are different ways of doing this.

John the Baptist took the direct approach. He didn't mince his words and he made the consequences of not listening abundantly clear. Through the rest of the New Testament we see other ways of being a messenger. Sometimes it is about persuasion (2 Corinthians 5.11); sometimes it involves argument (Acts 17.17); sometimes it is like snatching someone from a fire (Jude 23). Deciding what is right for any given context and people is one of the primary skills all followers of Jesus Christ need to learn. For we have all been commissioned as messengers (Matthew 28.18-20).

COLLECT

Almighty God,
by whose providence your servant John the Baptist
    was wonderfully born,
and sent to prepare the way of your Son our Saviour
by the preaching of repentance:
lead us to repent according to his preaching
and, after his example,
constantly to speak the truth, boldly to rebuke vice,
and patiently to suffer for the truth's sake;
through Jesus Christ your Son our Lord,
who is alive and reigns with you,
in the unity of the Holy Spirit,
one God, now and for ever.

Saturday 25 June

Judges 18.1-20, 27-end

'... as long as the house of God was at Shiloh' (v.31)

It is easy for us to dismiss idol worship as something belonging to ancient times or primitive peoples. The reality is, however, that we can all fall into the trap of worshipping a particular image of God, rather than God as revealed in the living Word.

The tabernacle, the place of God's presence among the people was in Shiloh. It was possible for people to approach God there and bring their petitions and questions. That should have been the focus for Micah and for the Danites; instead they both try to set up their own 'franchise' and, unsurprisingly, end up fashioning a god in their own image.

Consciously or unconsciously, all of us are prone to filtering out aspects of God's self-revelation that are uncomfortable for us. Our hymns, our liturgy, our Powerpoint images betray our desire for a god who will sooth every troubled brow and bless our every endeavour. We want to be in control of our worship and create our own tabernacle, just like the Danites, but self-made religion will always disappoint. Ultimately, it fails to let God be God and denies the personal aspect of our relationship with God. For in any personal relationship there will always be times when we are surprised and challenged. There is something wrong if we don't occasionally find ourselves contradicted, upset or put out.

O God, the protector of all who trust in you,
without whom nothing is strong, nothing is holy:
increase and multiply upon us your mercy;
that with you as our ruler and guide
we may so pass through things temporal
that we lose not our hold on things eternal;
grant this, heavenly Father,
for our Lord Jesus Christ's sake,
who is alive and reigns with you,
in the unity of the Holy Spirit,
one God, now and for ever.

COLLECT

Monday 27 June

Psalms **98**, 99, 101
I Samuel 1.1-20
Luke 19.28-40

Luke 19.28-40

'... the stones would shout out' (v.40)

I heard this passage read out when I was on retreat on Bardsey Island, the 'Island of saints' off the coast of Wales. It was an outdoor service set among weathered grey stones that formed the ruins of the old abbey. Our retreat group was joined for that service by a hermit who lived permanently on the island, as a solitary and in silence, but she had joined us for the service in order to receive communion. The priest who was leading our retreat had begun a little homily on this Gospel, and was just saying that of course Jesus could not mean literally that the stones would shout out but, rather that the building of the temple itself spoke metaphorically of the glory of God. 'Even these old stones ...' he began, and I expect he was going to talk about the 'silent witness' of the abbey ruins, but he got no further – the hermit interrupted him! 'But these stones do shout out,' she said, 'I have heard them!'

Those were the only words I ever heard her say, but I never have forgotten them.

Who am I to say what she heard in her intense life of prayer, but she reminded me, as does this passage, that even when the voice of the Church is stilled, or falters in its praise, the whole cosmos is alive with the glory of God, and when, at last, we remember to praise him, we are not making up a solo, but finally, and with humility, joining a chorus!

COLLECT

Almighty and everlasting God,
by whose Spirit the whole body of the Church
    is governed and sanctified:
hear our prayer which we offer for all your faithful people,
that in their vocation and ministry
they may serve you in holiness and truth
to the glory of your name;
through our Lord and Saviour Jesus Christ,
who is alive and reigns with you,
in the unity of the Holy Spirit,
one God, now and for ever.

Psalms **106*** (*or* 103)
I Samuel 1.21 – 2.11
Luke 19.41-end

Luke 19.41-end
'... he wept' (v.41)

There is gospel in these two little words, good news especially for a world that is both weary and wary of weeping, a world of compassion fatigue, of frozen tears and stiff upper lips. It is not just the world's oppressive consumer narrative telling us that we should all be shiny happy people having fun; the Church can mirror that same 'happiness diktat' too. Even, and sometimes especially, in church, people can be made to feel ashamed of tears and sorrow. Pastors can imply that they lack faith; well-meaning pastoral visitors can rush in to 'cheer up' the bereaved, and people suffering from depression can be made to feel that the Church of the man of sorrows is no place for them.

These two words blow all that away! Jesus has every cause to weep and so, often, have we. He loves Jerusalem and everyone in it, and he can foresee the coming disaster that fell upon it so horribly in 70 AD. When I was in seminary, we had to try and imagine what the siege and fall of Jerusalem would have been like; now we just turn on the TV. In Iraq, in Syria, in the Ukraine, we see it again and again: cities crushed to the ground, and their children within them. No wonder Jesus wept and still weeps. Perhaps, at last, his tears can unlock ours.

Almighty God,
send down upon your Church
the riches of your Spirit,
and kindle in all who minister the gospel
your countless gifts of grace;
through Jesus Christ our Lord.

COLLECT

189

Wednesday 29 June

Peter the Apostle

Psalms 71, 113
Isaiah 49.1-6
Acts 11.1-18

Acts 11.1-18

'... them and us' (v.12)

'The Spirit told me ... not to make a distinction between them and us' (v.12). Of all the things the Spirit tells us to do, perhaps this is the one we find the hardest. Thank God the Spirit got through on this occasion (even if it was after three attempts!), for everything turns on Peter's bold innovation in the face of criticism from the traditionalists. Without this move most of us would not be Christians. We might be interested outsiders, the God-fearers on the outer fringes of the synagogues, looking wistfully in on an attractive faith that excluded us.

The forces against which Peter made this move were strong then, and they are strong now. How deeply we still depend for self-esteem on judgemental distinctions between 'us' and 'them'. How pervasive still is the false and horrible theology of taint, of guilt by association, that lies behind this desire to stay pure, untouched by those whom we exclude and therefore do not understand.

Perhaps, as the sheet from Heaven was lowered a third time, and he was about to leave his kosher life behind, the great apostle reflected wryly on the way things come in threes, remembering his three denials, but also his three affirmations of the love that redeemed him. So Peter put his best foot forward and included us. Perhaps we might be bold enough to do the same with 'them', 'those other people', our current set of tainted outsiders.

COLLECT

Almighty God,
who inspired your apostle Saint Peter
to confess Jesus as Christ and Son of the living God:
build up your Church upon this rock,
that in unity and peace it may proclaim one truth
and follow one Lord, your Son our Saviour Christ,
who is alive and reigns with you,
in the unity of the Holy Spirit,
one God, now and for ever.

Psalms 113, **115**
1 Samuel 2.27-end
Luke 20.9-19

Luke 20.9-19

'I will send my beloved son' (v.13)

Jesus takes an old story and gives it a new twist, or shall we say that God himself takes a scriptural story and changes it utterly by uttering it, not in words, but in the flesh. The prophets had long since spoken of Israel as God's vineyard, and both Jesus and his hearers understood that he was in some way retelling Isaiah 5.1-7.

But now see the difference! In Isaiah, the absentee landlord remains absent, and the vineyard itself is destroyed, its hedge taken away, never to bear fruit for anyone again. In Jesus's story, the landlord remains fully engaged, and extraordinarily patient. He sends messenger after messenger; he is not deflected in his concern even by insult and violence, and at last he sends his beloved son in a final appeal, in an act of trust and vulnerability.

Even the last disaster, when the tenants kill the beloved son, is not final. The vineyard is not destroyed. There is a promise that it may yet bear fruit for others, but the real *coup de théâtre* is the parable coming to life. Jesus clearly identifies himself as the beloved son.

The story is not over, there is all to play for; even now salvation is on offer, even to those who plot his murder, then and now.

191

Friday 1 July

Psalm **139**
1 Samuel 3.1 – 4.1*a*
Luke 20.20-26

Luke 20.20-26

'Show me a denarius' (v.24)

'Let me see your money'! Surely this is the request we would least expect from Jesus! Just when we've got him safely cordoned off into a sanitized 'spiritual' segment of our lives, he walks into the living room and asks to look into our wallets. In our book he's not even supposed to know that money exists, and here he is asking for a gander.

I'm sure there was shock when he first said this too, shock and a certain shame-facedness, for by producing the coin, they confessed their own hypocrisy. This scene takes place in the temple, and the priests and the scribes should not have brought 'unclean' gentile money there!

Then comes the real question: who is being given their dues? Jesus' famous saying asks us to 'render ... to God the things that are God's' (Matthew 22.21), and we and his first hearers all know that 'the earth is the Lord's and all that fills it' (Psalm 24.1); everything our money could buy, all the resources and labour it represents, already belong to God! Our whole ruse of dividing the world between 'sacred' and 'secular', 'God' and 'Caesar', our 'spritual' life and our 'economy', has been blown away. No wonder they were amazed and silent.

After the silence, we and our money belong to another kingdom, and we honour a new head, no matter whose head is on our coins.

COLLECT

Almighty and everlasting God,
by whose Spirit the whole body of the Church
    is governed and sanctified:
hear our prayer which we offer for all your faithful people,
that in their vocation and ministry
they may serve you in holiness and truth
to the glory of your name;
through our Lord and Saviour Jesus Christ,
who is alive and reigns with you,
in the unity of the Holy Spirit,
one God, now and for ever.

Luke 20.27-40

'... all of them are alive' (v.38)

How often Jesus meets a loaded question with a glorious and unexpected answer, an answer that reframes the question altogether – and nowhere more so than here! The Sadducees' absurdly contrived 'trick question' (which sounds like a re-write of a Rogers and Hammerstein musical, 'One Bride for Seven Brothers') is met with a saying that goes to the heart of the gospel: 'Now he is God not of the dead, but of the living; for to him all of them are alive' (v.38).

Everything is reframed. Our lives are not a private, self-generated possession; they neither depend on, nor arise from, the biology and reproductive processes through which they are expressed in this age. We are alive now, and will be alive in the resurrection because we are alive to God and he to us. He loves us into life, and his love alone sustains us, for in him is life, and that life is the light of all.

These Sadducees who are trying to demonstrate life's termination are standing in the presence of Eternal Life himself, loving and sustaining them, as he does Abraham, Isaac and Jacob, as he does us! He has indeed 'spoken well', for even now the Word speaks us into being.

To know that, and to live from that is a liberation from anxiety now and a firm hope for the future.

Almighty God,
send down upon your Church
the riches of your Spirit,
and kindle in all who minister the gospel
your countless gifts of grace;
through Jesus Christ our Lord.

COLLECT

193

Monday 4 July

Luke 20.41 – 21.4

'... this poor widow has put in more' (21.3)

Now here is the outworking of the radical kingdom economics, which Jesus inaugurated with his earlier request to see a coin. Once again it is physical coins, the actual money, that prompt the revelation. This time it is not a token denarius in the hands of a scribe, but the widow's two copper coins. Render to God the things that are God's (Matthew 22.21) – yes, but everything we have belongs to God, and here, fulfilling the kingdom call, the poor and marginalized widow has 'put in all she had' (21.4).

The measures of the kingdom are not relative but absolute! Our whole economy of differentiation and differentials, of status conveyed in the obscene multiples of basic wages that CEOs receive, all falls to pieces before this simple truth. The only meaningful gift you can ever give God is everything, because everything is exactly what he has given you. It makes no difference whatsoever whether your everything is larger or smaller than anyone else's. Unless it's everything, it's nothing.

This is indeed good news for the poor, and a challenge for us as the rich. We may not, like the widow, be called to put all our money into the one temple treasury, but one way or another, we must find the faith to put it all into God's hands.

COLLECT

Merciful God,
you have prepared for those who love you
such good things as pass our understanding:
pour into our hearts such love toward you
that we, loving you in all things and above all things,
may obtain your promises,
which exceed all that we can desire;
through Jesus Christ your Son our Lord,
who is alive and reigns with you,
in the unity of the Holy Spirit,
one God, now and for ever.

Psalms **132**, 133
1 Samuel 6.1-16
Luke 21.5-19

Luke 21.5-19

'... do not be terrified' (v.9)

When we read this 'little apocalypse', we may well be thinking, 'it's all very well for Jesus to say "do not be terrified", but the things he lists here are frankly terrifying'. There has scarcely been a time between the day he said these words and our own when there have not been wars and insurrections, nations rising against one another and the even more dreadful civil and religious strife that divides nations and even families, the civil and religious wars through which intimacy is broken by persecution and betrayal. Why should we not be terrified?

What Jesus is calling for here is a kingdom vision that takes us through and beyond terror, a vision that meets terror with trust, faith and endurance. We can only rise to this if we rest and trust in that promise of life we heard earlier: the promise that even those who have met with death are alive to God, the God of the living; the promise that, in the final reckoning and new life inaugurated by the coming kingdom, we will indeed find that not a hair on our head has perished.

In light of that resurrection gospel, we can indeed discover, even in the chaos around us, even in persecution, not oppression, but what Jesus calls with beautiful audacity, a 'gift' of 'opportunity to testify' (v.13). What we testify to – what all the martyrs testify to – is the final triumph of Love, the final radiance of a light that no darkness can comprehend or extinguish.

> Creator God,
> you made us all in your image:
> may we discern you in all that we see,
> and serve you in all that we do;
> through Jesus Christ our Lord.

COLLECT

Wednesday 6 July

Psalm **119.153-end**
1 Samuel 7
Luke 21.20-28

Luke 21.20-28

'... your redemption is drawing near' (v.28)

We pick up the threads of yesterday's terrifying discourse and its paradoxical injunction that we should not be terrified, but today we make a transition from 'the bloody theatre of history' to that fulfilment and renewal that lie just beyond time, that moment when we turn from the theatre to Life itself. Precisely because they are beyond our experience, these things are hard to comprehend. I expressed that in a sonnet on this passage, which begins:

Now we begin to contemplate the End
With shadowed glimpses of apocalypse.
How can we even start to understand?
The heavens shaken, and the vast eclipse
Of everything that we have ever known.
Then, suddenly revealed, the power and glory
Once-veiled in symbols of the lamb and throne,
The all-revealing climax of our story.

Although in one sense we cannot understand, we can still trust and hope. If Jesus is unflinching about the bad news, he is also very clear that it is not the end of the story, and the key word here is 'redemption'. We have been redeemed. Redeemed is the opposite of abandoned. Whatever happens in the times through which we live and however time itself finally ends, we have been found, loved and valued at the price of God's own life-blood, and every day brings us nearer to the moment when that value is finally revealed and redeemed.

COLLECT

Merciful God,
you have prepared for those who love you
such good things as pass our understanding:
pour into our hearts such love toward you
that we, loving you in all things and above all things,
may obtain your promises,
which exceed all that we can desire;
through Jesus Christ your Son our Lord,
who is alive and reigns with you,
in the unity of the Holy Spirit,
one God, now and for ever.

Psalms **143**, 146
1 Samuel 8
Luke 21.29-end

Luke 21.29-end

'Look at the fig tree' (v.29)

This difficult discourse about the end of all things, which we have been following over these three days, ends today with the most unexpected of images: not with a sign of ending, but a sign of beginning; not the wars and pestilence, not the desolation, or the roaring of the sea that have filled yesterday's pages, but instead the first signs of spring, the year's turn, the trees coming into leaf.

'The trees are coming into leaf', wrote Philip Larkin, 'like something almost being said' and perhaps we have all had that feeling, when the year turns, the weather warms, the tender new green unfolds, that sense that all this is not only beautiful, but that it means something, it's trying to say something, almost promising something. That even though every spring and summer passes again into autumn and winter, the spring is somehow a sign of more than itself. Even the allegedly atheist Shelley spoke of 'the trumpet of a prophecy' before he ended his *Ode to the West Wind* with 'If Winter comes, can Spring be far behind?' Today's gospel confirms his intuition; the fig tree and all the trees are telling us something. The sonnet whose opening I gave you yesterday ends like this:

> You bid us, in the visions that you bring,
> To see the world's end as a sign of spring.

Creator God,
you made us all in your image:
may we discern you in all that we see,
and serve you in all that we do;
through Jesus Christ our Lord.

COLLECT

197

Friday 8 July

Luke 22.1-13

'... a man carrying a jar of water' (v.10)

The arrangements for this momentous Passover meal are fascinating and mysterious in equal measure. Mysterious in that they reveal a prior knowledge of events down to the smallest detail, down to the apparently chance-met stranger and what he carries. Fascinating because they reveal to us, and to Jesus' band of Galilean disciples, that we are not the only people with whom he has to do, not the only people who serve him. For the disciples, the whole journey to Jerusalem was in one sense a journey into hostile territory. Of course, Jerusalem was the venerated and holy city, a time-honoured place of pilgrimage, but it was also the stronghold of the Sanhedrin on the one hand, and the Roman occupiers on the other, both of whom were seeking to destroy Jesus and his followers.

Yet here is Jesus, casually telling them that he has other friends, other disciples, of whom they know nothing, right here in the city, people who are ready to receive him, who have even prepared a room.

It's so easy to divide the world into 'us' and 'them', to be hostile and suspicious towards those who don't belong to our group, to try and protect 'our Jesus' from the ideas and influence of outsiders. Yet Jesus himself has no such worries; he is always slipping through our ecclesial and doctrinal cordons and making friends in unexpected places. Maybe we should do the same.

COLLECT

Merciful God,
you have prepared for those who love you
such good things as pass our understanding:
pour into our hearts such love toward you
that we, loving you in all things and above all things,
may obtain your promises,
which exceed all that we can desire;
through Jesus Christ your Son our Lord,
who is alive and reigns with you,
in the unity of the Holy Spirit,
one God, now and for ever.

Psalm **147**
1 Samuel 9.15 – 10.1
Luke 22.14-23

Luke 22.14-23

'... he broke it and gave it to them' (v.19)

We will never come to the end of the mystery unfolded here, and it will take a lifetime of communion to have been even for a moment as utterly present to Christ as he is to us in this sacrament. He is present in our brokenness, even as the bread is broken; present when we feel our woundedness, even as the wine is poured like blood; present in our thankfulness, even as he give thanks; present in our joyfulness, even as he lifts the fruit of the vine, 'wine to gladden our hearts' (Psalm 104.16).

However, he is also present, to and in, and through our betrayals, for he invites his betrayer also to this table, and shares the bread and wine also with him. There is dark mystery here. 'Woe to that one by whom he is betrayed!' and yet 'it has been determined' (v.22).

None of us can be fully privy to what passes between Christ and Judas; we have enough to do to understand our own communion with him, our own recoveries from betrayal. But I think the gospel in its fullness entitles us to hope. What was Christ doing when he descended into hell? Perhaps he was looking for Judas in all his woe, so that he too could recover, like Peter, like the thief on the cross, and come with them to drink the wine, new with Christ, in the kingdom.

Creator God,
you made us all in your image:
may we discern you in all that we see,
and serve you in all that we do;
through Jesus Christ our Lord.

COLLECT

Monday 11 July

Psalms 1, 2, 3
1 Samuel 10.1-16
Luke 22.24-30

Psalm 1

'... but their delight is in the law of the Lord' (v2)

Our world is not short of words. Television, radio, newspapers, books, magazines, all compounded by Twitter and Facebook, mean we're never short of discourse. It's probably true to say that in our interactions with others, much of what we listen to, or say, is pretty meaningless. It's chatter, small talk, observations about the weather or the latest episode of our favourite soap opera. These oil the building of relationships but give us little really to ponder. 'Twitter' is, in truth, a rather accurate description.

Not so the law of the Lord. The word *torah* (law) comes from a verb that means to throw something so that it hits its target – not unlike a spear. The word of God is far from meaningless chatter. It's aimed, directional, targeted. The word of God pierces our hearts and minds and takes root, transforming us into the likeness of the one from whom it came.

But the word of God can only hit its target and do this transformational work if we deliberately put ourselves in its way, if we take such delight in God's chosen way of communicating with us that we do far more than simply study it as an intellectual exercise. Instead we're called to *meditate* on the word of God. To chew it over. To commit it to memory. To ponder it. To allow it to change us. Perhaps today's psalm is calling us to rediscover our *delight* in the law of the Lord.

Lord of all power and might,
the author and giver of all good things:
graft in our hearts the love of your name,
increase in us true religion,
nourish us with all goodness,
and of your great mercy keep us in the same;
through Jesus Christ your Son our Lord,
who is alive and reigns with you,
in the unity of the Holy Spirit,
one God, now and for ever.

Psalms **5**, 6 (8)
1 Samuel 10.17-end
Luke 22.31-38

Psalm 5

'For there is no truth in their mouth' (v.9)

It's easy to think we're the first generation of Christians to be told that our faith is irrelevant; the first generation to be undermined by the secular world seemingly going about its business and leaving us behind; the first to be told that faith has no place in the modern world and churchgoing is in terminal decline. The newspapers tell us this on almost a daily basis. It's easy to feel 'persecuted' (though few of us have ever actually been on the receiving end of true persecution).

Yet here is the centuries old psalmist praying to God for protection against lies and deception. We all grew up realizing that there was little truth in the old nursery rhyme: 'sticks and stones may break our bones, but words can never harm us'. Words can be used as weapons to undermine, to discourage, to inflict pain as sharp as a physical hurt, to cause us to lose confidence in ourselves and in our faith.

So how do we remain steadfast, calm, focused, when surrounded by those who would insist we're irrelevant and misguided? The psalmist brings us back to basics. He begins each day by asking God for protection and then steps out believing he is covered 'as with a shield' (v.14).

We can do no better than to pray each day for protection against verbal violence and then to go about our business, calm and confident, rejoicing in our faith. That way we become much more attractive witnesses, surely, than if we present ourselves as fearful, defensive Christians, forever complaining of being mistreated.

Generous God,
you give us gifts and make them grow:
though our faith is small as mustard seed,
make it grow to your glory
and the flourishing of your kingdom;
through Jesus Christ our Lord.

COLLECT

Wednesday 13 July

Psalm 119.1-32

'With my whole heart have I sought you' (v.10)

Today we read just the first 32 verses of the longest psalm in the Bible in order not to be late for whatever we're doing next, but these first few verses give us a flavour of the psalm as a whole. Some commentators have described it as 'terrible poetry' but for others, this psalm has proved to be treasured daily food for prayer.

Perhaps Psalm 119 can be summed up as a celebration of God's authoritative word, revealed to us through the Scriptures, in which we can have complete confidence and through which we can learn to trust God and discover how to live a life that reflects something of our Creator.

What shines through this psalm is the psalmist's *passion* for God's word. He doesn't read the Scriptures out of a sense of duty, or because he made an ordination or Confirmation promise to do so. He reads the Scriptures because he wants to know and understand and be fed by God's word – and he wants this with every ounce of his being.

How passionately do we care about God's word revealed to us through the Scriptures? Do we read out of a sense of duty, or with a real hunger for knowing more of God and learning God's ways? If our reading has become a little stale and 'routine', perhaps today we're being called to ask God to renew our passion for his word.

COLLECT

Lord of all power and might,
the author and giver of all good things:
graft in our hearts the love of your name,
increase in us true religion,
nourish us with all goodness,
and of your great mercy keep us in the same;
through Jesus Christ your Son our Lord,
who is alive and reigns with you,
in the unity of the Holy Spirit,
one God, now and for ever.

Psalms 14, **15**, 16
I Samuel 12
Luke 22.47-62

Psalm 15

'Lord, who may dwell in your tabernacle?' (v.1)

At first sight, this is a tricky psalm for those of us who know that we don't lead 'an uncorrupt life' (v.2). In fact, reading through the list of requirements for those who may enter God's presence, there can't be many of us who feel we qualify. And if anyone thinks they are always blameless, always do what is right, always speak the truth, never gossip, never blame others, we might be tempted to believe they are deluding themselves.

Fortunately, the psalm should not be interpreted legalistically. Ultimately we may only approach God through the death and resurrection of Jesus. But if Psalm 15 pulls us up short, pricks our consciences and makes us think, then all well and good. Sometimes it's all too easy to come crashing into God's presence with our list of intercessions and demands. Psalm 15 shouts 'Halt'! Before entering God's presence, we're asked to remember the holiness of God. We're called to pay service to him not just with our lips, but with our lives; not just with our words but with our actions.

Psalm 15 might be a good tool for self-examination before we present ourselves in Church each week. Are we guilty of crashing thoughtlessly into God's presence? How well do we prepare before receiving Holy Communion? This psalm is a reminder that our work and our walk are as important to God as our words when we come into his presence to worship him.

Generous God,
you give us gifts and make them grow:
though our faith is small as mustard seed,
make it grow to your glory
and the flourishing of your kingdom;
through Jesus Christ our Lord.

COLLECT

Ordinary Time

Friday 15 July

Psalm 19

'The heavens are telling the glory of God' (v.1)

We have every reason to be thankful for the producers of television programmes about the universe. They encourage us to turn our light-polluted city eyes back to the wonders of the star-lit heavens and cause us to be reminded of the vastness of the universe. It's a salutary lesson to be reminded of our relative insignificance.

The eminent scientist, Stephen Hawking, has dismissed God out of hand when postulating the origin of the cosmos. He has declared that his work shows there was no creator of the starry skies. Other scientists are less dismissive, recognizing that we still can't know for sure how the universe began.

No such ambivalence for the psalmist. As he watches the moon wane and the sun rise, he marvels at the wonder and beauty of creation, and lifts his heart to the Creator in praise and worship.

It's all too easy for the cares and troubles of daily life to cause us to become earthbound, eyes down, shoulders slumped, weighed down by the minutiae of our every waking hour. Perhaps we should resolve at least once a day, even in the concrete jungles of our cities, to take time out to lift up our eyes and to wonder at the vastness of creation. And then to praise the creator who cares for every hair on our tiny heads. Our troubles may seem not quite so significant in the context of eternity.

COLLECT

Lord of all power and might,
the author and giver of all good things:
graft in our hearts the love of your name,
increase in us true religion,
nourish us with all goodness,
and of your great mercy keep us in the same;
through Jesus Christ your Son our Lord,
who is alive and reigns with you,
in the unity of the Holy Spirit,
one God, now and for ever.

Psalms 20, 21, **23**
1 Samuel 13.19 – 14.15
Luke 23.1-12

Saturday 16 July

Psalm 23

'Though I walk through the valley of the shadow of death' (v.4)

Psalm 23 is quite possibly the best-known and best-loved passage of Scripture in the whole world, and for good reason. The imagery is profound, beautiful and timeless – faithful shepherd, green pastures, still waters, full table, anointing oil. Christian minds are immediately fast-tracked to Jesus, the Good Shepherd (John 10.11) who lays down his life for his sheep and who leaves the flock in order to seek out a single lost lamb. We know through this psalm and its gentle pastoral imagery that we are loved beyond measure.

The psalm isn't all sweetness and light, however. In verse 4 we are confronted by 'the valley of the shadow of death', and in verse 5 the presence of enemies is taken as given.

Anyone who has ever had the experience of an MRI scan, used in hospitals to detect a number of conditions including cancer, will have an understanding of what it might feel like to walk through the valley of the shadow of death. Closeted in a small white metal tunnel with only the clicks and bangs of the machinery for company, and knowing that the prognosis might not be good, the words of this psalm become very real indeed. But so does the confidence that comes with singing them out loud, even if it alarms the radiographers.

Our faith in God and our trust in his promises to bring us through even the valley of the shadow of death can give us the confidence to face the toughest of situations with calm and peace.

Generous God,
you give us gifts and make them grow:
though our faith is small as mustard seed,
make it grow to your glory
and the flourishing of your kingdom;
through Jesus Christ our Lord.

COLLECT

Psalm 30

'You have turned my mourning into dancing' (v.11)

At first sight, Psalm 30 is a song of thanksgiving for healing following a serious illness. The psalmist describes facing the possibility of his own death. Suddenly his easy confidence in God is challenged. He turns back to God and begs for forgiveness and healing, and as his health and vitality return, his relief and thanksgiving are expressed in song and dance.

It comes as something of a surprise then to see that the heading for this psalm in many English translations is 'A Song at the dedication of the temple'. The story attributed to an individual is in fact the story of a community. They have become complacent. They are spiritually dead. They call to God for help. He restores their life. They respond with singing and dancing. It is the story of the Christian life. It is the story of the Church.

In some churches, Christ's redeeming death and resurrection are well and truly celebrated. In others, the worship is dull and dreary – a little like wading through treacle. Where does the difference lie? In the joyful churches, each individual Christian celebrates their being restored to life from death. They follow the readings attentively, pray rather than listen to the intercessions, sing the hymns with a heartfelt passion, and the church is lifted up with praise.

Perhaps the solution for a seemingly dead church is for each individual to be helped to see just exactly what God in Christ has done for them so that with the psalmist they may sing, 'He did this for *me*.'

COLLECT

Almighty Lord and everlasting God,
we beseech you to direct, sanctify and govern
    both our hearts and bodies
in the ways of your laws
    and the works of your commandments;
that through your most mighty protection, both here and ever,
we may be preserved in body and soul;
through our Lord and Saviour Jesus Christ,
who is alive and reigns with you,
in the unity of the Holy Spirit,
one God, now and for ever.

Psalms 32, **36**
1 Samuel 15.1-23
Luke 23.26-43

Psalm 36

'There are they fallen, all who work wickedness' (v12)

Suicide bombers enter a school and gun down young children and their teachers. A vulnerable, elderly man is robbed at knifepoint in his own home. Teenage girls are kidnapped and trafficked. Yet another trusted teacher is arrested for downloading child pornography. 'There is no fear of God before their eyes' (v.1).

It's easy to despair. We live in a world that at times seems very dark indeed. The psalmist is not slow to point out that human beings without God are in a bad way, stumbling around, deaf and blind to the chaos they are wreaking.

People of faith – true faith in a God of goodness, mercy and light – need to speak up. This is *not* what God wants. Our God is a God of righteousness, faithfulness, steadfast love (vv.5-6). Even when it seems as if the flickering light of our faith is about to be extinguished completely by the darkness around us, we are called to stand firm and to witness to a God who draws close to those who are suffering, and who ultimately will be judge of all.

The psalmist encourages us to continue to worship the one whose righteousness is mountain high and whose judgements are seabed deep. And in worship to make real today the future promise of vindication when the 'foot of pride' (v.11) will no longer have force and the 'hand of the ungodly' will be stopped. 'Amen. Come, Lord Jesus.' (Revelation 22.20)

Lord God,
your Son left the riches of heaven
and became poor for our sake:
when we prosper save us from pride,
when we are needy save us from despair,
that we may trust in you alone;
through Jesus Christ our Lord.

COLLECT

Wednesday 20 July

Psalm **34**
I Samuel 16
Luke 23.44-56*a*

Psalm 34

'His praise shall ever be in my mouth' (v.1)

The psalmist begins confidently: 'I will bless the Lord at all times; his praise shall ever be in my mouth' (v.1). Blessing and praising God are straightforward when life is jogging along nicely. It's easy to have a thankful heart and to trust in God's promises when everything is good and we have nothing much to disturb us.

However, the psalmist is encouraging us to bless the Lord 'at all times'. To have 'his praise ever in my mouth'. To bless and praise the Lord when facing serious illness. To bless and praise the Lord in the depths of bereavement. To bless and praise the Lord when all around us seems dark and hopeless. To bless and praise the Lord when we've been let down and betrayed.

The psalmist reminds us that even in our very darkest moments, the Lord is 'near to the broken-hearted and will save those who are crushed in spirit' (v.18). So we bless and praise God *continually*, even when it's the very last thing we feel like doing, in recognition of the fact that God has not abandoned us, and ultimately, even if it feels impossible at the moment, all shall be well.

Perhaps the hope and confidence expressed in Psalm 34 can be summed up in the famous words of the former United Nations Secretary General, Dag Hammarskjöld: 'For all that has been, thanks. For all that will be, yes!'

COLLECT

Almighty Lord and everlasting God,
we beseech you to direct, sanctify and govern
    both our hearts and bodies
in the ways of your laws
    and the works of your commandments;
that through your most mighty protection, both here and ever,
we may be preserved in body and soul;
through our Lord and Saviour Jesus Christ,
who is alive and reigns with you,
in the unity of the Holy Spirit,
one God, now and for ever.

Psalm **37***
1 Samuel 17.1-30
Luke 23.56*b* – 24.12

Psalm 37

'Be still before the Lord and wait for him' (v.7)

Psalm 37 is a song of great encouragement. It is written by an elderly man (v.25) who, with all the benefit of hindsight, and with the advantage of a lifetime of experience to draw upon, reassures us that God is in control; that ultimately good will triumph over evil; and that we have no need to be anxious or afraid. Over the course of his long life, the psalmist has seen God triumph again and again, even if at the time it looked as if everything was falling apart.

In the light of this great assurance, there is only one thing needed of us. We are to 'be still before the Lord' and we are to 'wait for him' (v.7) – 'wait patiently', as some English translations render it. Being still and waiting patiently are perhaps not the most striking characteristics of most Christians. 'Be busy before the Lord' is more like it, with our committees and strategies and action plans. Somehow we've imbibed the world's values and have been deceived into believing that to be busy is to be seen to be important, but harried, anxious Christians are not a good witness to the God who is ultimately the Lord of all creation.

'Do not fret' says the psalmist in verse 7. God has everything under control. Our task is to wait on him, to sit still long enough to hear his voice and respond to his promptings – an original rendering of the ubiquitous advice to 'keep calm and carry on'.

Lord God,
your Son left the riches of heaven
and became poor for our sake:
when we prosper save us from pride,
when we are needy save us from despair,
that we may trust in you alone;
through Jesus Christ our Lord.

COLLECT

209

Friday 22 July

Mary Magdalene

Psalms 30, 32, 150
I Samuel 16.14-end
Luke 8.1-3

Psalm 32

'... you forgave the guilt of my sin' (v.6)

Mary Magdalene knew what it means to be forgiven. In her encounters with Jesus, she experiences at first hand the healing that comes with being told that your wrongdoing will not be held against you and that the slate is wiped clean. Mary Magdalene would almost certainly have sung, 'Happy the one whose transgression is forgiven' (v.1).

Mind and body are inextricably linked, and the psalmist describes in verses 3-4 the physical signs that result from unconfessed wrongdoing. Modern medicine has confirmed that worries, guilt and anxiety can all show in the form of physical symptoms. Then in verses 5-6, we are told of the relief that comes from confession and repentance. Interestingly the psalmist refers to God forgiving the 'guilt' of sin (v.6).

As Christians we know at head level that if we are truly sorry for the things we have done wrong, then God will forgive us. But how many of us continue to carry around the *guilt* of what we've done? It's almost as if despite God's forgiveness, we can't forgive ourselves. Isn't that rather presumptuous of us?

If we have confessed, then God has forgiven. That doesn't mean we forget what we did wrong, but we move on and refuse to allow it to define us. The fourteenth-century mystic Julian of Norwich went as far as to say that the spiritual wounds caused by our sin become 'badges of honour' – emblems of Jesus' forgiveness and love for us. We stagger on, rejoicing.

COLLECT

Almighty God,
whose Son restored Mary Magdalene to health of mind and body
and called her to be a witness to his resurrection:
forgive our sins and heal us by your grace,
that we may serve you in the power of his risen life;
who is alive and reigns with you,
in the unity of the Holy Spirit,
one God, now and for ever.

Psalms 41, **42**, 43
I Samuel 17.55 – 18.16
Luke 24.36-end

Psalm 42

'...when I think on these things, I pour out my soul' (v.4)

Sometimes our songwriters do us a disservice when they turn psalms such as this into gentle worship songs. The beginning of Psalm 42 is not gentle. It spells desperation. If the parched deer doesn't reach water soon, it will die. The suffering creature's gasps for water are used as an image of someone who is so desperate to know God's presence and help that they too feel almost as if they might die. 'My tears have been my bread day and night' (v.3). This is someone in deep, deep distress who feels abandoned and alone.

What does the psalmist do in such desperate circumstances? He doesn't give up. He doesn't give in to despair. He *remembers*. He thinks back to those many times when God has been very real to him. So he pulls himself up by his bootstraps, and, buffeted though he is by wind and waves (v.9), he clings on to the knowledge that if he hangs on in there and hopes in God, 'I will yet give him thanks, who is the help of my countenance, and my God' (vv.7,14)

When God feels very far away, when things aren't going right for us, when it seems as if everyone is against us, when we're tempted to despair, the psalmist encourages us to think back to the times when we knew without doubt that God was with us, and to know that, if we refused to be defeated, better times will surely come.

Almighty Lord and everlasting God,
we beseech you to direct, sanctify and govern
both our hearts and bodies
in the ways of your laws
and the works of your commandments;
that through your most mighty protection, both here and ever,
we may be preserved in body and soul;
through our Lord and Saviour Jesus Christ,
who is alive and reigns with you,
in the unity of the Holy Spirit,
one God, now and for ever.

COLLECT

211

Monday 25 July

James the Apostle

Psalms 7, 29, 117
2 Kings 1.9-15
Luke 9.46-56

Psalm 7

'Give judgement for me according to my righteousness, O Lord' (v.8)

'Judge me, O Lord' is an audacious thing to pray to the implacable judge portrayed in Psalm 7 who 'is provoked all day long' (v.11). However justified we might feel on the particular suit we bring before God, his forensic scrutiny of us is bound to expose our transgressions; more prudent, then, to pray 'forgive us our sins'.

To pray 'judge me, O Lord' is only conceivable because of the psalmist's other understandings of God: God is the psalmist's judge, but he is also his refuge (v.1); God is a warrior (vv.12-13), but he is also a shield (v.10).

The psalmist makes the highest possible claims for God: he is at once judgement and sanctuary from judgement; he is on the attack and in defence. He is, in other words, always and everywhere, the absolute expression of everything that is.

The Jewish scholar Robert Gordis expresses this totality of God, in Job's experience, as 'fleeing from God to God': it is God who pursues Job; it is God who is Job's redeemer from this pursuit.

We may have been content to define God using safe, consoling categories – Father, shepherd, gardener – and to allow these categories to delimit our engagement with him. How much more exhilarating to join the psalmist on his pilgrimage into the limitlessness of God and to discover that there is no end to this exploration.

COLLECT

Merciful God,
whose holy apostle Saint James,
leaving his father and all that he had,
was obedient to the calling of your Son Jesus Christ
and followed him even to death:
help us, forsaking the false attractions of the world,
to be ready at all times to answer your call without delay;
through Jesus Christ your Son our Lord,
who is alive and reigns with you,
in the unity of the Holy Spirit,
one God, now and for ever.

Tuesday 26 July

Psalm 48

'God has shown himself to be a sure refuge' (v.4)

Imagine gathering with countless others to sing this psalm in the temple that Solomon has just dedicated to God. Feel your spirit soar, your heart brim with hope. Here you see the truth of the words you sing: God is 'a sure refuge' (v.4); his right hand 'is full of justice' (v.10).

Now imagine yourself generations later gazing at the temple – in ruins – in the days after the Babylonians have ransacked Jerusalem. It is now not foreign kings who panic and tremble (vv.5-6) but you who are shaking with fear. This once-lauded symbol of God's invulnerability now better reflects your own brokenness. How can you sing that God is a sure refuge or is full of justice when you stand defenceless, with no one to vindicate you?

Many of us will not need to imagine this agonizing gap between the tenets of faith and lived reality for, at the worst of times, we may have experienced it; we may have sung of God's 'loving-kindness' (v.9) but felt abandoned; we may have spoken of God as 'our guide for evermore' (v.13) even as we wander in the wilderness.

The things that we have heard of God will not always be reflected in what we see (v.8), yet we are called to trust that they still hold true and that one day we will experience them. Don't despair: in impenetrable darkness, God still shines; in a world in free fall, God reigns.

COLLECT

Almighty God,
who sent your Holy Spirit
to be the life and light of your Church:
open our hearts to the riches of your grace,
that we may bring forth the fruit of the Spirit
in love and joy and peace;
through Jesus Christ your Son our Lord,
who is alive and reigns with you,
in the unity of the Holy Spirit,
one God, now and for ever.

Wednesday 27 July

Psalm **119.57-80**
I Samuel 20.18-end
Acts 2.1-21

Psalm 119.57-80

'At midnight I will rise to give you thanks' (v.62)

Sudden midnight wakefulness seldom feels like an occasion for thanksgiving: a child is crying in discomfort; a dog is barking in warning; a telephone is ringing heralding, you can only imagine, the worst kind of news. Or perhaps, more prosaically, your body has wrestled you to consciousness, insistent that you meet its demands, or your unquiet mind is asking of you, again, the unanswerable questions of yesterday.

Although we might feel, variously, aghast or exasperated at being jolted from sleep, in contrast the psalmist rises 'to give thanks' to God because of his 'righteous judgements' (v.62). Such a gift is God's blueprint for life that even at the precarious pivot from one day to the next, he is to be worshipped.

The poet–priest George Herbert prayed that God would give him 'a grateful heart ... Not thankful, when it pleases me; as if thy blessings had spare days: But such a heart, whose very pulse might be Thy praise'.

At midnight, at 6.00am when the alarm clock propels us beyond the duvet's embrace, on the fractious school run and in the lonely afternoon hours when no one comes and no one rings, do our hearts beat out the rhythm of praise?

Such regular, repeated, non-stop thanksgiving is not the fruit of emotion but of assent that God is good, always, and of a resolution that he is ever to be praised. God's blessings do not have spare days – or hours or minutes. Praise him!

COLLECT

Almighty God,
who sent your Holy Spirit
to be the life and light of your Church:
open our hearts to the riches of your grace,
that we may bring forth the fruit of the Spirit
in love and joy and peace;
through Jesus Christ your Son our Lord,
who is alive and reigns with you,
in the unity of the Holy Spirit,
one God, now and for ever.

Psalm 57

'... your loving-kindness is as high as the heavens' (v.11)

Arguably, this is a psalm appreciated most instinctively, not by a native of the mountains where snow-capped peaks punctuate the heavens, but by a worshipper from the flat-lands. Standing on these uninterrupted sweeps of land, gazing upwards into infinity, the worshipper feels as much as sees this image of God's loving-kindness reaching to the heavens. Here is an enveloping, over-arching benevolence that knows no limits.

Even the most painful experience cannot press pause on God's boundless compassion, as the structure of the psalm suggests, where the psalmist interweaves his cries of laments with shouts of praise. 'I lie in the midst of lions' (v.5) gives way to 'Be exalted, O God above the heavens' (v.6). 'They have laid a net for my feet' (v.7) is countered with 'I will sing and give you praise' (v.8). Through the purple and black tapestry of the psalmist's experience runs, uninterrupted, the gold thread of God's love.

Babies born very prematurely need, not just technology, but also the skin-to-skin contact with their parents known as 'kangaroo care'. Nestled against their parent, the baby's heartbeat steadies, taking up the rhythm of the greater heart that holds them. Likewise, when we rest on the assurance of God's loving-kindness, anxiety is replaced with faith, our heart takes up the unwavering beat of God's and we can say 'My heart is ready, O God, my heart is ready' (v.8).

Gracious Father,
revive your Church in our day,
and make her holy, strong and faithful,
for your glory's sake
in Jesus Christ our Lord.

COLLECT

Psalm 51

'Against you only have I sinned' (v.4)

In the NRSV and other versions of the Psalter, an editorial note places the composition of this psalm in the aftermath of David's adultery with Bathsheba. Whether or not such a gloss is historically accurate, this sordid episode provides a good test case for the psalmist's proposition, 'against you only have I sinned' (v.4).

After all, the list of those David has sinned against seems a long one. At the very least there are Bathsheba, spied upon in her privacy and preyed upon by power; Uriah, her husband, murdered in battle in an attempt to conceal adultery, and Joab, commander of the Israelite army, made an accessory to that murder. How, then, can such sin – or any of our own – be against God 'only'?

Confessing that God is the victim of our sinfulness cannot be a denial of the all-too-evident pain we inflict on others. Rather, it is an acknowledgement that how we conduct ourselves in relation to one another goes right to the heart of our relationship with God. In honouring others, as he requires, we honour him; in mistreating others, we show ourselves to be wide of the mark of his 'great goodness' and 'the abundance of [his] compassion' (v.1). When we harm others, we deny our kinship with God; we wound God with their pain.

God feels the full force of our sinfulness, but he is also the one to free us from its effects. It is God who washes, cleanses, purges and restores us. The one we hurt becomes our healer.

COLLECT

Almighty God,
who sent your Holy Spirit
to be the life and light of your Church:
open our hearts to the riches of your grace,
that we may bring forth the fruit of the Spirit
in love and joy and peace;
through Jesus Christ your Son our Lord,
who is alive and reigns with you,
in the unity of the Holy Spirit,
one God, now and for ever.

Psalm **68**
1 Samuel 23
Acts 3.1-10

Psalm 68

'Blessed be the Lord who bears our burdens day by day' (v.18)

Headlining this psalm are the eternal God's great interventions in time – his staggering, transfiguring victories where the earth has quaked (v.8), kings have fled (v.11) and doves been enamelled with silver and green gold (v.12). Recited in praise, these triumphs are also invoked as guarantors of future success: 'Send forth your strength, O God; establish, O God, what you have wrought in us' (v.27).

Almost hidden in the small print between gripping accounts of these wondrous events is the quieter miracle of God's continuous sustaining of us: 'Blessed be the Lord', the psalmist prays, 'who bears our burdens day by day' (v.18). God's power, then, is expressed not only in the epic moments of history sounded in the thunder of 'thousands upon thousands' of chariots (v.16), but also in his unseen sustaining of us where, at each moment, he is our salvation.

In the Lord's Prayer we ask for this ever-renewed miracle when we pray 'Give us today our daily bread' – a prayer not only for food, but also for Christ himself who is 'the bread of life' (John 6.48), our salvation.

Practised at asking for daily bread, how astute are we at tracing the answer we receive, at recognizing in the apparently ordinary round of our days, God's extraordinary bearing of us? How often is our morning petition 'give us today our daily bread' given its counterpoint in our evening prayer as we bless the God who bears our burdens day by day.

Gracious Father,
revive your Church in our day,
and make her holy, strong and faithful,
for your glory's sake
in Jesus Christ our Lord.

COLLECT

Psalm 71

'... you are my hope, O Lord God' (v.5)

In 1992, the US Democratic Party nominated Bill Clinton as their presidential candidate. He closed his acceptance speech with these words: 'I still believe in a place called Hope' – both a tribute to his home town of Hope in Arkansas and an allusion to all that he promised his presidency would deliver.

Despite everything he experiences, the psalmist, too, still believes in hope, although, for him, this is not located in a place or dependent on politics but present in God himself: 'you are my hope, O Lord God' (v.5). The psalmist's hope is personal, rooted in who God has shown himself to be through his 'righteousness' and 'mighty works' (vv.15,16).

Founded on God himself, the psalmist's hope is not dependent on favourable circumstances; he hopes despite all the odds being stacked against him. This is the quality of hope that Paul commends in Abraham who '[hoped] against hope' that he would become 'the father of many nations' (Romans 4.18). This is the hope 'for what we do not see' (Romans 8.25) that he encourages the Roman church to practise.

To consider hope as a 'practice', as a spiritual discipline, is an important corrective to contemporary understandings of hope as a mood or as a desire for something. For the faithful, hope is rather to be a matter of decision where, with the psalmist, we resolve that we 'will hope continually' (v.14) no matter what might come our way.

COLLECT

Let your merciful ears, O Lord,
be open to the prayers of your humble servants;
and that they may obtain their petitions
make them to ask such things as shall please you;
through Jesus Christ your Son our Lord,
who is alive and reigns with you,
in the unity of the Holy Spirit,
one God, now and for ever.

Tuesday 2 August

Psalm 73

'... you hold me by my right hand' (v.23)

When we first encounter him, the composer of this psalm seems to be the grumpy old man of psalmists: wonderfully tetchy, implacably incredulous, someone whose judgement on the world and its ways is exaggerated despair.

Once we engage with the words of our psalmist, however, we discover someone more rounded, more authentic, than this caricature might suggest. In his anguish, in his urgency, he is something of an Everyman who says what we, too, might have bemoaned: that the dishonest and the destructive prosper, leaving those who keep the rules to languish unrewarded and undefended, while God himself seems strangely absent. 'Where is God?' one elderly woman once asked me, distressed at what she had seen on the news, 'Where are the miracles?'

Here then, enshrined in Scripture, are our concerns, our experience. For this psalm is a wonderful honouring of what it is to be human and to reach out to God: that is, to live faithfully, but with frailty, trying to glimpse infinity from our fatally limited perspective.

In response to our frustration and our fears, God is incredibly tender, a constant presence who tolerates our tantrums, holds our hand and guides us through the windings of the world to the glory of heaven (vv.22-24). We may never arrive at a systematic answer to the problem of evil, but in the constancy of God there is a resolution of sorts: we are not abandoned, never forgotten, always held.

> Lord of heaven and earth,
> as Jesus taught his disciples to be persistent in prayer,
> give us patience and courage never to lose hope,
> but always to bring our prayers before you;
> through Jesus Christ our Lord.

COLLECT

Psalm 77

'I will remember the works of the Lord' (v.11)

In the closing lines of *The Waste Land*, the poet T.S. Eliot quotes from Dante's *Divine Comedy* and other great works of literature before commenting, so evocatively: 'These fragments I have shored against my ruins.'

The psalmist's own life is in ruins: he is anxious, comfortless, sleepless, beset by endless questions, which an apparently indifferent God does not answer. What can forestall further disintegration? What are the fragments he can shore against his ruins?

The answer, for the psalmist, is to 'remember the works of the Lord' (v.11), those wonders that speak of God's power, compassion and goodness. So the psalmist meditates on the Exodus, that defining moment when God turned slavery to freedom and the waters of the Red Sea to dry land. These are the fragments the psalmist shores against his ruins: if so God has been, so God is and will be.

Total collapse is prevented because the psalmist knows the story of salvation and is able to trace even God's unseen footprints (v.19) alongside those of his people. Can we, like the psalmist, readily 'remember the works of the Lord' retold in Scripture and find in those accounts the promise of our own salvation? Have we also noted those times when God led us by the hand, when his unseen footprints marked the sand beside ours, so that these fragments, too, we can shore against our ruins?

COLLECT

Let your merciful ears, O Lord,
be open to the prayers of your humble servants;
and that they may obtain their petitions
make them to ask such things as shall please you;
through Jesus Christ your Son our Lord,
who is alive and reigns with you,
in the unity of the Holy Spirit,
one God, now and for ever.

Psalm **78.1-39***
I Samuel 31
Acts 4.32 – 5.11

Psalm 78.1-39

'... that they might put their trust in God' (v.7)

In the fairy tale *Sleeping Beauty*, the princess's fairy godmothers give her beauty, wit, grace, dance, music and song, thereby equipping her to become a sure-fire winner of the X Factor. In a long-running British drama, a local chef and sharp practitioner promises to teach his new godson how to cook spaghetti carbonara and how to cheat the tax man. If you could give a child anything, what would it be?

The psalmist envisages engendering trust in a child – specifically, 'trust in God' (v.7). This immeasurably precious gift will form the bedrock for the child's life even at times of great upheaval; it will be the child's impetus for living purposefully and faithfully from here and to eternity. The vehicle for this gift of trust is telling the child the 'wonderful works' that the Lord has done (v.4) in accordance with Moses' instruction to the Israelites about their stewardship of God's laws: 'Recite them to your children and talk about them when you are at home and when you are away, when you lie down and when you rise' (Deuteronomy 6.7).

How are we sharing the wonderful works that God has done with the children in our care? At bedtime, are these the stories we tell them? Are 'the words of eternal life' (John 6.68) embedded in our children's vocabulary and written on their hearts? Have our children received from us their inheritance of faith 'so that they might put their trust in God' (v.7)?

Lord of heaven and earth,
as Jesus taught his disciples to be persistent in prayer,
give us patience and courage never to lose hope,
but always to bring our prayers before you;
through Jesus Christ our Lord.

COLLECT

Friday 5 August

Psalm 55

'... he will sustain you' (v.24)

Preparing a family for a funeral is a great privilege. It can also be profoundly sad, not only because people have been left bereft by the death of a loved one, but also because such conversations often bring to the surface the deep fractures in human relationships that occur long before death. A son is not to be mentioned, the family requests. A sister will be present, but must be seated separately. Behind the costly articulation of these words lies the distress that those who should be closest are distant in their estrangement or come all too near in vicious personal attack.

This is the sort of pain felt by the psalmist whose covenant with a companion has been violated (v.22). The psalmist is bewildered by the treatment he has received, reciting old endearments for their once beloved – 'you, one like myself, my companion and my own familiar friend' (v.15) – as if this incantation might somehow conjure back their old intimacy.

Standing in contrast to the fickleness of even the closest of human relationships is the faithfulness of God. He will not violate his covenant with his people to save, to hear, to redeem (vv.18-20) and to sustain (v.24). God remains steadfast.

The psalmist wants to flee the excruciating circumstances in which he finds himself in order to seek rest and shelter (vv.7-9). That sanctuary is God himself. '... my trust shall be in you, O Lord' (v.26), the psalmist concludes.

COLLECT

Let your merciful ears, O Lord,
be open to the prayers of your humble servants;
and that they may obtain their petitions
make them to ask such things as shall please you;
through Jesus Christ your Son our Lord,
who is alive and reigns with you,
in the unity of the Holy Spirit,
one God, now and for ever.

Psalms 27, 150
Ecclesiasticus 48.1-10
or 1 Kings 19.1-16
1 John 3.1-3

Psalm 27

'... be strong and he shall comfort your heart' (v.17)

On the mountain, Peter, James and John saw [Jesus'] glory (Luke 9.32) and witnessed in his transfigured face, in his dazzling white clothes, the truth they had only previously heard: that he is their light and their salvation.

Perhaps this revelation is to brace Peter, James and John for what is to come. When Jesus' enemies surround him, when they take his life and threaten their own, Jesus' disciples are to remember what they have seen and, remembering, are to 'be strong' (v.17).

Time and again the psalmist calls himself from fear to faith. This is not fearlessness in peace, or faith in tranquillity; it is confidence and courage under attack. In the Lord, his light and his salvation, the psalmist is surrounded by his enemies, yet secure (v.7); he is abandoned by his parents, yet adopted by God (v.13); at each twist and turn of the enemy's machinations, God outmanoeuvres them, whisking the psalmist away to hide in his shelter or his tent, lifting him above the fray to set him high on a rock (v.6).

Later, on another mountain, Jesus' disciples saw him surrounded by his enemies, set high on a cross. Even then, they heard him express not fear but faith, speaking not of abandonment but of embrace: 'Father, into your hands I commend my spirit' (Luke 23.46).

Be strong. Even in death, the Lord is your light and your salvation.

Father in heaven,
whose Son Jesus Christ was wonderfully transfigured
before chosen witnesses upon the holy mountain,
and spoke of the exodus he would accomplish at Jerusalem:
give us strength so to hear his voice and bear our cross
that in the world to come we may see him as he is;
who is alive and reigns with you,
in the unity of the Holy Spirit,
one God, now and for ever.

COLLECT

Monday 8 August

Psalm 80

'... show the light of your countenance, and we shall be saved'
(vv.4,8,20)

The psalmists are among those biblical writers that give us permission to say what we really think, not what we think we ought to – to 'speak what we feel, not what we ought to say', as Edgar says in King Lear (Act 5, Scene iii). How long, Oh Lord? Where are you, God? Why have you forsaken me? – these are the psalmists' cries of lament. Often these are placed in a poetic form where the lament has a mirroring statement of faith about the unchanging nature of God – 'For you are great and do wonderful things' (Psalm 86.10); 'For great is your steadfast love' (Psalm 86.13); 'For who among the clouds can be compared to the Lord?' (Psalm 89.6)?

The Psalms are also songs, and they use many devices that are similar to the songs of today – such as a chorus that is repeated. The repeating refrain of verses 4, 8 and 20 suggests that in order for God to restore the psalmist, something must happen to God too. 'Show the light of your countenance' does not imply that God's nature changes, but it does draw attention to the idea that God is not a monolithic, one-dimensional, unmoved deity. To be unchanging does not mean there is no variety of expression, no interest, no liveliness in God. 'Show the light of your countenance, and we shall be saved.' We are saved only as we see and experience a God who is alive, and in relationship with us.

COLLECT

O God, you declare your almighty power
most chiefly in showing mercy and pity:
mercifully grant to us such a measure of your grace,
that we, running the way of your commandments,
may receive your gracious promises,
and be made partakers of your heavenly treasure;
through Jesus Christ your Son our Lord,
who is alive and reigns with you,
in the unity of the Holy Spirit,
one God, now and for ever.

Tuesday 9 August

Psalm 89.1-18

'I will … build up your throne for all generations. [Selah]' (v.4)

The Psalms are poetry; some were probably songs, and many of them were clearly written for liturgical use. Often they are punctuated with the word *selah* (appearing after verse 4 of this psalm in most translations). The meaning of *selah* is not exactly clear; it could be a musical instruction for instrumentalists or singers, but another theory is that it refers to a weighted pause, an instruction to take a few moments to ponder the significance of what has just been sung or said.

It was 1887 when the German philosopher Nietzsche coined the phrase 'slow reading', describing a habit of reading that 'exacts from its followers one thing above all – to step to one side, to leave themselves spare moments, to grow silent, to become slow – the leisurely art of the goldsmith applied to language'. Since then, slow, contemplative reading has largely been overtaken by a trend for scanning for information. But the purpose of reading is not only to find information; it is also to absorb and invest meaning. Harvard scholar and publisher Lindsay Waters wrote, in 2007: 'The mighty imperative is to speed everything up, but there might be some advantage in slowing things down. People are trying slow eating. Why not slow reading?'

To read the scriptures well, we need to include slow reading: to allow the words to 'speak' to us – particularly with the Psalms, which so brilliantly capture the great range of human emotion. *Selah!*

God of glory,
the end of our searching,
help us to lay aside
all that prevents us from seeking your kingdom,
and to give all that we have
to gain the pearl beyond all price,
through our Saviour Jesus Christ.

COLLECT

Wednesday 10 August

Psalm 119.105-128

'I am troubled above measure; give me life, O Lord' (v.107)

How can a good God stand by and watch while innocent people suffer? What is the relationship between this and the apparent divine promise that the righteous will prosper? Theologians down the ages have puzzled over these questions, wrestling their reasoning onto the page, while poets (one thinks, for instance, of the agonized writing of Gerard Manley Hopkins) have reframed the questions and left them unresolved. The satisfying answers do not come from neat apologetics that seek to get God off the hook, but from those who admit that there is no comfortable answer. To eradicate suffering might make our lives pleasant, but would take the edges off our lived experience as the highs would disappear with the lows. Aldous Huxley's character, Savage, in *Brave New World*, put it starkly: 'I don't want comfort, I want God, I want poetry, I want real danger, I want freedom, I want goodness. I want sin.'

The idea that suffering mitigates against belief in God is not borne out in experience, for while some people do lose their faith over senseless suffering, others discover God in the midst of it. The psalmist – who is both poet and theologian – neither solves the question nor loses his faith. He reiterates his trust in God's goodness and his own good conscience that he has lived in the light of God's law. And in the midst of pain, he finds himself acutely alive and still in relationship with God.

COLLECT

O God, you declare your almighty power
most chiefly in showing mercy and pity:
mercifully grant to us such a measure of your grace,
that we, running the way of your commandments,
may receive your gracious promises,
and be made partakers of your heavenly treasure;
through Jesus Christ your Son our Lord,
who is alive and reigns with you,
in the unity of the Holy Spirit,
one God, now and for ever.

Psalms 90, **92**
2 Samuel 7.1-17
Acts 7.44-53

Psalm 92

'It is a good thing ... to sing praises to your name' (v.1)

'He that sings prays twice' is a saying often attributed to St Augustine. In fact, he never wrote that, but he did write, 'he who sings praise not only sings, but also loves Him whom he is singing to/for.' Rather than privileging singing over speech, Augustine described the difference between singing for its own sake and singing praise to God. His distinction is something like the difference between singing a serenade to win the heart of a beloved, and singing a love song to entertain others, or to get yourself into the pop charts.

For church musicians, whether volunteers or employees, there is always a temptation to treat the congregation as the audience. But if God is the beloved to whom we sing, the role of the musician is to sing (or play) for God, and by doing so to make a space for the congregation to enter into worship, so that all may offer praise to the Beloved. The technical demands of music make it nearly impossible for Church musicians to be 'lost in wonder, love and praise', as Wesley described it. But the test of true Church musicians is still whether they begin and end with the intent of giving praise to God, rather than singing for its own sake, or performing for personal benefit or glory. Music must be given as a gift, in order to reflect the love of which the psalmist speaks.

God of glory,
the end of our searching,
help us to lay aside
all that prevents us from seeking your kingdom,
and to give all that we have
to gain the pearl beyond all price,
through our Saviour Jesus Christ.

COLLECT

227

Psalm 88

'Lover and friend have you put far from me' (v.20)

The Psalms have no shortage of lament, but nearly all of them sound a note of hope along with their heartfelt cries, usually punctuated with phrases such as 'I believe that I shall see the goodness of the Lord' (Psalm 27.16). Psalm 88, though, is utterly bleak from start to finish. Here there is no reaching for the future, none of the expected 'yet will I praise the Lord', but an unbroken litany of despair. Not only has the psalmist lost his sense of God's presence, but he believes his lovers and friends have abandoned him too.

For those who really are in despair, it is perhaps a comfort to find an expression of abject misery within the pages of Scripture. There is no depth of feeling, no experience known to humanity, that cannot be spoken before God. Here we find permission not to pretend to be cheerful, permission – necessity even – to speak up when life is unbearable.

The psalm is also a reminder to listen for cries of despair from others, for they are often more like whispers than shouts. When friends and acquaintances express bleak thoughts, we should be brave enough to walk with them even when we don't know how to help, and kind enough not to impose hope and faith on them when they cannot believe it. Those who are in despair often seem to push their friends away. What they need is friends who will stubbornly refuse to leave.

COLLECT

O God, you declare your almighty power
most chiefly in showing mercy and pity:
mercifully grant to us such a measure of your grace,
that we, running the way of your commandments,
may receive your gracious promises,
and be made partakers of your heavenly treasure;
through Jesus Christ your Son our Lord,
who is alive and reigns with you,
in the unity of the Holy Spirit,
one God, now and for ever.

Psalms 96, **97**, 100
2 Samuel 9
Acts 8.4-25

Psalm 97

'The mountains melted like wax at the presence of the Lord' (v.5)

Belief in any deity involves the idea of power, not only for an infallible God, but even in the case of the Greek gods who, for all their foibles and failings, still had the power to intervene in human affairs. A serious problem occurs, however, when religious language seems either to give divine authority to human positions of power, or to imply that a God is as flawed as those unjust human purveyors of power. A recent response in religious language is to avoid over-emphasizing a negative reading of power, describing God in terms of love or kindness, and addressing God less as Lord or King, and more as Creator, Faithful One, or Comforter.

While this avoids privileging certain images of God, it also runs the risk of domesticating God. It is vital to correct a false impression that God is an authoritarian, paternalistic despot, but when we face real-life situations of injustice, a soft and cuddly God is of little use; justice cannot come without a stubborn demand for change, and a degree of anger against injustice.

However much we celebrate an intimate, forgiving, loving God, we should not lose sight of the vastness of God's justice. Faced with heavenly, holy glory we, like John on Patmos, would fall face down; like Zechariah we would be struck dumb; like the mountains, we too would 'melt like wax' before the Lord of all the earth.

God of glory,
the end of our searching,
help us to lay aside
all that prevents us from seeking your kingdom,
and to give all that we have
to gain the pearl beyond all price,
through our Saviour Jesus Christ.

COLLECT

Monday 15 August

The Blessed Virgin Mary

Psalms 98, 138, 147.1-12
Isaiah 7.10-15
Luke 11.27-28

Psalm 98

'Sing to the Lord a new song, for he has done marvellous things'
(v.1)

This psalm is the perfect choice for the feast of the mother of Christ, because it is echoed by the *Magnificat*, Mary's song in Luke 1, and songs by two other women, Deborah (Judges 5) and Hannah (1 Samuel 2). Despite the cultural expectations of women, all three of these female songwriters echo the psalmist in connecting joy with a robust view of God as judge. This connection seems slightly out of step with our cultural sensibilities. However, although the suggestion that God might be merciless or show unwarranted wrath is rightly called into question, the psalmist is joyful because he anticipates God by 'His own right hand and his holy arm' (v.2) restoring justice and equity to the world. Hearing the news headlines day after day, who would not rejoice at that?

The complexity, and the true joy, of understanding God as the judge of the earth lies in the fact that God's judgement is completely just, to the extent that he will not take our 'side' against other people. Those whom we perceive to be the worst of sinners may, in God's view, be as much victims as villains. God will judge rightly, says the psalmist; God may be a trickster, but will not play cruel tricks. A world filled with equity and justice is a matter for celebration for those who love God, for then the downtrodden will be lifted up and the hungry fed.

COLLECT

Almighty God,
who looked upon the lowliness of the Blessed Virgin Mary
and chose her to be the mother of your only Son:
grant that we who are redeemed by his blood
may share with her in the glory of your eternal kingdom;
through Jesus Christ your Son our Lord,
who is alive and reigns with you,
in the unity of the Holy Spirit,
one God, now and for ever.

Psalms **106*** (*or* 103)
2 Samuel 12.1-25
Acts 9.1-19*a*

Psalm 106

'He remembered his covenant with them' (v.46)

Psalm 106 begins by proclaiming God's endless love, and continues with a long list of the unfortunate mistakes, blunders and deliberate recklessness of God's people. In summing up, the psalmist explains that God 'remembered his covenant'. In most usages, the word covenant refers to a binding agreement that must be kept by both parties. If either side demonstrably breaks the covenant, the other is released from it. However, the repeated story of the biblical record is that, even though God's people repeatedly forget, flout or despise the covenant, God continues to keep it anyway.

Keeping a one-sided covenant is too much for most people to bear, and in human relationships it is not always right to maintain a broken covenant. Repeatedly broken promises can have an utterly dehumanizing effect on people, and God never calls us to be doormats. There is all the difference in the world between laying down your life for someone when the circumstances are purposeful, and just laying down your life for the sake of it.

Perhaps the best analogy for the covenant love the psalmist describes is that of the undying love (even if it is 'tough' love!) of parents for wayward children. The psalmist sees God's faithfulness to the covenant as inseparable from 'the greatness of his faithful love' (v.46). Even though God did not break the covenant, the compassion that flows from love always leads him to take the initiative in restoring it.

Almighty and everlasting God,
you are always more ready to hear than we to pray
and to give more than either we desire or deserve:
pour down upon us the abundance of your mercy,
forgiving us those things of which our conscience is afraid
and giving us those good things
which we are not worthy to ask
but through the merits and mediation
of Jesus Christ your Son our Lord,
who is alive and reigns with you,
in the unity of the Holy Spirit,
one God, now and for ever.

COLLECT

231

Wednesday 17 August

Psalms 110, **111**, 112
2 Samuel 15.1-12
Acts 9.19*b*-31

Psalm 111

'I will give thanks to the Lord ... in the congregation' (v.1)

Recent studies show that an increasing number of people claim to have faith, without adhering to traditional patterns of church attendance. The reasons include a suspicion of religious institutions and a sense that traditional worship is, in some way, not 'working' for people. Our responses have included reorganizing the hierarchy and attempting to make services more attractive in order to bring attendance up, but this somewhat consumerist response has its limitations and often comes with a severe cost to theological integrity.

In the midst of ongoing discussions about how best to revitalize congregations, we need to admit that patterns of religious affiliation have shifted beyond recognition. It is not enough to try to restore old patterns of churchgoing; we have to ask why people need to meet for fellowship and worship.

It remains the case that there is a basic human need to meet with others and share our commitments and beliefs. With a few exceptions, people generally do not flourish in isolation. Some do love traditional ritual, but the pattern of their lives makes Sunday worship impossible (this seems to be one reason why mid-week Cathedral worship is enjoying something of a renaissance). Alternative forms of church that have shed much of the baggage of institutional hierarchy are also proving successful in providing 'sacred space' for fellow pilgrims. Attendance at Sunday services may be in decline, but congregating with others to share and nurture faith still matters to people.

COLLECT

Almighty and everlasting God,
you are always more ready to hear than we to pray
and to give more than either we desire or deserve:
pour down upon us the abundance of your mercy,
forgiving us those things of which our conscience is afraid
and giving us those good things
    which we are not worthy to ask
but through the merits and mediation
of Jesus Christ your Son our Lord,
who is alive and reigns with you,
in the unity of the Holy Spirit,
one God, now and for ever.

Psalm 115

'... the earth he has entrusted to his children' (v.16)

From the very first pages of Genesis, the idea is woven all through the Bible that the stewardship of the earth was given to the human race (tend the earth, name the animals, be fruitful and multiply), and that the transgression of the boundaries set around creation had the result that tending the earth became a struggle, and not a joy.

This psalm mirrors the story of Genesis, reminding us that the earth is our God-given realm. If we fail to look after it, it will not automatically recover. There is a growing body of evidence that we are already in a very poor place ecologically. For people of faith, the only right response is to recover our sense of calling to take care of the earth, from the smallest individual act of energy saving or recycling to instigating vital larger scale changes to our society. If we don't do it, who will?

The psalmist draws a contrast with those who worship idols (vv.4-8) – those who gladly deceive themselves, imagining all is well when in reality they are investing their time and passion in things of no consequence. For Christians, the command to care for the earth is part and parcel of our covenant with God. If we fail to take notice of this, not only will the earth suffer, but our faith will increasingly take on a note of self-deception and irrelevance.

God of constant mercy,
who sent your Son to save us:
remind us of your goodness,
increase your grace within us,
that our thankfulness may grow,
through Jesus Christ our Lord.

COLLECT

Friday 19 August

Psalm **139**
2 Samuel 16.1-14
Acts 10.1-16

Psalm 139

'... where can I flee from your presence?' (v.6)

Readers of Psalm 139 usually take it to be a good thing that wherever they go, God's presence will always be there, but have you ever read these same words imagining a slight air of resignation? Plenty of people have tried to run from God's call (Jacob, Jonah and Saul, for instance), by going geographically to another place, or leaving their spiritual home, or trying to ignore the gifts God had given them and do something of their own choosing. But a true call simply will not go away, and the storm that overwhelmed Jonah is a good metaphor for the storm that brews in your soul if you try to run from God. 'You have made us for yourself, O Lord,' wrote Augustine in his Confessions, 'and our hearts are restless until they find their rest in you.'

Contemplating the extent of God's knowledge, and amazed that God holds a comprehensive grasp of the universe together with the intricate details of his own soul, the psalmist remains baffled as to why God doesn't do something about wicked people. (Yet again, psalms ask the difficult questions!) But the psalmist is not brash; rather than haughtily demanding that God gives an account of himself, he asks God to search his own heart. When I am angry about suffering and distress, it is worth pausing to ponder whether I, rather than God, am the one who lacks understanding.

COLLECT

Almighty and everlasting God,
you are always more ready to hear than we to pray
and to give more than either we desire or deserve:
pour down upon us the abundance of your mercy,
forgiving us those things of which our conscience is afraid
and giving us those good things
    which we are not worthy to ask
but through the merits and mediation
of Jesus Christ your Son our Lord,
who is alive and reigns with you,
in the unity of the Holy Spirit,
one God, now and for ever.

Psalms 120, **121**, 122
2 Samuel 17.1-23
Acts 10.17-33

Psalm 121

'I lift up my eyes to the hills' (v.1)

In the biblical narratives, the major revelations of God usually happen on mountains – Moses meets God on Mount Sinai, and Jesus is transfigured on the mountain top. For the psalmists, Jerusalem – the city of seven hills – is where God's presence is uniquely found. Look up from the heart of the city, and on all sides you see the rising slopes of seven hills. The grey-green of olive groves, the dusty roads and pathways lined with glinting white buildings, all lead into the city of God. The psalmist's strength comes from looking around and reminding himself that God's presence is with him. God is with him and all around him, just as the hills surround the city.

It is one of the foundations of Christian belief that God is everywhere, but we regularly find we cannot feel God's presence. So it is easy to fall into the habit of asking God to be present. I have heard people pray aloud, asking God to 'be present among us', or song leaders encouraging a congregation to sing in order to 'bring God's presence among us'. This is well intended, but it would be better to follow in the psalmist's footsteps. What the ancient songwriter did by looking to the hills was to recollect that God was already present. Nothing we or the psalmist could do would make God more present; all we need to do is look around us and remember.

God of constant mercy,
who sent your Son to save us:
remind us of your goodness,
increase your grace within us,
that our thankfulness may grow,
through Jesus Christ our Lord.

COLLECT

Monday 22 August

Psalms 123, 124, 125, **126**
2 Samuel 18.1-18
Acts 10.34-end

Psalm 126

'Those who sow in tears shall reap with songs of joy' (v.6)

Some of us find ourselves moved to tears quite quickly. For others, tears rarely well up in their eyes. Viewing our tears as seeds falling to ground is, however, a stimulating image. We're reminded of Jesus' teaching 'unless a grain of wheat falls into the earth and dies ...' (John 12.24).

The planting season is one of loss, sadness and deprivation. It's hard work, and there is little to show for it other than future promise. Then the time of waiting begins. Yet while the farmer waits, God is at work in the dark, subterranean world hidden from view. Cells grow and multiply, and the most amazing transformation takes place. The season of harvest brings great joy, laughter and abundance.

Jesus' teaching was about resurrection. The psalmist is remembering a time of restoration and longing for it to happen again. For both there is the recognition that only God can do this – that just as God turns the acorn into the mighty oak, so also only God can turn our tears and our longings into songs of joy. This is why the Psalms are so important, for they teach us how to sing songs of lament as well as joy. They remind us that life is made up of many seasons and there is wisdom in simply recognizing where we are in the cycle.

COLLECT

Almighty God,
who called your Church to bear witness
that you were in Christ reconciling the world to yourself:
help us to proclaim the good news of your love,
that all who hear it may be drawn to you;
through him who was lifted up on the cross,
and reigns with you in the unity of the Holy Spirit,
one God, now and for ever.

Psalms **132**, 133
2 Samuel 18.19 – 19.8*a*
Acts 11.1-18

Psalm 132

'Let us enter his dwelling place' (v.7)

The 2010 film *The Way* is the story of a father who undertakes a pilgrimage in memory of his son. It's a beautiful study both of grief and of the place of pilgrimage, as the father completes the Camino de Santiago.

Psalm 132 is included in the Songs of Ascents (Psalms 120 to 134) and as such is a pilgrimage psalm. It would most likely have been sung by people as they made their way towards Jerusalem. It reminds them of how Zion was chosen as the sacred place of the divine presence and the place where God's chosen one rules over his people.

As I write this, my daughter has just returned from a Christian summer festival. She wouldn't use the word 'pilgrimage' to describe what she's just done, but I am struck that she has journeyed with many thousands of others to a special place where she has encountered God in a new way. She's been reminded of God's promises, and she has pledged herself to honour God in her life. It's exciting to see the way pilgrimage is being rediscovered in a new way in our times, but important also to set it in historical context. Alongside the significance of journeying together to a sacred place, is the memory of all God has done in the past, and the hope that God will once again bring renewal.

Almighty God,
you search us and know us:
may we rely on you in strength
and rest on you in weakness,
now and in all our days;
through Jesus Christ our Lord.

COLLECT

Wednesday 24 August

Bartholomew the Apostle

Psalms 86, 117
Genesis 28.10-17
John 1.43-end

Psalm 86

'... you alone are God' (v.10)

The TV cartoon *Tom and Jerry* contains a good lesson in spirituality. The cat Tom is forever chasing the mouse Jerry, who always manages to find some way of evading capture. Although, like any cartoon character, Jerry performs all sorts of gravity-defying tricks to avoid Tom, his basic tactic is simple. When being chased he makes straight for the hole in the skirting board.

'Let us keep our eyes fixed on Jesus' (Hebrews 12.2, GNT). When in trouble or when facing temptation, the trick is to keep looking ahead and not look back over our shoulder.

This psalm is notable for its emphasis on 'you'. The psalmist refers continually to the character of God rather than the detail of his own difficult situation. There are many who hate him and try to shame him, and even seek his life, but this is a prayer to the God who is 'good and forgiving, abounding in steadfast love' (v.5). Again and again he speaks of God and reminds himself (and the community) of God's character. This is why Christian songs and prayers that focus on 'me' and 'my needs' miss the point. Christian worship is about refocusing on God, lifting our eyes above all that clamours for our attention, not looking back at the temptations that chase us, but looking straight ahead at the One who is our only rescuer.

COLLECT

Almighty and everlasting God,
who gave to your apostle Bartholomew grace
    truly to believe and to preach your word:
grant that your Church
may love that word which he believed
and may faithfully preach and receive the same;
through Jesus Christ your Son our Lord,
who is alive and reigns with you,
in the unity of the Holy Spirit,
one God, now and for ever.

Psalms **143**, 146
2 Samuel 19.24-end
Acts 12.1-17

Psalm 143

'I flee to you for refuge' (v.9)

If you are familiar with Myers-Briggs personality type indicators, you will know that alongside the basic personality types, there is also a theory about 'shadow functions'. This theory suggests that when a person is under stress, they will often respond in a manner directly opposite to their normal pattern. So, for example, an introvert will start to function as an extrovert.

Other writers have applied this idea more generally and talk about our 'shadow mission'. Under stress we are diverted from our true mission to a shadow one. I observe this in myself – under stress I simply get busy and cram my life with more and more activity (presumably to stop myself thinking about what is causing the stress). Someone I know well turns to shopping when times are hard. When working in Africa, I noticed various Church leaders reverting to practices from their tribal religion when they were at their wits' end.

The psalmist is clearly under great strain. This 'psalm of complaint', as it is known, is undoubtedly written by someone who does not know where else to turn. He has reached the end of his human resources and so cries out to God. This in itself is hugely significant. Instead of turning to his shadow mission, he turns to God. Instead of defaulting to a different function, he maintains his faith and trust in God. So what is your shadow mission?

Almighty God,
who called your Church to bear witness
that you were in Christ reconciling the world to yourself:
help us to proclaim the good news of your love,
that all who hear it may be drawn to you;
through him who was lifted up on the cross,
and reigns with you in the unity of the Holy Spirit,
one God, now and for ever.

COLLECT

239

Friday 26 August

Psalms 142, **144**
2 Samuel 23.1-7
Acts 12.18-end

Psalm 144

'O Lord, what are mortals that you should consider them ...?' (v.3)

The term 'status anxiety' has become a common expression for the desperate search for prestige and honour displayed by many in our society. Whether it is recognition for professional achievements or whether it is celebrity popularity, there can be little doubt that many of us suffer from deep insecurities about our status in the world.

The word status can be translated literally as standing place. It asks of us: where do we stand in relation to the world, our fellow human beings and in relation to God?

This psalm gives a clear and helpful answer to those questions: we stand in a place of need (bringing our petitions to God), but we also stand in a place of gratitude (bringing our praise to God). To put this another way: we stand in-between need and gratitude; petition and praise. The first is all-important. Recognizing our need of God and expressing this continually in prayers of petitions gives us a healthy view of ourselves. However, we also recognize that we have already received much from God and we join with all heaven in expressing gratitude and praise. So we give thanks for the skills, talents and gifts God has given each one of us, and acknowledge that using them to the full, in an attitude of petition and praise, gives us the only status we need.

COLLECT

Almighty God,
who called your Church to bear witness
that you were in Christ reconciling the world to yourself:
help us to proclaim the good news of your love,
that all who hear it may be drawn to you;
through him who was lifted up on the cross,
and reigns with you in the unity of the Holy Spirit,
one God, now and for ever.

Psalm 147
2 Samuel 24
Acts 13.1-12

Psalm 147

'Sing praise to the Lord' (v13)

There is a strange power in beauty. Sometimes I gaze on a painting, or absorb myself in music, or enjoy a good book, and know that something deep within me has been touched. Beauty has many dimensions. Today's psalm is a hymn of praise, part of a group of doxologies that conclude the Psalter. One commentator points out that the key assertion is that God is gracious (the word itself is not used in this translation but it is in others). The commentator points out that the Hebrew word for 'gracious' suggests 'an anaesthetic dimension of beauty'.

It is worth reflecting for a while on the way beauty can have the properties of a 'pain killer'. There are poems and paintings from the First World War trenches that seek to capture beauty in the midst of horror, pain and great suffering. In the concentration camps of the Second World War, men and women would sing to one another. There is something within human nature that desperately searches for beauty, and this search cannot be suppressed even by the most terrible evil.

So when the psalmist talks of the outcasts, the broken-hearted, and the downtrodden, he does so in the context of this search for beauty. He finds beauty in the gathering, the healing and the lifting action of God, together with the blessing of children, the granting of peace, the sending of his word. God is gracious and God's beautiful actions bring us life even in the midst of death. So let us sing praise to the Lord.

Almighty God,
you search us and know us:
may we rely on you in strength
and rest on you in weakness,
now and in all our days;
through Jesus Christ our Lord.

COLLECT

Monday 29 August

Acts 13.13-43

'... by this Jesus, everyone who believes is set free' (v.39)

When I attended a training course on working with the press, I was taught the ABC of being interviewed. The technique involves 'acknowledging' the question, before 'bridging' to what it is you want to 'communicate'. Once trained in this technique, it's great fun observing the different ways interviewees do this on different TV and radio programmes.

Paul's speech in Antioch shows that this technique is far from new. He starts by connecting with his audience (vv.16-22) and acknowledging their shared story and background. He then bridges (vv.23-26) to the new story he wants to tell. Finally, he speaks of Jesus, emphasizing how he is good news for his listeners (vv.27-41).

There are of course dangers to such techniques, and the task of telling the story of Jesus has to be done sensitively, personally and with great respect for our listeners. Yet in the UK today, so many people are ignorant of this story, and there is a real need to go beyond the media's interest in the the Church as an organization, Christians as attendees, and Jesus as no more than a historical figure or moral teacher. It is only fair to acknowledge these interests, but we must then learn how to bridge to the real story of Jesus, by whom 'everyone who believes is set free from all those sins from which you could not be freed by the law' (v.39).

COLLECT

Almighty God,
whose only Son has opened for us
a new and living way into your presence:
give us pure hearts and steadfast wills
to worship you in spirit and in truth;
through Jesus Christ your Son our Lord,
who is alive and reigns with you,
in the unity of the Holy Spirit,
one God, now and for ever.

Psalms **5**, 6 (8)
1 Kings 1.32 – 2.4; 2.10-12
Acts 13.44 – 14.7

Acts 13.44 – 14.7

'... we are now turning to the Gentiles' (13.46)

We should not be surprised that the story of the growth of the Church shows clearly how the seed of faith grows differently in diverse soils. From the whole city gathering to hear the word of the Lord (13.44), and many becoming believers (13.48), through to those who contradicted Paul (13.45), those who stirred up persecution (13.50), and those who tried to stone the apostles (14.5). All this is very reminiscent of Jesus's parable of the sower (Matthew 13).

This is an important lesson for those of us who are prone to look over our shoulder and wonder why church X is growing when our own church isn't. It is all too easy to blame ourselves or blame a particular group within the Church for our apparent 'failure'. However, the reality is that the great tectonic plates of Western society are shifting under our feet and rather than trying to work out who is to blame, we rather need to exercise spiritual discernment in knowing how to respond. When is it right to move on and shake the dust off our feet in protest (13.51) and when is it right to remain for a long time (14.3)? When should we speak boldly and when should we let our actions do the talking (14.3)? There are no rules to this, simply walking in step with the Spirit.

Merciful God,
your Son came to save us
and bore our sins on the cross:
may we trust in your mercy
and know your love,
rejoicing in the righteousness
that is ours through Jesus Christ our Lord.

COLLECT

243

Acts 14.8-end

'... they strengthened the souls of the disciples and encouraged them' (v.22)

When I played football regularly, I learnt that there are many different ways of encouraging the team. Some team captains would shout a lot, barking orders and generally trying to direct the play. Others were good at saying just a few, well-chosen words as they ran past a player. Others led by example, showing by the way they tackled and passed the ball what they expected from colleagues.

The same is true of encouragement in the Church. There are so many different ways of spurring people on and motivating them to give their best. Paul and Barnabas set an example: the healing, the rejection of adoration, the endurance of great suffering and pain, and then the time given to revisit the disciples. Arguably the most striking encouragement is their statement: 'It is through many persecutions that we must enter the kingdom of God' (v.22). Sometimes the best encouragement we can give people is to be completely honest about what to expect from the Christian life. If we talk only of joy, fruitfulness and blessings, we are telling only half the story and we set people up for a fall. In reality we know there will be dark days, times of questioning, occasions when we will be ridiculed and mocked. How good to know then that we are following in the footsteps of Jesus and the saints.

COLLECT

Almighty God,
whose only Son has opened for us
a new and living way into your presence:
give us pure hearts and steadfast wills
to worship you in spirit and in truth;
through Jesus Christ your Son our Lord,
who is alive and reigns with you,
in the unity of the Holy Spirit,
one God, now and for ever.

Thursday 1 September

Acts 15.1-21

'... no small dissension and debate' (v.2)

One of my first experiences of chairing a Church Council meeting involved intervening between two members who squared up to each other, voices raised and clearly nearing the point when fists would fly. One of my first deanery meetings involved two vicars having a shouting match across the room. Maybe that's the effect I have on people! Or maybe it's an indication that the Church struggles with conflict.

There was no avoiding conflict in the early Church. First, Paul and Barnabas discussed the matter with those who took a different view. When there was no resolution, they referred the matter to those with greater authority. There they recounted their experience, debated Scripture, explored tradition and used reason.

Everything about this passage says that the debate was heartfelt and passionate. Yet there is also a clear sense of genuine listening and a desire to come to a common mind. We know that not everyone accepted the final decision, but we can safely assume that no one questioned the process of decision-making. There is much for us to learn here, not least that passion and strong feelings should be encouraged and not stifled. However, they should be focused on core issues, and they should be accompanied by good process, based on sincere listening, honest speaking and openness to God's guidance.

Merciful God,
your Son came to save us
and bore our sins on the cross:
may we trust in your mercy
and know your love,
rejoicing in the righteousness
that is ours through Jesus Christ our Lord.

COLLECT

Friday 2 September

Psalms 17, **19**
1 Kings 6.1, 11-28
Acts 15.22-35

Acts 15.22-35

'... to impose on you no further burden than these essentials' (v.28)

'Believe, belong, behave': the phrase has been much used in recent years, ever since the sociologist Grace Davie first explored the idea that many people in the UK might 'believe' without 'belonging' to any Church. However, this begs the very difficult question of 'behaving': when and how should we expect faith and Christian community to shape our behaviour?

The curious phraseology of the letter to Gentile believers is usually understood as urging them to have nothing further to do with pagan religion and idol worship (often associated with acts of sexual immorality). No doubt the envoys who carried the letter would have expanded further on the detail, but we are not given this information. The clear implication is that we must explore for ourselves (under the guidance of the Holy Spirit) what it means 'to impose on you no further burden than these essentials' (v.28).

Churches that operate with blurred boundaries around 'belonging' are often rightly concerned about not imposing undue burdens on people. However, we can then struggle to discern the essentials that should be imposed, such as how should new Christians break with pagan religion and idol worship in our own day? No wonder the early Church debated long and hard and then pronounced: 'it has seemed good to the Holy Spirit and to us' (v.28).

COLLECT

Almighty God,
whose only Son has opened for us
a new and living way into your presence:
give us pure hearts and steadfast wills
to worship you in spirit and in truth;
through Jesus Christ your Son our Lord,
who is alive and reigns with you,
in the unity of the Holy Spirit,
one God, now and for ever.

Saturday 3 September

Acts 15.36 – 16.5

'Barnabas took Mark with him' (15.39)

I couldn't understand why our youth worker was opposing the change. He was usually very open to new ideas and often the first to adopt innovation, but on this occasion he dug his heels in. As I vented my frustration to a colleague, she challenged me to reflect on what motivated this youth worker in his ministry. 'You know' she said 'that he always puts the interests of the young people first. Could it be that, far from being obstinate, he simply feels this change isn't right for them?'

Knowing what motivates people in ministry is all-important to developing their gifts and talents. It is probably simplistic to say that Barnabas was people-orientated while Paul was task-orientated, but it is certainly clear that Barnabas could see potential in Mark which Paul could not. It is noteworthy that both of them took companions with them on their journey, but they had different ways of choosing them and working with them.

So much of ministry in the Church is about discerning the gifts of people round us and then developing those gifts, but there is far more to this than meets the eye. Understanding motivation, knowing preferred styles of working, being skilled in delegation, offering second chances: all these things are key tasks for the minister who knows they cannot go it alone, but can only do what they see their Father doing.

Merciful God,
your Son came to save us
and bore our sins on the cross:
may we trust in your mercy
and know your love,
rejoicing in the righteousness
that is ours through Jesus Christ our Lord.

COLLECT

Monday 5 September

Acts 16.6-24

'God had called us to proclaim the good news' (v.10)

Does the Christian faith belong to the East or the West? Is Christianity for the rich or the poor? The answers will not surprise you, but the circumstances might.

Paul was at Troas, a port on the Aegean Sea. Travelling east would take him into Asia. Travelling west would take him into Europe. He had a deep conviction that God's intention was that he should go west. Most of Asia did not hear the Good News for another thousand years. It was carried eastward from Europe by missionaries and traders. Today we rejoice to hear of Asian Christians, missionaries and migrant workers, travelling westward and introducing Jesus to those in Europe who have grown up without hearing his story.

Arriving in Europe, Paul met two women. The first was an entrepreneur whose trade had brought her across the sea. She sought out the Jewish community, too small to have an indoor synagogue, and stumbled upon the Saviour. The second was not a trader but someone who had been traded – a slave trafficked to provide an income for pimps. She too recognized the way of salvation, and it calmed her frenzy. It cost Paul his freedom and it cost her ... who knows? History has sadly not dignified her with a name.

The life-changing gospel of Jesus Christ is good news for East and West, for rich and poor. Somewhere among all that, it is good news for you.

COLLECT

God, who in generous mercy sent the Holy Spirit
    upon your Church in the burning fire of your love:
grant that your people may be fervent
in the fellowship of the gospel
that, always abiding in you,
they may be found steadfast in faith and active in service;
through Jesus Christ your Son our Lord,
who is alive and reigns with you,
in the unity of the Holy Spirit,
one God, now and for ever.

Tuesday 6 September

Acts 16.25-end

'Believe on the Lord Jesus, and you will be saved' (v.31)

Extreme events often make people think about their eternal destiny. A new birth can prompt a person to wonder whether there is a Creator. A severe illness can prompt a person to ask whether there is a Saviour. In Philippi, a jailer survived a tremor and assumed his captives had escaped through the smashed doors. An immediate suicide seemed preferable to a drawn-out execution.

But what drew him to faith was not extreme at all. It was the integrity of Paul and Silas who, rather than scamper, had chosen to wait for justice to be seen to be done. You and I do not need miracles or jail sentences in order to relate to this story. We don't even need to draw attention to ourselves with hymns at midnight. All we need for our neighbours to notice that people of Christian faith are distinctive is integrity. The way we dignify outsiders, the way we take responsibility for unloved areas of housing estates, the way we recognize and respond to needs – these things are observed.

When integrity has broken down barriers between Christians and unchurched people, the next step is shared experience. Out of the storage vessels came water for the jailer to clean the prisoners' wounds. Out of the same vessels came water to baptize the jailer's family. It doesn't require an earthquake for you or me to introduce someone to Jesus. It's much simpler than that.

Lord God,
defend your Church from all false teaching
and give to your people knowledge of your truth,
that we may enjoy eternal life
in Jesus Christ our Lord.

COLLECT

Wednesday 7 September

Acts 17.1-15

'... people who have been turning the world upside down' (v.6)

Why is a *Reflections for Daily Prayer* reader like a Jew from Beroea? (I apologise that this sounds like a riddle from a Christmas cracker!) Because they both 'examine the Scriptures every day' (v.11).

When the concept of Christians using a methodical scheme to familiarize themselves with the Bible was first popularized a century ago, the converts in Beroea were the inspiration. They were sympathetic to Paul's message that Jesus was the Messiah who had been anticipated in the Hebrew Scriptures. But if they were to make the change of life that following Jesus involved, they needed to be convinced by their own study.

I have a 1930s precursor of *Reflections* on the desk next to me. Called *Daily Notes*, its cover boldly states: 'Written by university men'. There are several reasons why an aid to studying the Bible would not advertise itself like that today, but at the time it was important to stress how thoroughly researched the information was.

The combination of personal knowledge of the Bible and reliable guidance through its difficulties is still extremely important. Why? Because the alternative is people rushing emotionally after rumours and misunderstandings. It happened in Thessalonica where a crowd of 'ruffians in the market places' weren't interested in considering what might be true, but were hankering after a fight (v.5). Uninformed religion can still have that impact. At this very moment, Bible in hand, you are standing against it.

COLLECT

God, who in generous mercy sent the Holy Spirit
upon your Church in the burning fire of your love:
grant that your people may be fervent
in the fellowship of the gospel
that, always abiding in you,
they may be found steadfast in faith and active in service;
through Jesus Christ your Son our Lord,
who is alive and reigns with you,
in the unity of the Holy Spirit,
one God, now and for ever.

Psalm **37***
1 Kings 11.1-13
Acts 17.16-end

Acts 17.16-end

'... he is not far from each one of us' (v.27)

In Athens, Paul did something he hadn't done before. Of course, he went to the synagogue and talked with local Jews about the Hebrew Scriptures (our Old Testament). But then he went to the marketplace and spoke to anyone who happened to be there. There was no point in discussing the Scriptures as his way of introducing Jesus. The Greeks would not have understood what he was talking about. So instead he began to chat about their contemporary culture – poets, statues, popular ideas. They joined the conversation, sarcastically at first, but then with interest.

The reason they engaged is that Paul didn't tell them that everything they yearned after was worthless. Instead, he told them to go on yearning because Jesus offered the fulfilment of those hopes.

It makes me wonder how Paul would begin a conversation today with someone who has never been to church. I'm sure he would not ask, 'Have you heard of The Acts of the Apostles?' Instead he might ask, 'Have you heard of *Game of Thrones*?' (It is, after all, the world's most pirated and watched TV drama.) I can imagine him continuing, 'You know how the characters speak of the gods of death? Well, I've made a life-changing discovery that there is a God of Life.'

Have you seen anything on television that you are eager to chat about? Go ahead! See whether God makes himself known in the conversation.

Friday 9 September

Psalm **31**
1 Kings 11.26-end
Acts 18.1-21

Acts 18.1-21

'... speak and do not be silent; for I am with you' (vv.9-10)

Where does the Christian faith belong?

It belongs outside church walls. Corinth was a seaport whose economy depended on servicing the most basic desires of sailors ashore. Like Jesus himself, Paul witnessed to God's love in places where it was neither comfortable nor easy. In fact, Paul got so frustrated by his reception in the respectable places of worship that he stomped elsewhere with his message (v.7).

It belongs in the workplace. Priscilla and Aquila had been driven from their home by religious persecution. Paul had been driven from his home by a conviction that he must let the world know about Jesus. They all needed to make a living in Corinth, and came together to do so. When Silas and Timothy arrived with a gift from Christians elsewhere, Paul could devote himself to evangelism full-time and still afford to eat.

Where does the Christian faith not belong?

It doesn't belong in the courts. Gallio's judgement was that lawyers were the wrong people to settle theological disputes. It's not clear whether wisdom or lethargy lay behind his decision (v.15). More is known about Gallio because his brother was the writer Seneca. He described Gallio as 'charming and gracious', so perhaps he should have the benefit of the doubt. Either way, since this precedent it is hard to think of any occasion when Christians squaring up in court has brought anything but disrepute in the view of outsiders.

COLLECT

God, who in generous mercy sent the Holy Spirit
    upon your Church in the burning fire of your love:
grant that your people may be fervent
in the fellowship of the gospel
that, always abiding in you,
they may be found steadfast in faith and active in service;
through Jesus Christ your Son our Lord,
who is alive and reigns with you,
in the unity of the Holy Spirit,
one God, now and for ever.

Psalms 41, **42**, 43
1 Kings 12.1-24
Acts 18.22 – 19.7

Saturday 10 September

Acts 18.22 – 19.7

'... burning enthusiasm' (18.25)

Jesus was an educated man. He was able to read, and even as an adolescent his brain impressed academics, but he surrounded himself with people who were not like that – fishermen and women of a humble background. These were the people who established the first churches.

Twenty years later something new was happening. Intellectuals were coming to faith and sharing the leadership of Christian communities. There was Paul, of course, from the university town of Tarsus. Like Jesus, he had both a craftsman's skill and a knowledge of philosophy. Now there was Apollos too. He came from Alexandria in Egypt, also a university town, and was saturated in scriptural knowledge, but his encounter with the teaching of Jesus was not just cerebral – he spoke with 'burning enthusiasm' (v.25).

Nobody can blame Apollos for what he didn't yet know about what is now accepted Christian theology. Very little was written down. From Jerusalem to Rome there must have been many conversations like the one he had with Priscilla and Aquila (v.26). Out of these, orthodox theology emerged – rooted in what had been learnt from those who met Jesus, and tested by experience. What Apollos newly discovered about baptism and perhaps about the Holy Spirit was taken to Corinth, where he became a leader of the church. In his letter to the Corinthian church, Paul commented on Apollos' teaching, so it is still having an impact on Christians to this day.

> Lord God,
> defend your Church from all false teaching
> and give to your people knowledge of your truth,
> that we may enjoy eternal life
> in Jesus Christ our Lord.

COLLECT

Monday 12 September

Psalm **44**
I Kings 12.25 – 13.10
Acts 19.8-20

Acts 19.8-20

'... the word of the Lord grew mightily' (v.20)

In some ways, the spiritual climate of 2016 is not very different from Ephesus in AD 52. You don't need to keep the television on for long before someone 'publicly maligns the Way' (v.9, NIV). And in any city you will find a shop like 'Sceva and Sons' where you can buy something claiming to put you in touch with supernatural darkness.

However, there are some ways in which Ephesus all those years ago was unique. Miracles in which God's healing was conveyed by a handkerchief were not a routine part of Christian experience. The Bible describes them as extraordinary (v.11), and they come in contrast to Paul's experience in Athens or Corinth, where there are no accounts of God healing people.

Is it right to pray for healing for those who are sick, mentally or physically, in these days when medicine has advanced immeasurably? Of course it is! If we recognize that the spiritual climate of the world hasn't changed, then the part God plays in healing hasn't changed either. God is listening to our cry for him to drive out all that keeps people from a fulfilled life. In Ephesus, notorious for occult practices, it required a dramatic gesture like setting fire to all that held the believers back. Tonight in my second-floor flat, where this Bible passage has brought to mind half a dozen friends with mental illnesses, lighting a candle seems a more appropriate expression of my prayer.

COLLECT

O Lord, we beseech you mercifully to hear the prayers
    of your people who call upon you;
and grant that they may both perceive and know
    what things they ought to do,
and also may have grace and power faithfully to fulfil them;
through Jesus Christ your Son our Lord,
who is alive and reigns with you,
in the unity of the Holy Spirit,
one God, now and for ever.

Psalms **48**, 52
I Kings 13.11-end
Acts 19.21-end

Acts 19.21-end

'... gods made with hands are not gods' (v.26)

Those who care that our descendants should inherit a planet that can support human life plead for an end to the way we are exhausting its natural resources. But it's difficult for their voices to be heard because those who make an immediate profit from those resources shout persuasively about not wanting to sacrifice our comforts.

Those whose lives have been damaged by intrusive or untrue media revelations implore the press to act in a different way. But corporations need to sell newspapers, and they know the public will part with their money because we have an appetite for reading salacious stories.

Farmers in the developing world work extremely hard and yet remain in unjust poverty because the world's trade systems are stacked against them. But supermarkets and food manufacturers need to squeeze their suppliers because we, their customers, want a bargain and go elsewhere if we don't get it.

Christians in a first-century Greek city thrill people with the news that the living God has walked and talked among them. A relationship with him is life-enhancing and without cost. But silversmiths whip up riotous opposition because their businesses will collapse if people realize there is a free alternative to purchasing their religious trinkets.

You are not powerless to make a stand on protecting the environment, rejecting irresponsible media and favouring goods that have been traded fairly. Make your choice, as the followers of Jesus have had to do for two thousand years.

Lord of creation,
whose glory is around and within us:
open our eyes to your wonders,
that we may serve you with reverence
and know your peace at our lives' end,
through Jesus Christ our Lord.

COLLECT

Wednesday 14 September

Holy Cross Day

Psalms 2, 8, 146
Genesis 3.1-15
John 12.27-36*a*

Genesis 3.1-15

'What is this that you have done?' (v.13)

How are we to recognize evil? In Hollywood fantasy films it's easy to spot, because the baddies are scaly, ugly and horned. In life it's harder to identify because wickedness does not advertise itself. Racist political parties do not begin their terror with secret police and internment; they start by announcing engagingly, 'We know you're concerned that it's all getting too much'. Abusers of children rarely pounce with weapons; they wheedle their way into lives with charm.

The Bible's great metaphor of the serpent-tempter teaches us that this is so. Adam and Eve were not lured into rebellion against God because they were attracted by war, rape or hatred. Instead evil introduced itself with winsome visions of a life more exciting or rewarding than the way God had planned (vv.1-5).

In J.K. Rowling's *Harry Potter* novels, Dumbledore is the headmaster of Hogwart's Academy and adolescent Harry's mentor. He foresees 'dark days ahead' when a choice will have to be made 'between what is right and what is easy'.

The choice between what's right and what's easy is one we have to make every single day. Those actions can eventually lead to the ruin of the environment, the poverty of those in the developing world, the fracturing of our closest relationships. But at the moment of decision, we can persuade ourselves that our choices are as inconsequential as biting a piece of fruit.

COLLECT

Almighty God,
who in the passion of your blessed Son
made an instrument of painful death
to be for us the means of life and peace:
grant us so to glory in the cross of Christ
that we may gladly suffer for his sake;
who is alive and reigns with you,
in the unity of the Holy Spirit,
one God, now and for ever.

Thursday 15 September

Acts 20.17-end

'... a message that is able to build you up' (v.32)

I've been a member of my church for 40 years. Every few weeks I preach a sermon there. It's a privilege, but also a challenge. From the pulpit I dare not advocate anything I don't do myself. People who have known me since I was a teenager are entirely aware of whether or not I live up to those standards.

In the world's longest-running children's television programme, *Blue Peter*, the presenters demonstrate live how to create something, then reach for a perfect and complete version with the catchphrase, 'And here's one I made earlier'. If only every preacher could say that about himself or herself at the end of every sermon!

After more than two years with the Christians of Ephesus, Paul gave his final message to the leaders of the church he had nurtured. The responsibility was passing to them and Paul offered himself as a role model. These were the qualities he hoped future leaders would emulate: being a servant who did not give up in hardship (v.19), being able and willing to account for why he followed Jesus (v.21), caring vigilantly for those entrusted to his protection (v.28), and living simply while being devoted to the needs of the poor and vulnerable (v.35).

In fact, not just leaders but every Christian could pray for the Holy Spirit to increase those selfless qualities. If only we could point to ourselves, saying, 'And here's one God made earlier'.

O Lord, we beseech you mercifully to hear the prayers
of your people who call upon you;
and grant that they may both perceive and know
what things they ought to do,
and also may have grace and power faithfully to fulfil them;
through Jesus Christ your Son our Lord,
who is alive and reigns with you,
in the unity of the Holy Spirit,
one God, now and for ever.

COLLECT

Friday 16 September

Psalms **51**, 54
1 Kings 18.21-end
Acts 21.1-16

Acts 21.1-16

'The Lord's will be done' (v.14)

Well-meaning Christians can sometimes give you the wrong advice. It happened to Paul, so you and I are not exempt. It is, let's be honest, sometimes very hard to be sure what God wants us to do on any particular occasion.

Paul had made up his mind to go to Jerusalem because he had a conviction about it so captivating that he was sure the Holy Spirit of God was responsible (20.22). He felt the task that God had entrusted to him could not be considered complete until he reported to the believers in the birthplace of Christianity that gentiles were coming to faith in their hundreds.

The Christians in Tyre told Paul that the Holy Spirit had told them he should not go (v.4). That must have been unsettling because Paul believed God had told him the very reverse. Agabus, renowned for revealing what God's will was, acted out in the style of an Old Testament prophet that going to Jerusalem would lead to Paul's arrest (v.11). Paul's reply was that, true though it may be, persecution was no reason to quit when God had given him his life's work.

In the end Paul did the only thing any of us can do. He listened to the advice. He prayerfully asked God to show him what to do. He made up his mind. And he stepped out decisively knowing that he had to take responsibility for whatever happened next.

COLLECT

O Lord, we beseech you mercifully to hear the prayers
    of your people who call upon you;
and grant that they may both perceive and know
    what things they ought to do,
and also may have grace and power faithfully to fulfil them;
through Jesus Christ your Son our Lord,
who is alive and reigns with you,
in the unity of the Holy Spirit,
one God, now and for ever.

Psalm **68**
1 Kings 19
Acts 21.17-36

Acts 21.17-36

'... thousands of believers' (v.20)

James was the leader of the Christians in Jerusalem. He was the kind of leader whose calm presence had given the Christian Church a fine public reputation. In particular, the Jews had come to respect those of their number who had become followers of Jesus – thousands of them (v.20). James' greatest achievement was chairing a council in which decisions were made about whether gentiles who converted to Christianity would have to become Jews as well. Despite strongly held views, the discussion concluded in a peaceful agreement (Acts 15.19). Deciding that gentile followers of Jesus did not have to obey the Jewish law was the resolution that led to Christianity becoming a worldwide religion.

Now Paul arrived in Jerusalem. James was a diplomat; Paul was an activist. James was worried that his arrival would upset the balance. Paul might have preached that not only were gentile Christians free from having to obey Jewish laws, but that Jewish Christians should renounce them too. James suggested that Paul should take part in a Jewish purification custom in order to show his respect in an explicit way. Paul saw the wisdom of this (v.26).

It didn't work out the way they hoped. Malicious and untrue rumours spread that Paul had done something offensive (v.28). Violence ensued. The account pointedly identifies a gentile soldier as the one who rescued the situation. The advance of the Christian faith was unstoppable, but the personal stakes were now very high for Paul.

Lord of creation,
whose glory is around and within us:
open our eyes to your wonders,
that we may serve you with reverence
and know your peace at our lives' end,
through Jesus Christ our Lord.

COLLECT

259

Monday 19 September

Psalm **71**
1 Kings 21
Acts 21.37 – 22.21

Acts 21.37 – 22.21

'I beg you, let me speak to the people' (21.39)

Paul has set out for Jerusalem. He is initially welcomed by the Christians there, but, true to form, he soon causes upset and is almost killed in the ensuing riot. Saved by Roman soldiers, Paul uses the opportunity to tell of his conversion.

The story of Paul's dramatic conversion on the road to Damascus is well known, but what stands out in this account is the way in which he tells his story. He witnesses to his faith clearly, warmly, personally. He gives little details ('about noon', 22.6) that help the listener to see that this is a personal account. He doesn't use jargon. He speaks eloquently of the way in which his life was turned around and of the Jesus whose followers he once persecuted but has now joined.

How do we respond when asked about our faith? How would you respond to the question, 'Why do you go to church?' A mumbled, 'Errrm, because I always have,' or 'Well I'm not sure,' doesn't really cut the mustard. We should always be prepared to speak up for our faith and be able to explain quietly, clearly, personally what it means to us.

If we're not able to do so, perhaps it's time to seek out a wise and trusted friend to help us articulate 'who Jesus Christ is to me'.

COLLECT

Almighty God,
you have made us for yourself,
and our hearts are restless till they find their rest in you:
pour your love into our hearts and draw us to yourself,
and so bring us at last to your heavenly city
where we shall see you face to face;
through Jesus Christ your Son our Lord,
who is alive and reigns with you,
in the unity of the Holy Spirit,
one God, now and for ever.

Psalm **73**
1 Kings 22.1-28
Acts 22.22 – 23.11

Acts 22.22 – 23.11

'Keep up your courage!' (23.11)

To say that Paul was a controversial character is probably something of an understatement. Bold and brash, as zealous for Christ as he once was for persecuting Christians, he finds himself the centre of riots and dissension time and time again. This time he divides the Sanhedrin (the supreme court in Judea) along party lines: on one side, the Pharisees who believed in the resurrection of the dead; on the other, the Sadducees who didn't.

Chaos ensues once more, violence breaks out, and Paul is dragged from the melee into the barracks, the door slammed firmly closed. It's entirely possible that Paul was by this time feeling more than a little weary, but that night, the Lord draws near and encourages him to keep going.

If we are true to our faith, we will upset people. No matter how gently we might witness to our faith, we will from time to time touch raw nerves and cause offence. The truth isn't always easily received. It might be good when this happens to ask ourselves, 'Is this person angry with me because what I've said is untrue? Or are they angry because what I've said *is* true?'

If the latter, we need to stay calm and listen quietly to that still, small voice whispering, 'Keep up your courage! You have testified for me before. You must witness to me again' (23.11). And then take a big deep breath and dive back in.

> Gracious God,
> you call us to fullness of life:
> deliver us from unbelief
> and banish our anxieties
> with the liberating love of Jesus Christ our Lord.

COLLECT

Psalms 49, 117
1 Kings 19.15-end
2 Timothy 3.14-end

Wednesday 21 September

Matthew, Apostle and Evangelist

1 Kings 19.15-end

'Then he set out and followed Elijah' (v.21)

The call of Elisha has echoes of the call of Jesus' first disciples. Elijah calls Elisha away from his daily work of ploughing. Invested with Elijah's mantle, Elisha recognizes that his life is about to take on a new direction. He says farewell to his family, deals with his oxen, and leaving everything behind, he follows Elijah, 'and became his servant' (v.21).

Jesus' call to Matthew, the tax collector, is not to be his servant but his disciple, and that is our calling too. Like those first disciples, in response to Jesus' promptings, we're asked to be prepared to leave the vestiges of our own life behind, to follow him and then, as a disciple, to spend the rest of our lives as apprentices.

As disciples we are called to learn from Jesus, but not simply in an academic way. Instead we're asked to walk and work alongside him, learning as we go, watching and imitating. There is no 'fast track' to success as a disciple. We must sit at Jesus' feet, listen to his teaching, watch what he does and learn to do likewise. It's a life-long apprenticeship.

As today we remember the call of Matthew, and God's calling of prophets and saints throughout the centuries, perhaps we may consider again our own calling, and seek to rededicate ourselves to a lifetime of discipleship in his service.

COLLECT

O Almighty God,
whose blessed Son called Matthew the tax collector
to be an apostle and evangelist:
give us grace to forsake the selfish pursuit of gain
    and the possessive love of riches
that we may follow in the way of your Son Jesus Christ,
who is alive and reigns with you,
in the unity of the Holy Spirit,
one God, now and for ever.

Thursday 22 September

Acts 24.1-23

'... they ought to be here before you to make an accusation' (v.19)

In celebrating Matthew yesterday we missed the rest of Chapter 23 of Acts. In summary, the Jews decide they have really had enough of Paul and plot to kill him. The tribune gets to hear of their conspiracy and thwarts them by sending Paul to Caesarea, to Felix the Roman Governor. Paul is kept under guard in Herod's quarters. So, here at the beginning of chapter 24, Paul is called once again to witness to his new faith.

Paul launches into his defence, we note 'cheerfully' (v.10). He must have taken to heart God's instruction to keep up his courage. Unlike Ananias, Tertullus and the elders, he doesn't use charm and flattery to butter up the Governor. He simply speaks the truth – and at the same time points out that as the accusers from Asia haven't appeared to witness against him, under Roman law the charges ought to be dropped.

Despite the weakness of the case against Paul, Felix isn't strong enough to bring it to a close, and Paul is put under house arrest. Sometimes being in the right doesn't guarantee that we will be treated fairly. Our accusers may well not be strong enough, or big enough, to admit that they are wrong, or may be fearful of what their 'friends' will say. In such cases, we have little option but to follow Paul's example and to sit tight, keeping up our strength and courage and trusting that ultimately God will vindicate us.

Almighty God,
you have made us for yourself,
and our hearts are restless till they find their rest in you:
pour your love into our hearts and draw us to yourself,
and so bring us at last to your heavenly city
where we shall see you face to face;
through Jesus Christ your Son our Lord,
who is alive and reigns with you,
in the unity of the Holy Spirit,
one God, now and for ever.

COLLECT

Friday 23 September

Psalm **55**
2 Kings 2.1-18
Acts 24.24 – 25.12

Acts 24.24 – 25.12

'Go away for the present' (24.25)

The Roman Governor Felix is a master of procrastination. He simply can't decide what to do with Paul, and is also quite hopeful that if he keeps him under house arrest for long enough, Paul may well offer him a hefty bribe. So two years pass, and still Felix fails to come to a decision, repeatedly thrown off track as he is by the penetrating power of Paul's proclamations about justice, self-control and judgement. Felix shows himself to be weak, fickle and cowardly.

Before we dismiss Felix, however, perhaps we ought to learn a little from him. How good are we at putting things off: decisions we should make; a difficult conversation; an action that will make us unpopular but which we know in our heart of hearts to be the right thing to do? I suspect that Felix isn't alone in mastering the art of procrastination.

So often we procrastinate because we fear failure, criticism and sometimes even our own perfectionism. But in putting off decisions that need to be made, and failing to do things that must be done, we can end up being deeply unfair to others. Paul endured two years of house arrest because of Felix's inability to act. Who are we imprisoning by our failure to get something done? Is there a decision we know we must make? Something we know we must do? Perhaps today is the day to hand it over to God in prayer, and then to take the first tiny step to make it happen.

COLLECT

Almighty God,
you have made us for yourself,
and our hearts are restless till they find their rest in you:
pour your love into our hearts and draw us to yourself,
and so bring us at last to your heavenly city
where we shall see you face to face;
through Jesus Christ your Son our Lord,
who is alive and reigns with you,
in the unity of the Holy Spirit,
one God, now and for ever.

Saturday 24 September

Acts 25.13-end

'Tomorrow ... you will hear him' (v.22)

King Agrippa and his sister, Bernice, arrive in Caesarea on a courtesy visit to welcome the new governor Festus. Festus confesses that, like Felix before him, he can make neither head nor tail of the accusations against Paul. He asks for Agrippa and Bernice's help in deciding what to say to the Emperor Caesar, to whom Paul wishes to appeal. Festus' problem is that he can see that there isn't really a case to answer.

With Agrippa and Bernice in their royal purple robes and golden crowns, Felix in his scarlet state finery, the military in their uniforms and the great and the good, all suited and booted, Paul, a prisoner of two years and probably looking a little the worse for wear, is called to speak.

We are reminded of Jesus' warning that, 'you will be dragged before governors and kings because of me' (Matthew 10.18). But we should remember too Jesus' promise that we shouldn't worry about what to say in such circumstances because, 'what you are to say will be given to you at that time' (Matthew 10.19).

Sometimes we have to speak up for our faith when really what we'd rather do is run and hide. The people we have to address may seem intimidating and important in worldy terms. Paul inspires us to be bold, be brave, put ourselves in God's hands and trust that he will speak through us. His words, not ours.

Gracious God,
you call us to fullness of life:
deliver us from unbelief
and banish our anxieties
with the liberating love of Jesus Christ our Lord.

COLLECT

Acts 26.1-23

'... the Gentiles – to whom I am sending you' (v.17)

Paul recounts once again the story of his conversion, embellishing his narrative this time with detail that would make sense to Agrippa, one of the Herod dynasty, one who was very familiar indeed with Judaism. Paul is very clear that God has commissioned him to be an apostle (v.16) but an apostle to the Gentiles, 'to open their eyes so that they may turn from darkness to light' (v.18). With those words we are instantly reminded of Simeon who, receiving the infant Jesus in the temple, proclaimed that he would be 'a light to lighten the Gentiles' (Luke 2.32).

Though initially hesitant when non-Jews such as Cornelius were converted (Acts 10), the early Church soon accepted the equality of Jews and Gentiles in the sight of God, and understood that the good news of the gospel is for absolutely everyone, regardless of race or class. For those more steeped in tradition, it must have been hard to listen to Paul and to see that the barriers they had so painstakingly erected between themselves and the non-believing Gentiles were to be torn down.

In theory we understand that the Gospel is for everyone, absolutely everyone, but do we live this out in practice? Do we restrict our circle of friends to those who attend our church? Or do we mix with and gently witness to a wide range of people?

Are there those we choose to ignore because we've already concluded that they are 'no-hopers'? Paul challenges us today to think again.

COLLECT

Almighty and everlasting God,
increase in us your gift of faith
that, forsaking what lies behind
and reaching out to that which is before,
we may run the way of your commandments
and win the crown of everlasting joy;
through Jesus Christ your Son our Lord,
who is alive and reigns with you,
in the unity of the Holy Spirit,
one God, now and for ever.

Tuesday 27 September

Acts 26.24-end

'Are you so quickly persuading me to become a Christian?' (v.28)

Paul concludes his defence, and such is his passion and conviction, Governor Festus and King Agrippa are lost for words. Festus can only bluster around and accuse Paul of madness. Agrippa swiftly moves out of Paul's reach before he can challenge him further.

Paul is so full of joy, so enthusiastic, so convinced of his conversion that those who hear him are challenged to make their own response to this account of the risen Jesus. 'Are you so quickly persuading me to become a Christian?' demands Agrippa. Words I suspect we don't often hear in our own context today!

Witnessing to our faith is a tricky balance. We all know those who corner others and attempt to force them to believe, verbally battering them with the Bible, blinding them with certainties. Perhaps in response to this, the majority of us go the other way and rarely utter a word about our faith and what it means to us.

What difference might it make if we were so visibly joyful and at home with our faith that those around us were challenged and encouraged to find out more about the risen Jesus? If someone wandered into our church service on a Sunday morning, would they leave again unmoved? Or would our joy and delight in the God whom we worship prove infectious? Perhaps today Paul is challenging us to rekindle that spark of faith into a vivacious flame.

God, our judge and saviour,
teach us to be open to your truth
and to trust in your love,
that we may live each day
with confidence in the salvation which is given
through Jesus Christ our Lord.

COLLECT

Psalm 119.105-128
2 Kings 9.1-16
Acts 27.1-26

Acts 27.1-26

'I urge you now to keep up your courage' (v.22)

Paul, still under arrest despite Agrippa's conviction of his innocence, joins a group of prisoners being escorted under guard to Rome. Despite Paul's warnings not to leave shore, the ship sets sail and is caught in a severe storm. No one could accuse Paul of a quiet life.

Surrounded on all sides by tempestuous winds, cruel and angry seas, frightened and panicky men, Paul remains calm. An angel, a messenger from God, has appeared to him and has promised him that his life will be saved and that he will stand trial before Caesar, and that the lives of his fellow passengers will also be saved. We hear echoes of Jesus' calm and commanding presence when the disciples were terrified during a storm on the Sea of Galilee. 'Why are you afraid, you of little faith?' (Matthew 8.26)

If we know that we have a task to do, one for which we know that God has called us, we cannot let even the most severe of storms push us off course. It may look to all intents and purposes as if our plans will be shipwrecked, not least if others initially refuse to listen to us, but Paul teaches us by example to remain calm and focused, confident in the one whom we serve: the one who can calm even the most savage wind and waves; the one who has promised to bring us safely back to shore.

COLLECT

Almighty and everlasting God,
increase in us your gift of faith
that, forsaking what lies behind
and reaching out to that which is before,
we may run the way of your commandments
and win the crown of everlasting joy;
through Jesus Christ your Son our Lord,
who is alive and reigns with you,
in the unity of the Holy Spirit,
one God, now and for ever.

Psalms 34, 150
Tobit 12.6-end *or* Daniel 12.1-4
Acts 12.1-11

Thursday 29 September

Michael and All Angels

Daniel 12.1-4

'Michael, the great prince' (v.1)

Daniel has been given a vision of a terrible future war. He asks God for more details, and God sends an angel messenger to explain. Not just any old angel; God sends Michael, 'the great prince, the protector of your people', whose name means, 'who is like God?' A specific angel with a specific name, assigned to a specific task.

When an angel appears to Mary to tell her she is to bear God's son, it isn't Michael who arrives; God sends Gabriel, whose name means 'strength of God'. A specific angel with a specific name, assigned to a specific task.

Despite the immeasurable host of angels and archangels alluded to in the Bible and celebrated today, it would appear that angels have names. They are each known to God, individually, by name. We do not worship an objective, detached God, who acts impersonally to create and sustain the world around us. We worship a God who knows each of us by name and who acts personally and individually according to a specific situation.

The angels are not just a magnificent 'heavenly host'; they are individual creatures with names. We are not simply anonymous members of the human race; we are individuals, unique, loved for who we are, known personally to God by name.

Do we treat others with the same individual care and attention we receive from God?

Everlasting God,
you have ordained and constituted
the ministries of angels and mortals in a wonderful order:
grant that as your holy angels always serve you in heaven,
so, at your command,
they may help and defend us on earth;
through Jesus Christ your Son our Lord,
who is alive and reigns with you,
in the unity of the Holy Spirit,
one God, now and for ever.

COLLECT

Friday 30 September

Acts 28.1-16

'Paul had gathered a bundle of brushwood' (v.3)

In celebrating Michael and the angels yesterday we missed the end of chapter 27 of Acts, and the recounting of the shipwreck Paul warned would happen. The shipwrecked prisoners find themselves on the island of Malta, where they are welcomed by the islanders with a warming and comforting fire. Paul busies himself collecting kindling for the fire before joining the others.

You couldn't blame Paul for being thoroughly fed up by now. He's been unjustly imprisoned for over two years, and just when he can finally see the chance to vindicate himself before the Emperor in Rome, the ship on which he's travelling goes down in a storm and he's delayed for what turns out to be three months, though at that time Paul could not have known how long his journey would be delayed.

We all know the frustration of thwarted plans. We write our to-do lists, plan our time productively, and then with a ring of the doorbell or the ting-ting of a text message all our carefully laid plans can be demolished. In such circumstances we have two options. We can moan and complain and sigh and grumble. Or we can go and collect some firewood, join in the party, and apply ourselves wholeheartedly to whatever happens to have come our way, trusting that God's timing is not our timing, and God's timing is more likely to be right.

COLLECT

Almighty and everlasting God,
increase in us your gift of faith
that, forsaking what lies behind
and reaching out to that which is before,
we may run the way of your commandments
and win the crown of everlasting joy;
through Jesus Christ your Son our Lord,
who is alive and reigns with you,
in the unity of the Holy Spirit,
one God, now and for ever.

Psalms 96, **97**, 100
2 Kings 17.1-23
Acts 28.17-end

Acts 28.17-end

'For this people's heart has grown dull' (v.27)

As we reach the end of the Acts of the Apostles, we leave Paul still under arrest in Rome. He still hasn't appeared before Caesar, but he takes the lead and invites the local Jewish leaders to hear his case. He doesn't want to give up on his own. They want to hear what Paul has to say because they've heard about this strange new sect and the trouble it has been causing. They listen hard. Some are convinced about Jesus. Others refuse to believe. Then as they depart, Paul, probably in exasperation at their unwillingness to comprehend, flings after them verses from Isaiah, accusing them of spiritual death and decay.

The religious leaders have lost their spark. Overfamiliarity with their religion, unthinking routine, bogged down by the day-to-day paraphernalia of religious duty, they have become blind and deaf to the truth, life and vitality of the God they worship. Customs and traditions, rules and regulations, religious duty and force of habit have replaced their faith in the God of life. They are cautious, negative and narrow in their religion. The contrast with Paul's open, welcoming, inviting, inclusive, lively faith in the risen Jesus is too much. They are too comfortable or too set in their ways to respond.

Dull, dutiful, narrow, restricting religion? Or lively, engaging, open, life-giving faith? Which do we possess?

Monday 3 October

Psalms **98**, 99, 101
2 Kings 17.24-end
Philippians 1.1-11

Philippians 1.1-11

'... constantly praying with joy' (v.4)

It is striking how many discipleship courses are based on Paul's Letter to the Philippians. That is probably because Philippians really does seem to contain all the essentials for a life lived in Christ, as we shall see in the coming days. It is an upbeat letter full of warmth, reassurance, challenge, sound doctrine and with a quotable quote on almost every other line.

I have lost count of the number of encouraging messages and greetings cards I have received that have written on them a verse from Philippians. That is somewhat surprising, because Paul wrote the letter while in prison. I am not sure that if I were to be chained up, falsely accused, I would be quite so full of hope and positivity.

Right at the start of the letter Paul tells the small church in Philippi that he is praying for them 'with joy'. The source of his joy is the fact that, even though they are not physically present with him, these brothers and sisters hold out to him the encouragement of a shared passion and focus – the grace of God and the truth of Christ's gospel. Paul's prayer for them is no less encouraging, that their 'love may overflow more and more with knowledge and full insight to help you to determine what is best' (vv.9,10).

Today, we might follow Paul's example by praying 'with joy' for our friends and supporters, those who encourage us with their very being.

COLLECT

O God, forasmuch as without you
we are not able to please you;
mercifully grant that your Holy Spirit
may in all things direct and rule our hearts;
through Jesus Christ your Son our Lord,
who is alive and reigns with you,
in the unity of the Holy Spirit,
one God, now and for ever.

Philippians 1.12-end

'... that Christ is proclaimed in every way' (v.18)

One has to admire Paul's single-minded determination. He seems to be able to see everything that happens to him, for good or bad, even his own imprisonment at the hands of an oppressing power, as an opportunity to proclaim the gospel. That is his number one priority. Everything else that is happening to him, even the painful stuff of life, serves that one end. 'What does it matter?' (v.18), he is even able to say. Paul had an almost reckless confidence in preaching the gospel that got him into a great deal of trouble.

Organizations and companies these days are encouraged to have a simple, clear vision statement that sums up what they are all about and tells their customers what they exist to do. If Paul had written a vision statement for himself, it might be something like this: 'to proclaim Christ'. Paul exhorts the Philippians likewise to live out their whole lives in a way that glorifies and honours Christ.

There are parts of the worldwide Church today where proclaiming Christ with the same boldness as Paul will land you in similar peril. For those of us fortunate enough not to live in contexts of real persecution, the danger might take another form. We might fail to develop that single-minded passion for proclaiming Christ. We might fail to make that our 'vision statement', not because of fear necessarily, not because it's too difficult, but because it's too easy.

Faithful Lord,
whose steadfast love never ceases
and whose mercies never come to an end:
grant us the grace to trust you
and to receive the gifts of your love,
new every morning,
in Jesus Christ our Lord.

COLLECT

Wednesday 5 October

Psalms 110, **111**, 112
2 Kings 18.13-end
Philippians 2.1-13

Philippians 2.1-13

'... in humility regard others as better than yourselves' (v.3)

It's a funny thing, being humble. It's like a visual trick that you only see if you don't quite look at it. If you think you've mastered being humble, you probably haven't. If you start to feel proud about how humble you are, you're obviously not!

Humility is a much-misunderstood virtue. It is tempting to think that being humble is simply all about thinking badly about yourself in comparison with others. Here, Paul paints a picture of what it truly looks like to live a life of humility. And what it looks like – is Jesus. Jesus chose humility. He 'emptied *himself*' (v.7) and 'humbled *himself*' (v.8). Only because Jesus knew that he was 'in the form of God' (v.6) was he able to make the powerful choice to lay down his own heavenly status in order to become human.

Being humble is not putting yourself down. It's just not needing to promote yourself. The Christian writer C.S. Lewis said: 'The thing about a truly humble person is not that they think less of themselves, but that they think of themselves less.' Humility is not self-deprecation. It's not about being a doormat. It's not thinking of yourself as rubbish and awful. In fact, only those with a really strong, true, firm, accurate sense of their identity in Christ are able really to make the powerful choice to humble themselves. So perhaps becoming humble is something we can choose to do, and practise getting better at, following the way of Christ.

COLLECT

O God, forasmuch as without you
we are not able to please you;
mercifully grant that your Holy Spirit
may in all things direct and rule our hearts;
through Jesus Christ your Son our Lord,
who is alive and reigns with you,
in the unity of the Holy Spirit,
one God, now and for ever.

Psalms 113, **115**
2 Kings 19.1-19
Philippians 2.14-end

Thursday 6 October

Philippians 2.14-end

'I think it necessary to send to you Epaphroditus' (v.25)

There is much travelling back and forth in this section of the letter: Timothy to Philippi and then back to Paul with news; Epaphroditus on a return journey back to Philippi having been sent by the Philippians to help Paul in prison; and Paul himself hoping to travel to Philippi soon.

How encouraging it is when someone you love and trust comes to visit you, especially when you're going through hard times. Paul obviously knew the power of presence. He knew that sending Timothy to the Philippian church would encourage and build them up. Epaphroditus is described as 'longing' for them (v.26), and presumably the feeling is mutual, since his visit to them will cause them to 'rejoice' (v.28).

My teenage son is away for a week on a trip with friends, and although it is so easy for me to be in contact with him through email, texts and messages, they are no substitute for the joy of seeing him face to face when he returns in person. I truly will 'rejoice at seeing him again, and ... be less anxious' (v.28)!

In these days when it is so easy to 'message' someone, we don't have the same need to send people as messengers back and forth as Paul and the Philippians did. However, I wonder whether we do need to hold on to the thought that in order to really encourage someone, a personal visit, with support, help, news, ministry or service might be just what is required.

Faithful Lord,
whose steadfast love never ceases
and whose mercies never come to an end:
grant us the grace to trust you
and to receive the gifts of your love,
new every morning,
in Jesus Christ our Lord.

COLLECT

Philippians 3.1 – 4.1

'I regard everything as loss' (v.8)

Paul here lists all his credentials that, looked at from one perspective, afford him the highest standing in his culture and society. In themselves, these things are not 'nothing'; they are significant aspects of who Paul is. However, compared with the value of knowing Christ as Lord, he says that they are 'loss'.

There are several things in my past and my background I am (perhaps justifiably) quite proud of. They include the education I have been given, the qualifications I have worked hard for, the job opportunities I have enjoyed, the churches and communities I have had the privilege to be part of, the family and friends who have nurtured me and in whom I delight. These are all things I count 'as gain' and that have given richness and purpose to my life.

However, I know too that these things should in no way privilege me above others who have not had the same chances and opportunities. I know also that none of these things makes me a Christian or even, necessarily, a better person. I know that compared to the huge gain of Jesus 'making me his own' (v.12) through his cross and resurrection, they pale in comparison. It's all a matter of perspective. They are all good things, but they are not good enough to earn my right standing before God, and they never will be. Only Christ can do that.

COLLECT

O God, forasmuch as without you
we are not able to please you;
mercifully grant that your Holy Spirit
may in all things direct and rule our hearts;
through Jesus Christ your Son our Lord,
who is alive and reigns with you,
in the unity of the Holy Spirit,
one God, now and for ever.

Saturday 8 October

Philippians 4.2-end
'Do not worry about anything' (v.6)

'Do not worry about anything' is a command much easier said than done. On one level it is obvious. God is sovereign and will provide for all my needs so there should be no need to worry. The trouble is, it's not always that easy to allow that head knowledge to invade my heart and mind.

Worry, anxiety, stress, fear is something that besets us so readily and is so difficult to stop doing by ourselves. I remember when I was ill a few years ago and I was told that 'worrying would only make it worse'. That made me worry all the more!

Paul seems to have cracked it. He has learned to be content in every situation. 'Rejoice!' has become his byword. But note that he has 'learned' to be content (v.11). That implies that it was not always so. For Paul, the absolute belief that there really is no need to worry is hard won from living through the good times and the very, very bad. Paul has *learned* that God is faithful, and his resurrection perspective helps him to see the challenges of life in the light of eternity.

Not worrying is something we cannot easily do by ourselves. But we can learn over time to trust God, increasingly bringing *everything* (large and small) to him in prayer, letting the knowledge that he is near seep into our hearts and souls bringing peace, gradually allowing him to turn our worry into his contentment.

Faithful Lord,
whose steadfast love never ceases
and whose mercies never come to an end:
grant us the grace to trust you
and to receive the gifts of your love,
new every morning,
in Jesus Christ our Lord.

COLLECT

Psalms 123, 124, 125, **126**
2 Kings 21.1-18
1 Timothy 1.1-17

1 Timothy 1.1-17

'Christ Jesus came into the world to save sinners' (v.15)

Paul writes his letter to Timothy as his mentor, to instruct and encourage him in his leadership of the church at Ephesus. The letter is full of sound advice about how lead the church in 'love that comes from a pure heart, a good conscience, and sincere faith' (v.5). Paul, however, does not set himself up as a faultless paragon of virtue. On the contrary, he wears openly his own shameful history as a persecutor of the very Christians he now seeks to build up.

It is exactly *because* Paul sees himself as the 'foremost' of sinners (v.15), rescued by the grace, faith, love and mercy of Christ that he is able to offer himself as any kind of example. This is not an example of perfection but an example of redemption.

On the news yesterday evening there was an interview with a man who had once been a drug dealer, addicted to heroin. He now works as a counsellor and advocate for those also struggling with similar addictions. What made him so effective was his understanding of the depths in which his clients now found themselves. He had been there too and so was able to offer effective help. Paul's knowledge of himself as 'chief amongst sinners' (v.15) enables him all the more to recognize the overflowing effectiveness of God's mercy, and to encourage his young friend Timothy, as he holds out an offer of that same mercy to others.

COLLECT

God, the giver of life,
whose Holy Spirit wells up within your Church:
by the Spirit's gifts equip us to live the gospel of Christ
    and make us eager to do your will,
that we may share with the whole creation
    the joys of eternal life;
through Jesus Christ your Son our Lord,
who is alive and reigns with you,
in the unity of the Holy Spirit,
one God, now and for ever.

Psalms **132**, 133
2 Kings 22.1 – 23.3
1 Timothy 1.18 – end of 2

1 Timothy 1.18 – end of 2

'... a quiet and peaceable life in all godliness and dignity' (2.2)

Paul writes his letter to Timothy in order to help him to live out his calling as a minister in the Church of Christ 'having faith and good conscience' (1.19). One of the main ways to achieve this, it seems ('First of all then ...', 2.2), is through prayer and learning. Both men and women should pray and learn, but they are to pray and learn in a particular manner – quietly and peaceably, not angrily or arrogantly.

The same Greek word is used three times in this passage, in verses 2, 11 and 12 of Chapter 2. The first time, when it relates to living a peaceful life, Bible translators invariably use the word 'quiet', suggesting an ordered life free from disturbance and disruption. However, when it relates to women learning, teaching or holding authority, the translators tend to use a different word, 'silence'. But it is the same word in all three places!

This passage has been used over the centuries to silence women and prevent them from taking leadership roles in the Church. Instead, it could be argued that Paul is simply encouraging all Christian people, men and women, lay and ordained, bishops, priests and deacons, to live a life of prayer and learning together in the Church in a way that is dignified, godly and 'quiet', rather than angry and confrontational.

This passage does not advocate silence, from either women or men. It does, however, encourage peaceful and prayerful learning in partnership together.

God, our light and our salvation:
illuminate our lives,
that we may see your goodness in the land of the living,
and looking on your beauty
may be changed into the likeness of Jesus Christ our Lord.

COLLECT

Wednesday 12 October

1 Timothy 3

'... how one ought to behave in the household of God' (v.15)

In the ordination service of priests in the Church of England, the person being ordained is asked, 'Will you endeavour to fashion your own life and that of your household according to the way of Christ?' It has always been of great comfort to me that the response '... I will' is firmly preceded by the words 'By the help of God ...' I am reassured that God is going to help me with this – and with all the other promises I made at ordination.

The expectation that a minister's household – husband, wife, children, wider family members, close friends – is somehow included in their charge of ministry is a daunting one. Any of us who have children know that, although we take responsibility for their care and wellbeing, we cannot always be responsible for how they will turn out. Much as we might like our children to be paragons of virtue, good manners and godly living, in practice we know that they are human as we are, and they don't always get it 'right'. That is why it is sobering to read that an element of the qualifications to be a bishop or deacon is good management of one's own household and children. In the family, as in the Church, it might not always work out the way we had hoped, but with love, grace, patience, forgiveness and a large dose of 'the help of God', we do our best at both.

COLLECT

God, the giver of life,
whose Holy Spirit wells up within your Church:
by the Spirit's gifts equip us to live the gospel of Christ
    and make us eager to do your will,
that we may share with the whole creation
    the joys of eternal life;
through Jesus Christ your Son our Lord,
who is alive and reigns with you,
in the unity of the Holy Spirit,
one God, now and for ever.

Thursday 13 October

1 Timothy 4

'... everything created by God is good' (v.4)

Paul's words to Timothy here warn him to avoid petty-minded and deceitful attitudes that attempt to control people by making them avoid certain foods and practices. Paul puts forward an alternative, life-affirming view that gives great liberty to Christians to enjoy with grateful thanks the world God has created by his loving hand. His words do not constitute permission to over-indulge in food or any other of God's good gifts of creation intended for pleasure, but to live to the full in the world in which we are placed.

Paul is careful to point out that whilst nourishment for the body comes from food that is given for our enjoyment, nourishment for the soul comes from 'words of faith' and 'sound teaching' (v.6). Some people put a lot of time and effort into honing their bodies with physical training and eating the right things. All well and good. But here Paul encourages Timothy to pay equal attention to training himself in godliness, through reading and teaching Scripture.

I wonder whether we experience our reading of the Bible, even these daily readings and reflections, as 'training'? Sometimes we might not feel like getting up and doing it; sometimes it may tire us. Difficult bits might even make us ache in mind or spirit. But over time, if we 'continue in these things (v.16)', our efforts at reading and understanding will reap their own reward and we will become fitter in the things of the living God.

God, our light and our salvation:
illuminate our lives,
that we may see your goodness in the land of the living,
and looking on your beauty
may be changed into the likeness of Jesus Christ our Lord.

COLLECT

1 Timothy 5.1-16

'Do not speak harshly' (v.1)

The fifth of the Ten Commandments (Exodus 20.12) is: 'Honour your father and mother'. Here that command is extended further in the new household of God, so that all people in the Church are to treat each other as though they are members of the same family. Older women become mothers, older men fathers and those of the same age sisters and brothers. In this new household, older people are to be spoken to with dignity, honoured, provided for and respected for the contribution they have made to society.

'Elder abuse' has become a real and disturbing facet of modern life. Many older people in our society today find themselves neglected, ignored or, worse still, hurt mentally, physically and emotionally. Paul has very strong words for people in the Church who do not care for older people in need.

How might we show the respect, care and consideration Paul advocates here to someone who is in need today? It will not always be easy. Just as families have their 'awkward characters', so do churches. The challenge for each of us it to consider ourselves as part of a wider family in the Church, and to see those with whom we do not share a blood relationship as our 'family' and therefore our responsibility to honour and respect.

COLLECT

God, the giver of life,
whose Holy Spirit wells up within your Church:
by the Spirit's gifts equip us to live the gospel of Christ
    and make us eager to do your will,
that we may share with the whole creation
    the joys of eternal life;
through Jesus Christ your Son our Lord,
who is alive and reigns with you,
in the unity of the Holy Spirit,
one God, now and for ever.

Saturday 15 October

1 Timothy 5.17-end

'... do not ordain anyone hastily' (v.22)

I smile when I read this line from Paul's letter to the young leader, Timothy. I work at a theological college where women and men study and train for ordination and leadership in the Church. Students arrive at college after many months, often years, of a 'process of discernment', during which their sense of calling is prayerfully explored. Most experience this as a positive process, but some complain that the wheels of the Church grind far too slowly and that the whole thing takes an inordinately long time.

Paul's warning not to fast-track the process has a good common-sense basis. Thinking back over the things Timothy, leader and overseer of this new church in Ephesus, has been expected to attend to as outlined in this letter – instructing, countering false teaching, organizing the household of God, setting an example in word and deed, organizing social care, adjudicating in conflicts – it is no wonder that Paul advises against rushing into it without due consideration and preparation.

The Church in this day, as in Paul's, will do well to pay attention to the careful selection and training of men and women who offer themselves to be leaders. Perhaps today you might spend some time praying for those in your part of the Church who are engaged with the process of discerning and testing vocations to ministry, that they would do so with the good timing of the gracious God who calls people to serve him as faithfully as Timothy did.

God, our light and our salvation:
illuminate our lives,
that we may see your goodness in the land of the living,
and looking on your beauty
may be changed into the likeness of Jesus Christ our Lord.

Monday 17 October

1 Timothy 6.1-10

'... trapped by many senseless and harmful desires' (v.9)

The opening words about slavery are disturbing: 'Let all who are under the yoke of slavery regard their masters as worthy of all honour' (v.1). Slavery is not praised here as a good thing in itself, but neither is it attacked as an evil. The tone is of upholding the status quo, since rocking the boat could impede the spread of the gospel. That does not make the accommodation to slavery in this passage any easier to read.

Press ahead, however, and we come to a principle that would eventually overturn slavery as an acceptable institution in the Christian world: 'the love of money is a root of all kinds of evil' (v.10). We are to meet any desire to be rich with the utmost suspicion, since it is apt to lead to destruction and spiritual desolation. Riches belong further down the pecking order of what makes for a good human life than was generally thought in biblical times, and far further than they typically feature today.

Such thoughts eventually tilted the Christian mind against slavery: it could not be tolerated once we saw slavery as the perfect example of putting money before people, and riches above values. 1 Timothy 6 might start out quiescent enough when it comes to slavery, but it soon sows the seeds for its undoing, and that goal, we should remember, is by no means a goal already achieved. Slavery is with us still, an evil driven by 'love of money'.

COLLECT

Grant, we beseech you, merciful Lord,
to your faithful people pardon and peace,
that they may be cleansed from all their sins
and serve you with a quiet mind;
through Jesus Christ your Son our Lord,
who is alive and reigns with you,
in the unity of the Holy Spirit,
one God, now and for ever.

Psalms 145, 146
Isaiah 55
Luke 1.1-4

Luke the Evangelist

Luke 1.1-4

'... so that you may know the truth' (v.4)

The opening of each of the Gospels gives us a good sense of the character of its writer. Matthew wants to situate Jesus within his Jewish lineage and jumps in with a genealogy. Energetic Mark hits the road running, with John the Baptist's preaching. Mystical, philosophical John opens with a prologue about the pre-existent Word, eternally in the Father's bosom, and now made flesh. From the prologue of Luke's Gospel, that evangelist emerges as a learned and organized man. Unlike some of his sources, he was not an 'eyewitness' to Christ, but, like them, all the same, Luke *was* certainly 'a servant of the word' (v.2). Luke deals courteously with those writers and teachers who have gone before him, but he clearly also sets himself the task of pressing further than most of them had been able. Sure enough, so excellent was the product of Luke's labours that his Gospel survives, while most of Luke's source material does not, apart from Mark's Gospel (and Matthew's, if Luke knew Matthew's Gospel, which is quite likely).

Luke's position should strike a chord with us today. Like us, he was not an eyewitness, and, like most of us, he belonged to an already somewhat Christianized community: his audience was familiar with the basics (or at least, his primary recipient was, this 'most excellent Theophilus', v.3). Luke had people like us in mind, and today we thank God for him, whose toil has set before us such an ideal text for educating ourselves about the good news concerning Christ.

Almighty God,
you called Luke the physician,
whose praise is in the gospel,
to be an evangelist and physician of the soul:
by the grace of the Spirit
and through the wholesome medicine of the gospel,
give your Church the same love and power to heal;
through Jesus Christ your Son our Lord,
who is alive and reigns with you,
in the unity of the Holy Spirit,
one God, now and for ever.

COLLECT

285

Wednesday 19 October

2 Timothy 1.1-14

'I know the one in whom I have put my trust ...' (v.12)

This passage lays out two central ideas about the structure of the Christian life: that it is characterized both by receiving and by giving; we both receive and entrust. The former notion, reception, turns up when Paul reminds Timothy about the story of his faith, grounded in his own family history. We are even given the names of two principal characters in Timothy's spiritual formation: his grandmother Lois and his mother Eunice. Reception is also present when Paul talks about how Timothy took up his ministry: it was a gift, something received from God through a human intermediary. Timothy has this gift 'through the laying on of my hands' (v.6).

If that is receiving, then the theme of passing on comes in as Paul talks about his own situation. He meets suffering for Christ's sake with confidence. Paul knows that what he has entrusted to God, God will keep safe, namely Paul's whole self. Further still, at God's bidding, Paul has entrusted the young man, Timothy, with the message of the gospel and care of the churches.

For each of us, every present moment stands forever poised between the past and the future. Our reading today helps to form a Christian attitude to both. The past has the character of reception: God has given; we have received. The future has the character of entrustment: we hand ourselves back to God, and commit the ongoing work of his service to others after us.

COLLECT

Grant, we beseech you, merciful Lord,
to your faithful people pardon and peace,
that they may be cleansed from all their sins
and serve you with a quiet mind;
through Jesus Christ your Son our Lord,
who is alive and reigns with you,
in the unity of the Holy Spirit,
one God, now and for ever.

Psalms 14, **15**, 16
Judith 7.19-end *or* Leviticus 9
2 Timothy 1.15 – 2.13

2 Timothy 1.15 – 2.13

'... what you have heard from me ... entrust to faithful people' (2.2)

Today we encounter the same dynamic that we encountered yesterday: of receiving and entrusting. In the passage before us, we find it in the idea of *tradition*, which derives from the Latin for 'handing over'. The life of the Church has been marked by tradition in this way from the beginning, as Paul's words make clear: 'what you have heard from me through many witnesses entrust to faithful people who will be able to teach others as well' (2.2). This is what tradition is all about.

Passing on like this creates a lineage and, in the early Church, knowing who had taught your teacher was an important part of keeping to the orthodox faith. As an example, St Irenaeus of Lyons was celebrated and trusted, as having been taught by the martyr St Polycarp, who had himself been a disciple of the Apostle John. The truth of the faith was passed on from person to person.

We also see in the passage today that lineage is not only about ideas: 'Remember Jesus Christ, raised from the dead, a descendent of David' (2.8). In Christ, God came to have a human lineage, to be descended from David. That makes lineage not only part of the *way* in which the faith is passed on, but also part of the message itself. At the heart of the theological *tradition*, which Paul and Timothy were so committed to handing on – as well as John, Polycarp and Irenaeus – lies the proclamation that in the incarnation of the Son of God, the origin of all things entered a human lineage for our sake.

Almighty God,
in whose service lies perfect freedom:
teach us to obey you
with loving hearts and steadfast wills;
through Jesus Christ our Lord.

COLLECT

287

Friday 21 October

Psalms 17, **19**
Judith 8.9-end *or* Leviticus 16.2-24
2 Timothy 2.14-end

2 Timothy 2.14-end

'... avoid wrangling over words ... Have nothing to do with stupid and senseless controversies' (vv.14,23)

Today we are warned not to engage in idle disputes about words, which chimes with the status of 2 Timothy as one of the 'pastoral epistles', alongside 1 Timothy and Titus. These are pastoral letters because they are about the care of the flock of Christ, and they are pastoral letters because they are exchanges between the shepherds of that flock, the pastors of the early Church. As we peer over the shoulders of these Church leaders to learn their concerns, we see just how much they cared about unity among the people of God. That is why 'wrangling over words' (v.14) and 'stupid and senseless controversies' (v.23) are so much to be avoided: they weaken the unity of the body.

Present Church disagreements are obvious enough. Alongside our history of disunity lies the threat of further breaking apart. That makes the task of praying and working for unity one of the Christian's primary duties, alongside preserving the measure of unity that we already have, even when that is disagreeable. These responsibilities belong particularly to the leaders of the Church. The canons of the Church of England, for instance, conclude their short definition of the duties of a bishop with the words that he or she is 'to set forward and maintain quietness, love, and peace'. We might not envy them their task, but we can pray for them.

COLLECT

Grant, we beseech you, merciful Lord,
to your faithful people pardon and peace,
that they may be cleansed from all their sins
and serve you with a quiet mind;
through Jesus Christ your Son our Lord,
who is alive and reigns with you,
in the unity of the Holy Spirit,
one God, now and for ever.

Psalms 20, 21, **23**
Judith 9 *or* Leviticus 17
2 Timothy 3

Saturday 22 October

2 Timothy 3

'... you have observed my teaching, my conduct, my aim in life, my faith, my patience, my love, my steadfastness' (v.10)

In verse 16 of this chapter we find one of the few occasions where Scripture takes a step back and says something about itself as Scripture: 'All scripture is inspired by God and is useful for teaching, for reproof, for correction, and for training in righteousness' (v.16). The rest of the chapter in which this verse sits helps us to understand what is being said. The overall setting is one of distress, temptation and persecution. Against that background, the role of Scripture becomes all the more clear. It provides stability, right judgement, and a plumb line in uncertain times.

Our passage also sets its statement about Scripture within the context of Timothy's wider human experiences. In particular, it sets Scripture within the story of the various examples who have helped him to faith and theological understanding: both Paul ('you have observed my teaching, my conduct' and so on, v.10) and Timothy's family ('continue in what you have learned... knowing from whom you learned it, and how from childhood you have known the sacred writings', vv.14-15).

2 Timothy 3.16 sets out an important statement about the authority and usefulness of the Bible. In the rest of the passage, we learn why this 'teaching ... reproof ... correction, and ... training in righteousness' is important, and why the family of the Church is the natural and best place to receive the truths of the Scriptures with full understanding.

Almighty God,
in whose service lies perfect freedom:
teach us to obey you
with loving hearts and steadfast wills;
through Jesus Christ our Lord.

COLLECT

Monday 24 October

2 Timothy 4.1-8

*'I have fought the good fight, I have finished the race,
I have kept the faith' (v.7)*

Today, Paul instructs Timothy about how he is to proclaim the message of the gospel, which is with faithfulness and patience. Look elsewhere in the New Testament, and we find that these are not only the *means* of preaching but also part of the message itself. The good news is that God is faithful (1 Corinthians 1.9, for instance, or 1 Thessalonians 5.24); the good news is that God is patient (2 Peter 3.9).

Read on a little further in 2 Timothy and we see Paul putting himself forward (not for the first time) as an illustration for his own message. The apostle shines as an example and image of faithfulness and patience. He looks back over his long life and ministry and can say of himself what we might all also aspire to be able to say of ourselves one day: 'I have fought the good fight, I have finished the race, I have kept the faith' (v.7).

Patience and faithfulness start with God. They flow from him, but the way in which they reach us is often through others and their example. Finally, if we have lived up to our Christian vocation, we can reach the end of our lives saying both that we have lived by faith and patience, and that we have modelled them, and in that way have helped to fix them in others.

COLLECT

Blessed Lord,
who caused all holy Scriptures to be written for our learning:
help us so to hear them,
to read, mark, learn and inwardly digest them
that, through patience, and the comfort of your holy word,
we may embrace and for ever hold fast
    the hope of everlasting life,
which you have given us in our Saviour Jesus Christ,
who is alive and reigns with you,
in the unity of the Holy Spirit,
one God, now and for ever.

2 Timothy 4.9-end

'The Lord be with your spirit. Grace be with you' (v.22)

Doubts have been raised over the authorship of the pastoral epistles: were they written by Paul or by someone else, later on, in the Pauline tradition? After a sceptical century, the reasons to deny that Paul himself wrote them seem thinner once again. Certainly, these closing verses present us with a story of pathos and community that rings true to what we know of Paul. The overall tone is of confidence: 'the Lord stood by me and gave me strength... I was rescued from the lion's mouth' (v.17). The final words are an invocation of grace, which is the deepest message of the whole body of the Pauline letters.

There is also pathos here and a window onto the humanity of the apostle. Winter is coming and he languishes in a cold prison. 'Bring the cloak' (v.13), he urges, and 'Do your best to come before winter' (v.21). These requests are set within a tapestry of names, some familiar and others otherwise unknown. Just as grace has been a keynote of Paul's message, and is present here right to the end, so also the importance of the Church and Christian community has been present throughout his writing, and is found here, to the end.

Paul was also emphatic about reconciliation, and we find that here too. Earlier, Paul had parted ways with Mark, but now we find them reconciled. Reconciliation is in the details of Paul's story as well as in his message: 'Get Mark and bring him with you, for he is useful in my ministry' (v.11).

Merciful God,
teach us to be faithful in change and uncertainty,
that trusting in your word
and obeying your will
we may enter the unfailing joy of Jesus Christ our Lord.

COLLECT

Wednesday 26 October

Titus 1

*'... in due time he revealed his word through the proclamation
with which I have been entrusted' (v.3)*

The Greek of the New Testament has several, subtly different, words for time. Two are deployed in our passage today, in verses 2 and 3. *Chronos* is the more usual word for time: it is the succession of one moment after another. It is translated in verse 2 as 'ages'. The Christian hope had been 'promised before the ages began', that is, promised before the succession of time began. From *chronos* we have our word 'chronology'.

The other word for time is *kairos*. It is precisely *not* the regular succession of one moment after another. Rather, *kairos* is a time in contradistinction to the rest of time, not part of 'the ages' but time that stands apart from the usual flow. *Kairos* is the 'due time' of verse 3. It is the opportune time, the time of God's initiative: what Paul calls 'the acceptable time... the day of salvation' (2 Corinthians 6.2) and what Isaiah announced as 'the year of the Lord's favour' (Isaiah 61.2).

When, therefore, we read of the proclamation of this 'due time', more is in mind than just that this is the time for its proclamation. Rather, the proclamation itself is *about* this time. The Christian message is the proclamation of this 'now': this moment of grace, this time of gifts. It contains both a warning, not to delay, and a glad announcement, ultimately connected to the resurrection of Christ. As St John of Damascus put it, ''Tis the spring of souls today; Christ has burst His prison'.

Blessed Lord,
who caused all holy Scriptures to be written for our learning:
help us so to hear them,
to read, mark, learn and inwardly digest them
that, through patience, and the comfort of your holy word,
we may embrace and for ever hold fast
    the hope of everlasting life,
which you have given us in our Saviour Jesus Christ,
who is alive and reigns with you,
in the unity of the Holy Spirit,
one God, now and for ever.

Titus 2

'... so that they may encourage the young women' (v.4)

In our reading today, we again encounter the importance of setting a good example. Particularly, in this passage, we see the importance of that across age differences: those who are older should be an example to those who follow behind them in age. We read about older women setting an example for younger women, and about Titus setting an example for the younger men. The general principle is that we are to 'model' what it means to be a Christian.

That probably sounds sensible enough, but we should not take it for granted. Generations are more segregated today than perhaps they have ever been. Young people may have relatively few opportunities to associate with older role models or sources of wisdom: extended families tend to be further flung than before, and voluntary groups where older people worked with younger people have declined precipitously.

The Church bucks this trend to some extent. Not all congregations, admittedly, contain many young people, but those that do can provide a rather countercultural opportunity for the young and old to mix. That is worth bearing in mind when we think about how to organize Church life. Groups segregated by age can be an important part of Christian fellowship and discipleship – youth groups, pensioners' groups and so on – but we miss something precious, and distinctly biblical, if we keep different groups of people too far apart, and not least the older and the young.

Merciful God,
teach us to be faithful in change and uncertainty,
that trusting in your word
and obeying your will
we may enter the unfailing joy of Jesus Christ our Lord.

COLLECT

293

Friday 28 October

Simon and Jude, Apostles

Psalms 116, 117
Wisdom 5.1-16
or Isaiah 45.18-end
Luke 6.12-16

Isaiah 45.18-end

*'Turn to me and be saved, all the ends of the earth!
For I am God, and there is no other' (v.22)*

For this feast of the apostles St Simon and St Jude, we have a reading from the most 'apostolic' of Old Testament Books. Isaiah, and especially the section taking in chapters 40 to 55, is full of calling and sending (an apostle is someone who has been sent), and of announcing (which is an apostle's great task). Obviously, there would be differences between the message of this Old Testament book and the message of the New Testament apostles, but those differences should not be overdone.

In today's passage from Isaiah we read the proclamation that there is one God, and only one God, who created and rules all things, who has spoken to us, who is concerned with all people, and who is to be honoured by all people. This God is righteous and demands righteousness, and he is also the saviour. We cannot be sure where Simon or Jude preached, although there are legends, or how long they did so before they met, as it is also said, a martyr's death. We can be sure, however, that in a polytheistic world, their message of the One God was like that of Isaiah; that in a pessimistic world (as the world of the first century was), their message was, like Isaiah's message, one of hope; and that like Isaiah they preached about God's self-communication, now perfectly known in Jesus, the Word made flesh.

COLLECT

Almighty and eternal God,
you have kindled the flame of love
in the hearts of the saints:
grant to us the same faith and power of love,
that, as we rejoice in their triumphs,
we may be sustained by their example and fellowship;
through Jesus Christ your Son our Lord,
who is alive and reigns with you,
in the unity of the Holy Spirit,
one God, now and for ever.

Psalms 41, **42**, 43
Judith 15.14 – end of 16
or Numbers 6.1-5, 21-end
Philemon

Philemon

'... no longer as a slave but as more than a slave, a beloved brother'
(v.16)

The Letter to Philemon brings us back to the topic of slavery. The central character is Philemon's slave Onesimus. The letter is so delicately worded that the exact problem is not clear: perhaps Onesimus was a runaway who had stolen something, but we are not quite sure. Nor is the proposed remedy crystal clear: Onesimus is to become 'more than a slave', a brother, but does that mean released from slavery? We do not know.

As with 1 Timothy, slavery as an institution receives no censure here. The whole logic of the letter, however, is part of what would eventually overturn slavery. We find here the idea that a slave can be, and should be, an equal, a 'beloved brother', and that a slave could be honoured even as Paul is honoured by Philemon: 'welcome him as you would welcome me' (v.17).

The implications of this letter for a specific ethical question, namely slavery, took time to become clear. Its implications for the general structure of Christian ethics are more straightforward. Paul mentions both the idea of *duty* and the idea of *love*, but love clearly has the upper hand. Love touches on the heart of the message about Christian life, not duty: 'though I am bold enough in Christ to command you to do your duty, yet I would rather appeal to you on the basis of love' (vv.8-9).

Blessed Lord,
who caused all holy Scriptures to be written for our learning:
help us so to hear them,
to read, mark, learn and inwardly digest them
that, through patience, and the comfort of your holy word,
we may embrace and for ever hold fast
the hope of everlasting life,
which you have given us in our Saviour Jesus Christ,
who is alive and reigns with you,
in the unity of the Holy Spirit,
one God, now and for ever.

COLLECT

Monday 31 October

Daniel 1

*'[King Nebuchadnezzar] placed the vessels in the treasury
of his gods' (v.2)*

The beginning of the story of Daniel may sound familiar. We are reminded of another tale featuring a Jewish boy who makes good in a foreign court: Joseph at the court of Pharaoh. In both cases it is wisdom and skill in interpretation that makes the difference.

However, the similarity is misleading. It suggests that we are launching into an account of a rapid rise to fame and fortune. In fact, the story of Daniel is much darker and more dangerous. Daniel is not alone in being at risk in a strange place; his whole people are in the same situation. The nation has been overrun, their king deposed, their city burned to the ground and their temple destroyed. The temple treasures, dedicated to the worship of the God of Israel, are now, horror of horrors, in a pagan temple. It is the end of everything.

Unless – perhaps faith in God can be sustained. Perhaps there is some courage left, some steadfastness, some wisdom that will help a group of young men negotiate their way through the minefield of the Babylonian court and out the other side. Daniel and his friends are already playing a dangerous game, with their insistence on keeping to their own diet. They may not survive. Babylonian names notwithstanding, they remain true to their Jewish identity. Their story shows how it is possible, with God, to stand tall at the end of everything.

COLLECT

Almighty and eternal God,
you have kindled the flame of love
in the hearts of the saints:
grant to us the same faith and power of love,
that, as we rejoice in their triumphs,
we may be sustained by their example and fellowship;
through Jesus Christ your Son our Lord,
who is alive and reigns with you,
in the unity of the Holy Spirit,
one God, now and for ever.

Psalms 15, 84, 149
Isaiah 35.1-9
Luke 9.18-27

Tuesday 1 November

All Saints' Day

Isaiah 35.1-9

'... make firm the feeble knees' (v.3)

Today we widen our thinking about saints. The book of Daniel features young men who surely qualify, remaining true to their faith and identity in the face of extreme danger. They are able to behave as if they know God will rescue them, even when they think they may actually die. Our reading from Isaiah shows us the kind of vision that keeps them strong.

The place of danger this time is not an alien court but a waterless waste. God's people stand at the edge of a desert. In front of them all is heat and dust and danger. Moving forward means walking into death. 'Be strong, do not fear!' they must exclaim (v.4). For God's people there are paths, there is water, there are even flowers. God's presence changes everything; it turns a deathly journey into a triumphal procession.

God's saints are not immune to human suffering. What makes them different is their faith in what lies beyond. Isaiah sings of everlasting joy in the presence of the God who redeems his people, where the blind see and the lame dance, and we are reminded of Jesus' words about the kingdom of God. There is a different world order in which there is joy for God's people, despite everything. For Isaiah it was Jerusalem. For Christians it is the heavenly Jerusalem, where we know we will, at the end, join all God's saints around his throne.

Almighty God,
you have knit together your elect
in one communion and fellowship
in the mystical body of your Son Christ our Lord:
grant us grace so to follow your blessed saints
in all virtuous and godly living
that we may come to those inexpressible joys
that you have prepared for those who truly love you;
through Jesus Christ your Son our Lord,
who is alive and reigns with you,
in the unity of the Holy Spirit,
one God, now and for ever.

COLLECT

297

Wednesday 2 November

Psalms **9**, 147.13-end
or **119.57-80**
Daniel 2.25-end
Revelation 2.12-end

Daniel 2.25-end

'... the God of heaven will set up a kingdom that shall never be destroyed' (v.44)

The king of Babylon is today revealed as the tyrant he is. The king has demanded that his wise men tell him not only what his dream means, but the forgotten dream itself. The king's execution order is of course totally unreasonable, even more so because it includes Daniel and his friends, who have not even been involved in the consultation.

What happens next does not surprise us. Again it reminds us of the story of Joseph in Genesis. God reveals to Daniel the dream and its meaning, and Daniel recounts it to the king, earning for himself and his companions not only life but promotion.

The meaning of the dream, though, takes us far beyond the scope of anything in Genesis. It encompasses the future of the whole area in which Judaea was set, ruled successively by the Babylonians, the Persians, the Greeks and the Romans. The history of the period is complicated, and it is made more so here by the allusive way in which it is recounted. What really matters is the climax of the interpretation, intended to be read by those who are persecuted and in danger. All kingdoms fall, in the end, to the rule of the God of heaven. That is what people living at the whim of a tyrant need to hear, whether the tyrant is Nebuchadnezzar or any of his more recent counterparts.

COLLECT

Almighty and eternal God,
you have kindled the flame of love
    in the hearts of the saints:
grant to us the same faith and power of love,
that, as we rejoice in their triumphs,
we may be sustained by their example and fellowship;
through Jesus Christ your Son our Lord,
who is alive and reigns with you,
in the unity of the Holy Spirit,
one God, now and for ever.

Psalms 11, **15**, 148 *or* 56, **57** (63)
Daniel 3.1-18
Revelation 3.1-13

Thursday 3 November

Daniel 3.1-18

'... we will not serve your gods' (v.18)

This passage needs to be read aloud. The repetitive lists at first make us smile, but soon they become deeply sinister. They lead inexorably, word by word, to a terrible choice for our heroes, as the king's arbitrary and ridiculous command provides an opening for the enemies of these upstart Jews.

'You shall have no other gods before me' – this is the first commandment, essential to Jewish faith, and the commandment explains why: 'I am the Lord your God, who brought you out of the land of Egypt, out of the house of slavery' (Exodus 20.2-3). Without God there is no Israel, just a bunch of slaves. Faithful Jews cannot turn their backs on this God even to save their lives.

Shadrach, Meshach and Abednego voice the doubt in the minds of God's persecuted people down the ages; they do not know whether their God can save them. The doubt is there, but it makes no difference. They will choose the flames.

We know what is going to happen, but readers of this book have not always known. In times of danger some saw their fellow Jews, members of their families, people they loved, thrown into furnaces without any miraculous rescue. We all at some time face a choice: do we turn our backs on the God who permits our suffering? Or do we grit our teeth and praise him anyway?

God of glory,
touch our lips with the fire of your Spirit,
that we with all creation
may rejoice to sing your praise;
through Jesus Christ our Lord.

COLLECT

Friday 4 November

Daniel 3.19-end

'Blessed be the God of Shadrach, Meshach, and Abednego' (v.28)

So we have our happy ending. The brave heroes are miraculously saved; the king is converted by this convincing display of power; the God of the Jews becomes the God of Babylon, and Shadrach, Meshach and Abednego are once again promoted. A tyrant is still a tyrant, however, and one who can change his religious allegiance so easily can change it again. The rescue from danger is dramatic but, we suspect, temporary.

For its original Jewish readers, this is a story of hope against the odds. There have been many tyrants down the ages willing to kill Jews, and they have not often been rescued. This story tells of a presence in the fire, walking with the three men, all of them comfortable and safe in the flames. It offers hope that even when things seem hopeless, God's presence somehow makes a difference.

For Christian readers, however, the story takes on a new resonance. We are reminded of one who longed for rescue from painful death, but still walked steadfastly towards it, who went through the flames of hell and emerged victorious on the other side. Salvation, we remember, comes not instead of suffering but rather in and through suffering and death. There will always be tyrants, but their power is always, despite appearances, reduced to nothing in the face of the power of God in Christ.

COLLECT

Almighty and eternal God,
you have kindled the flame of love
    in the hearts of the saints:
grant to us the same faith and power of love,
that, as we rejoice in their triumphs,
we may be sustained by their example and fellowship;
through Jesus Christ your Son our Lord,
who is alive and reigns with you,
in the unity of the Holy Spirit,
one God, now and for ever.

Saturday 5 November

Daniel 4.1-18

'... in order that all who live may know that the Most High is sovereign' (v.17)

Daniel's skill in the interpretation of dreams is once more put to the test. He is 'chief of the magicians' (v.9), so much is expected. Daniel's problem this time is not going to be in understanding the dream, but rather in presenting uncomfortable truths to the one who has power of life and death.

King Nebuchadnezzar is very pleased with himself. He is ruler of a secure empire. He has the backing of the gods of Babylon, and has now brought over to his side even the powerful God of the Jews. He has a palace full of courtiers to do his bidding. He sees himself as a benevolent ruler, protecting his subjects from harm, but we know that Nebuchadnezzar is dangerous. We have already seen what happens when he lets power go to his head, and turns his subjects into victims. A benevolent tyrant is still a tyrant, and absolute power, as we know, corrupts absolutely. The king needs to be taught a lesson, and even before Daniel delivers his interpretation, we can tell what his dream is about. The all-powerful is about to have his power taken away.

What we are about to see is a demonstration of an alternative, real power, that is genuinely benevolent, gracious, forgiving, willing the good of all. The power of 'the Most High' will be set against the power of the king, and all will see that there is no contest.

God of glory,
touch our lips with the fire of your Spirit,
that we with all creation
may rejoice to sing your praise;
through Jesus Christ our Lord.

COLLECT

301

Monday 7 November

Psalms 19, **20** *or* **71**
Daniel 4.19-end
Revelation 5

Daniel 4.19-end

'... he is able to bring low those who walk in pride' (v.37)

So now we know. Daniel delivers his interpretation, and surprisingly is not executed or even demoted. What happens to Daniel is not, for once, the point. This chapter is about an even more serious topic, and distractions are not allowed. We are asked to focus our whole attention on the question of who runs the universe.

Nebuchadnezzar believes he does. He is ruler of all the known world, and thinks rather highly of himself as a result. As well he might – the Babylonians were extremely efficient conquerors and oppressors, it seems. But this is a classic case of pride coming before a fall, and a much-improved emperor eventually emerges as a result.

Who runs the universe? Is it those with their fingers on the buttons of weapons of mass destruction? Is it big business, or the banks? Is it the scientists, with their increasing capacity to save us or destroy us? Is it some new deadly virus? The writer of Daniel has for us the same message as for the ancient Jews. There is only one ruler in this universe, and all other claims to ultimate power fall before the claim of the God of Israel. In our fragile and insecure world, it is the task of believers to declare, against all the evidence to the contrary, that 'his sovereignty is an everlasting sovereignty, and his kingdom endures from generation to generation' (v.34).

COLLECT

Almighty Father,
whose will is to restore all things
in your beloved Son, the King of all:
govern the hearts and minds of those in authority,
and bring the families of the nations,
divided and torn apart by the ravages of sin,
to be subject to his just and gentle rule;
who is alive and reigns with you,
in the unity of the Holy Spirit,
one God, now and for ever.

Daniel 5.1-12

'... they brought in the vessels ... and drank from them (v.3)

Another emperor, another need for Daniel's interpretation skills. Not a dream this time, but the writing on the wall.

Another emperor, another tyrant, willing to trample on the sensitivities of his subjects. His hubris more than matches that of his father before him. For Jewish readers, he has committed terrible sacrilege: the treasures of the house of the God of Israel are not for showing off at a party. We who have read the last four chapters are not surprised to find that the king's self-indulgent, drunken behaviour has immediate consequences.

The king and his guests drink their sacrilegious toasts to the 'gods of gold and silver, bronze, iron, wood and stone' (v.4). But there is an uninvited guest at this feast, a God not made with hands, a presence that will not be mocked. This God cannot be held or seen or touched, is not static and controllable. This God is alive and active. This God communicates, in words that demand careful attention. This God does not need to be represented by an object, but needs nothing more than a word to reduce the most powerful king in the world to a quivering wreck of terror and confusion.

Enter Daniel, who we imagine to have retired from public service. He will be summoned back to court, and back into danger. We wait to see whether another Babylonian ruler is about to get his comeuppance.

God, our refuge and strength,
bring near the day when wars shall cease
and poverty and pain shall end,
that earth may know the peace of heaven
through Jesus Christ our Lord.

COLLECT

303

Wednesday 9 November

Psalms **23**, 25 or **77**
Daniel 5.13-end
Revelation 7.1-4, 9-end

Daniel 5.13-end

'... the God in whose power is your very breath' (v.23)

In case we, like the emperor, have not yet learned who is in charge, yet another story shows us what happens to tyrants who set themselves up against 'the Most High God' (v.21), as this book likes to call the God of Israel. Belshazzar has already recognized the sinister and alarming nature of the words that have appeared on his wall. Now he learns their meaning. They are words connected with weights and measures. His reign has been evaluated, and found to be inadequate. He will be replaced.

We know something about the transition of power between the Babylonians and the Persians, and there are good historical reasons why it happened, but our writer is not interested in them. This book wants to show us, above all, that God controls everything and everyone. If there is a regime change, then God is behind it and God has his reasons. Its readers are encouraged to believe this, even when it is not easy to see, and to know that ultimately they can feel safe in God's world

And what of Daniel? He has once again been promoted to a position of power, but this book has already taught us about the temporary nature of the goodwill of tyrants. The empire may be under new and more benign rule, but let us not imagine for one moment that Daniel is safe.

COLLECT

Almighty Father,
whose will is to restore all things
in your beloved Son, the King of all:
govern the hearts and minds of those in authority,
and bring the families of the nations,
divided and torn apart by the ravages of sin,
to be subject to his just and gentle rule;
who is alive and reigns with you,
in the unity of the Holy Spirit,
one God, now and for ever.

Daniel 6

'It pleased Darius' (v.1)

Of course it pleased Darius. Who would not enjoy being the only god in the world for a month? The courtiers of this new tyrant know exactly how to appeal to him. Darius is caught in the net of his own vanity.

Let's try to forget the children's story, with its smiling Daniel and its cuddly lions. Let's instead see the claws and hear the roar; let's feel the terror. Let's notice the deaths of innocent women and children. Let's remember other believers who faced lions and were not saved. This is not a children's story; it is a horror story.

At the end, of course, our hero is alive and more powerful than ever, his enemies defeated and his God installed as the God of the Persian empire. In some ways this story mirrors those that have gone before. It establishes the identity of true divine power. However, there is a human dimension to this story that makes it all too real in our imaginations: a whole night in the dark with the lions, a night Daniel has brought on himself by his insistence on praying in public, and the mauled children that haunt us.

Daniel is a brutal book. It makes us face danger over and over again. It tells us there will always be another tyrant. It challenges us to consider our own faithfulness, our own courage in the service of 'the living God, enduring forever' (v.26).

God, our refuge and strength,
bring near the day when wars shall cease
and poverty and pain shall end,
that earth may know the peace of heaven
through Jesus Christ our Lord.

COLLECT

Friday 11 November

Psalms 28, **32** *or* **55**
Daniel 7.1-14
Revelation 9.1-12

Daniel 7.1-14

'... his kingship is one that shall never be destroyed' (v.14)

The book of Daniel changes at this point. We have been reading stories, but now we are seeing visions and dreaming dreams. The themes, however, remain the same: the identity of the ruler of the universe, and the stark choices imposed on his followers.

The language is symbolic. It draws on the myths of other nations as well as the traditions of Israel. The animals represent the powers that have ruled over Judaea: Babylon, Persia and Greece. It is likely that the original readers of the book of Daniel were living under the rule of the Greek Antiochus IV, who was particularly arbitrary and brutal. Being a Jew and staying alive became a minefield of negotiation and danger.

All is not lost, however. The Ancient One (v.13) is still on his heavenly throne, and in his courtroom justice is still done. Before him stands one in human form who is given delegated authority over the world. Who is it? Christian readers inevitably see here the figure of Christ, who reigns in God's kingdom, but this ancient text is enigmatic. It tells its readers that all human kingdoms will ultimately fall before God's kingdom, and that God will share his rule with a representative of humanity. How precisely that will happen is shrouded in mystery. Even now we cannot know how and when the tyranny of evil will eventually be overthrown, but Daniel encourages us to trust that it will.

COLLECT

Almighty Father,
whose will is to restore all things
in your beloved Son, the King of all:
govern the hearts and minds of those in authority,
and bring the families of the nations,
divided and torn apart by the ravages of sin,
to be subject to his just and gentle rule;
who is alive and reigns with you,
in the unity of the Holy Spirit,
one God, now and for ever.

Saturday 12 November

Daniel 7.15-end

'Then I desired to know the truth' (v.19)

When you no longer feel at home in your homeland; when the government is arbitrary and cruel, and there is no other power out there who can come to the rescue; when danger lurks on every street corner; when you no longer know who you can trust; when families are divided and careless talk costs lives; how do you survive? How do you stay faithful to your identity and your God? How do you live with integrity? How do you not give in to despair?

You gather secretly with others of your faith. You read the ancient stories of the God who protects and saves his people. And you are given a new resource, the stories and visions of Daniel, a hero faithful in the face of death many times, a visionary who sees beyond the present horror.

Daniel tells you that everything has been mapped out by the all-powerful God. Tyrants have been allocated their time, but judgement will inevitably come, even to Antiochus. It is too dangerous to write this down, or to speak it openly, but you understand the book's code. And you get the big picture: there is only one ruler in the universe, and nothing happens without his permission.

Does it help? Perhaps. It is a way of making sense of chaos and despair. In our sometimes chaotic and brutal world, perhaps it can help us too.

God, our refuge and strength,
bring near the day when wars shall cease
and poverty and pain shall end,
that earth may know the peace of heaven
through Jesus Christ our Lord.

COLLECT

307

Monday 14 November

Psalms 46, **47** or **80**, 82
Daniel 8.1-14
Revelation 10

Daniel 8.1-14

'... then the sanctuary shall be restored to its rightful state' (v.14)

There is a connection between the right ordering of worship and the just ordering of the world according to every strand of the Old Testament. In Exodus, the people of God travel with the sanctuary in their midst. Kings and Chronicles tell the story of God's temple, while the prophets foretell its rebuilding. Here the book of Daniel reflects on the cosmic significance of worship.

As modern readers, we get lost in the details of the vision and the variety of horns. To decode them now, you need particular expertise in ancient Near Eastern history. However, the core of the message remains the same. All conflict between the nations and the rise and fall of empires have at their root one complex human emotion: pride – the desire to be pre-eminent and to lord it over others.

The only antidote to pride known to humankind is worship: to humble yourself before God is the best route to being able to humble yourself before others. Regular, sustained worship and prayer at the heart of any community enables humility, critical reflection, justice and the restoring of core values as part of the regular rhythm of its life.

What is true on a cosmic scale is true also of the individual human heart. What place does regular worship have in checking pride in your own life?

COLLECT

Heavenly Father,
whose blessed Son was revealed
    to destroy the works of the devil
and to make us the children of God and heirs of eternal life:
grant that we, having this hope,
may purify ourselves even as he is pure;
that when he shall appear in power and great glory
we may be made like him in his eternal and glorious kingdom;
where he is alive and reigns with you,
in the unity of the Holy Spirit,
one God, now and for ever.

Tuesday 15 November

Daniel 8.15-end

'So I, Daniel, was overcome ...' (27)

The ministry of a prophet, an intercessor, a pastor or a preacher is very costly. Daniel was all of these, yet his day job was none of them; it was to be a senior civil servant and counsellor, going about the king's business in a land far from home.

Learning to live in that place of exile was demanding enough. Yet Daniel is also called to the profoundly uncomfortable place of being able to see the eternal realities at the heart of history.

That ability to see is a combination of human and spiritual disciplines kept over a lifetime and God's particular anointing and help, given in this passage through the interpreter Gabriel. This may seem at first sight an attractive and even glamorous calling, central to the purposes of God.

Yet Daniel found this ministry exhausting. He was overcome and lay sick for several days. Understanding and writing down the vision took all of his strength.

You may be called to be a prophetic ministry, or to be an intercessor or a pastor or a preacher. Be realistic about the great demands of this ministry if exercised well. If you are not so called, then you will know someone who is. Pray for strength for those called to bear the weight of God's word today.

Heavenly Lord,
you long for the world's salvation:
stir us from apathy,
restrain us from excess
and revive in us new hope
that all creation will one day be healed
in Jesus Christ our Lord.

COLLECT

Daniel 9.1-19

'O Lord, hear; O Lord, forgive;
O Lord, listen and act and do not delay!' (v.19)

Prayer is being with God daily with the people on your heart (according to Michael Ramsey, a former Archbishop of Canterbury).

Intercession for others can take many different forms. Often it will be a quiet, regular bringing of individuals to mind before God in all the different circumstances of their lives. A list of names of those we remember in these ways is a vital aid to personal prayer. Sometimes intercession will be passionate when someone we love is passing through crisis, when people we know are in danger, when tragedy strikes.

Sometimes intercession will mean, as here, discerning what is deeply wrong at the heart of a community and seeking God's grace on its behalf. For Daniel, this meant leading his own people in prayers of repentance and confession, for centuries of wrongdoing. This repentance was an essential element in the healing and spiritual renewal that were needed.

Reflect for a few moments this day on the ways in which you pray for individuals and communities in the light of Daniel's great prayer. Are your prayers for others regular? Are they disciplined? Do you pray for your enemies as well as for your friends? Are you praying for communities as well as people? Are you passionate in your prayer for others?

COLLECT

Heavenly Father,
whose blessed Son was revealed
   to destroy the works of the devil
and to make us the children of God and heirs of eternal life:
grant that we, having this hope,
may purify ourselves even as he is pure;
that when he shall appear in power and great glory
we may be made like him in his eternal and glorious kingdom;
where he is alive and reigns with you,
in the unity of the Holy Spirit,
one God, now and for ever.

Thursday 17 November

Daniel 9.20-end

'... for you are greatly beloved' (v.23)

Sometimes in the second half of Daniel, we can become lost in the detail and miss the meaning. The detailed answers to Daniel's prayers, like the vision in chapter 8, bemuse us today. The rise and fall of long-forgotten empires can confuse contemporary saints of God.

So listen today, instead, not to the great game of thrones being played out here but to the simple words of Gabriel, God's messenger, to Daniel his servant. Especially, hear these words by which Daniel is known in heaven: 'greatly beloved'. The phrase will be repeated twice in the very next chapter (Daniel 10.11,19).

Ponder the phrase as it is applied to Daniel here, towards the end of a long and difficult life of prayerful service in exile from his homeland. Then, ponder here the phrase spoken not to Daniel alone but, through Christ, to all those who respond to God's call. For each of us, through Christ, is greatly beloved in the grace of God.

Finally (and this is often the really hard part), hear the words spoken to you, again as you stand in Christ: 'for *you* are greatly beloved'. You may need some moments of quiet repetition really to hear the word that is being spoken. For once we have heard that word fully, our ears are open to the rest of what God might say in our generation.

Heavenly Lord,
you long for the world's salvation:
stir us from apathy,
restrain us from excess
and revive in us new hope
that all creation will one day be healed
in Jesus Christ our Lord.

COLLECT

311

Psalms **63**, 65 *or* **88** (95)
Daniel 10.1 – 11.1
Revelation 13.1-10

Daniel 10.1 – 11.1

'... the sound of his words like the roar of a multitude' (v.6)

We draw to the end of our journey through Daniel. Daniel 10 introduces the longest sequence of visions in the entire book, running through to the end of Chapter 12. In terms of genre, we have left the tales of Daniel and his companions in Babylon behind us. We are in the land of apocalyptic visions.

'Apocalyptic' means revealing or uncovering something. The apocalyptic writings pull back the curtain on spiritual and eternal realities and reveal the eternal truths and patterns behind them. The apocalyptic style of writing developed after the exile as God's people suffered and wrestled with the reality of being a small community gathered around the temple in an often hostile world.

There are some examples of apocalyptic writing in the Old Testament (including Daniel 7-12 and much of Zechariah) and many more in the apocrypha and literature written after the Old Testament and before the New. It is present in the New Testament in some of the Gospel passages and, of course, in the Book of Revelation.

The great truth at the heart of the genre is that there are spiritual realities and battles that we cannot see underlying the great events in the world. In these realities, however difficult, God is at work to bring about his kingdom. God's people are called to be faithful, courageous, to hold fast and to pray.

COLLECT

Heavenly Father,
whose blessed Son was revealed
    to destroy the works of the devil
and to make us the children of God and heirs of eternal life:
grant that we, having this hope,
may purify ourselves even as he is pure;
that when he shall appear in power and great glory
we may be made like him in his eternal and glorious kingdom;
where he is alive and reigns with you,
in the unity of the Holy Spirit,
one God, now and for ever.

Daniel 12

'... you shall rise for your reward at the end of the days' (v.13)

A belief in the resurrection from the dead emerges only gradually in the Old Testament. There is throughout an acknowledgement that death is a bad thing, as well as a thirst for eternity. There are individuals, such as Enoch and Elijah, who are snatched away to be with God forever, but a general hope of resurrection emerges slowly as God's people wrestle with the call of eternity in their hearts.

That Old Testament faith reaches something of a high point in Daniel 12. Here are several key ideas that will be at the foundation of the resurrection in the New Testament: death is like sleep; there will be an awakening – some to everlasting life and some to shame; the righteous will live for ever; God knows their names – they are written in the book of life; we do not know the day or the time when these things will come to pass.

There is much here that is neither filled out nor explained – particularly the question of how human beings can share in eternal life. Daniel is able to see but still through a glass darkly. The world must wait and watch and pray and long for the birth of the one who will come to bring life in all its fullness.

Heavenly Lord,
you long for the world's salvation:
stir us from apathy,
restrain us from excess
and revive in us new hope
that all creation will one day be healed
in Jesus Christ our Lord.

COLLECT

Monday 21 November

Psalms 92, **96** *or* **98**, 99, 101
Isaiah 40.1-11
Revelation 14.1-13

Isaiah 40.1-11

'Then the glory of the Lord shall be revealed' (v.5)

One of the greatest of the Old Testament prophets begins his song with his life's message from God: 'Comfort, O comfort my people' (v.1). His songs continue (most think) until the end of Isaiah 55. These 15 chapters are the most powerful words of hope in Scripture, addressed to the second generation of exiles to prepare them for salvation.

We do not know this prophet's name. He values gentleness and humility in God and God's servants. Perhaps for that reason he refers to himself only as 'a voice' (vv.3,6). I like to call him 'Col' (from the Hebrew *q'ol* meaning voice).

Col's words throughout are full of contrasts. In this opening song he contrasts past and present: we are at a crisis, a turning point in God's dealings with his people. He contrasts the weightiness and permanence of God's power and glory breaking in (vv.4-5) with the lightness and fragility of human lives (flowers and grass, vv.6-7). The Hebrew word 'glory' means something heavy, dense and immensely powerful.

The Christian's task and calling in Advent is to prepare the way of the Lord: to so witness to those around us that a way is opened for them to hear God's message of comfort and forgiveness and come home. As we prepare for Advent, what will your life message be? How will it be read?

COLLECT

Eternal Father,
whose Son Jesus Christ ascended to the throne of heaven
    that he might rule over all things as Lord and King:
keep the Church in the unity of the Spirit
and in the bond of peace,
and bring the whole created order to worship at his feet;
who is alive and reigns with you,
in the unity of the Holy Spirit,
one God, now and for ever.

Psalms **97**, 98, 100 *or* **106*** (*or* 103)
Isaiah 40.12-26
Revelation 14.14 – end of 15

Tuesday 22 November

Isaiah 40.12-26

'To whom then will you compare me ...?' (v.25)

The question is asked in every generation: who created the heavens and the earth, the universe in all its majesty? Did God truly create the world and all that is in it? Or are the gods themselves a human creation? The way we experience life will turn upon our answer.

In earlier generations, the gods of Babylon were, quite literally, made with human hands (vv.19-20). In modern times, the philosophers have told us, the gods are merely a projection of human need, human power, human insecurity.

Col's second song lifts the eyes of exiles above the temples of Babylon, away from the everyday and takes us back to the beginnings of creation, to the edge of the world. Our own science takes us back further to the origins of time and matter and the entire universe. But the fundamental questions remain the same. Is the universe created by a loving God, more powerful and merciful than we can imagine? How do we account for the world's order and beauty, humanity's sense of purpose, our consciousness of who we are, our longing for happiness, our need of forgiveness?

If we are to take God seriously, we need to revisit these fundamental questions. We need to regain our perspective as the evenings close in at the end of the year. The tame idols in our hearts need to be replaced with a fresh vision of the living God.

COLLECT

God the Father,
help us to hear the call of Christ the King
and to follow in his service,
whose kingdom has no end;
for he reigns with you and the Holy Spirit,
one God, one glory.

Wednesday 23 November

Isaiah 40.27 – 41.7

'... they shall mount up with wings like eagles' (40.31)

Exhaustion distorts perspective. All manner of things can drain our vitality: illness, bereavement and stress, sheer hard work sustained over a number of months, a number of different demands coming all at once with no chance to draw breath and recover.

Whatever the cause, we should recognize that tiredness will affect us spiritually as well as physically. When our inner batteries are drained, we begin to live less joyfully, less adventurously in our discipleship. Step by step, we make the easier choices and take the less demanding road. We become more vulnerable to temptation and harder to rouse. As the old collect for last Sunday has it: 'Stir up O Lord the wills of your faithful people'.

The Christian life is demanding and requires strength and resilience. The whole purpose of these chapters is to pass on a message of comfort and gentleness to those who are weary. We need to hear them in that way, but Col has words that require action as well. To advance, when we are tired, there is always a need to retreat.

The promise is sure: 'those who wait for the Lord shall renew their strength' (40.31). When you are tired, get off the treadmill of overactivity. Press the pause button. Take time to wait on God. Spread your wings like an eagle and wait for the warm thermal currents to lift you up.

COLLECT

Eternal Father,
whose Son Jesus Christ ascended to the throne of heaven
    that he might rule over all things as Lord and King:
keep the Church in the unity of the Spirit
and in the bond of peace,
and bring the whole created order to worship at his feet;
who is alive and reigns with you,
in the unity of the Holy Spirit,
one God, now and for ever.

Psalms **125**, 126, 127, 128
or 113, **115**
Isaiah 41.8-20
Revelation 16.12-end

Isaiah 41.8-20

'You are my servant ...' (v.9)

What does it mean to be the servant of the Lord in a time of change and turmoil? The prophet of Isaiah 40–55 now introduces one of his strongest themes. The nation of Israel has a special destiny and calling. That calling is rooted not in Israel's special qualities but in the grace and mercy of God. The calling is not to be special for Israel's own sake but for the purposes of God.

The identity of the servant in this passage is clear. The servant is Israel, the personification of the nation. This identity will change and intensify in the next chapters, as we will see. Here, the exiles in Babylon are being encouraged to reflect on their identity, to remember who they are. That means remembering where they have come from. They are the offspring of Abraham, God's friend, and Jacob, his servant.

God promises to be with his servant in all circumstances, even the most challenging and dangerous. God's presence has the power to drive away fear, to bestow grace sufficient for this day's trials, to give courage, to make the desert bloom.

Who do you think you are? Reflect today on your identity. Hear God's call: 'You are my servant ... do not fear, for I am with you' (vv.9-10). You are part of the Church, God's new Israel, called by the grace of God, not because we are special but for the purposes of God.

God the Father,
help us to hear the call of Christ the King
and to follow in his service,
whose kingdom has no end;
for he reigns with you and the Holy Spirit,
one God, one glory.

COLLECT

317

Friday 25 November

Isaiah 41.21 – 42.9

'... a bruised reed he will not break' (42.3)

The servant of Lord in the past is Israel, descended from Abraham and Jacob. The servant in the present are the exiles, called to serve God's purposes, to sing the Lord's song still in a strange land.

There is another servant, however, described in yet more personal language in at least four of Col's songs, and the first is here in 42.1-9. This servant is still to come. He is the agent of God's deliverance and God's salvation not for Israel alone but for the whole earth.

From earliest times, Christians have seen in these servant songs a prophecy of God's Messiah, fulfilled in Jesus Christ. He it is who claimed to be the light of the world, who opened the eyes of the blind, who set free those bound by evil and sickness and death (42.6-7). He it is who is given not just for Israel but to bring justice in the earth.

He it is who comes, indeed, as a servant, according to each of the gospels, not to be served but to serve. He it is who ministers with gentleness and tenderness to those who are poor and hurting and in need.

In the power we exercise as God's servants today, how will we take care of the bruised reed and nurse the dimly burning wick?

† *The two Psalm cycles coincide at this point.*

COLLECT

Eternal Father,
whose Son Jesus Christ ascended to the throne of heaven
    that he might rule over all things as Lord and King:
keep the Church in the unity of the Spirit
and in the bond of peace,
and bring the whole created order to worship at his feet;
who is alive and reigns with you,
in the unity of the Holy Spirit,
one God, now and for ever.

Saturday 26 November

Isaiah 42.10-17

'Sing to the Lord a new song...' (v.10)

Col's language is steeped in the language and style of the psalms. He is almost certainly one of the sweet psalmists of Israel. It's a remarkable testimony to his faith and vision of God that in the second generation of exile, his own vision of God's glory cannot be contained but bursts out in overflowing songs of joy. This is a song that summons not Israel alone to worship but the whole creation, the coastlands, the inhabitants all along the route from Babylon back to Jerusalem.

This great call to worship would be set to music and sung by a choir with trumpets and lyres, cymbals and drums. It acts here as a preface to a prophetic oracle in which God speaks to all who will listen.

Like the great hymn of praise, the prophet cannot contain the living word he is called to bring. The oracle bursts forth upon the world, a vital life-giving force able to accomplish that which it describes (see Isaiah 55.11).

We read the prophecy therefore as one heralded with a fanfare and announced with trumpets: God will deliver his people; God will lead us home; God will demonstrate his goodness and his greatness; God will make the way clear.

Let this sweet psalm and this oracle resound in your heart as you prepare for Advent tomorrow. Christ comes as King to bring us home. Rejoice.

God the Father,
help us to hear the call of Christ the King
and to follow in his service,
whose kingdom has no end;
for he reigns with you and the Holy Spirit,
one God, one glory.

COLLECT

Seasonal Prayers of Thanksgiving

Blessed are you, Sovereign God of all,
to you be praise and glory for ever.
In your tender compassion
the dawn from on high is breaking upon us
to dispel the lingering shadows of night.
As we look for your coming among us this day,
open our eyes to behold your presence
and strengthen our hands to do your will,
that the world may rejoice and give you praise.
Blessed be God, Father, Son and Holy Spirit.
Blessed be God for ever.

Christmas Season

Blessed are you, Sovereign God,
creator of heaven and earth,
to you be praise and glory for ever.
As your living Word, eternal in heaven,
assumed the frailty of our mortal flesh,
may the light of your love be born in us
to fill our hearts with joy as we sing:
Blessed be God, Father, Son and Holy Spirit.
Blessed be God for ever.

Epiphany

Blessed are you, Sovereign God,
king of the nations,
to you be praise and glory for ever.
From the rising of the sun to its setting
your name is proclaimed in all the world.
As the Sun of Righteousness dawns in our hearts
anoint our lips with the seal of your Spirit
that we may witness to your gospel
and sing your praise in all the earth.
Blessed be God, Father, Son and Holy Spirit.
Blessed be God for ever.

Blessed are you, Lord God of our salvation,
to you be glory and praise for ever.
In the darkness of our sin you have shone in our hearts
to give the light of the knowledge of the glory of God
in the face of Jesus Christ.
Open our eyes to acknowledge your presence,
that freed from the misery of sin and shame
we may grow into your likeness from glory to glory.
Blessed be God, Father, Son and Holy Spirit.
Blessed be God for ever.

Passiontide

Blessed are you, Lord God of our salvation,
to you be praise and glory for ever.
As a man of sorrows and acquainted with grief
your only Son was lifted up
that he might draw the whole world to himself.
May we walk this day in the way of the cross
and always be ready to share its weight,
declaring your love for all the world.
Blessed be God, Father, Son and Holy Spirit.
Blessed be God for ever.

Easter Season

Blessed are you, Sovereign Lord,
the God and Father of our Lord Jesus Christ,
to you be glory and praise for ever.
From the deep waters of death
you brought your people to new birth
by raising your Son to life in triumph.
Through him dark death has been destroyed
and radiant life is everywhere restored.
As you call us out of darkness into his marvellous light
may our lives reflect his glory
and our lips repeat the endless song.
Blessed be God, Father, Son and Holy Spirit.
Blessed be God for ever.

Blessed are you, Lord of heaven and earth,
to you be glory and praise for ever.
From the darkness of death you have raised your Christ
to the right hand of your majesty on high.
The pioneer of our faith, his passion accomplished,
has opened for us the way to heaven
and sends on us the promised Spirit.
May we be ready to follow the Way
and so be brought to the glory of his presence
where songs of triumph for ever sound:
Blessed be God, Father, Son and Holy Spirit.
Blessed be God for ever.

Blessed are you, creator God,
to you be praise and glory for ever.
As your Spirit moved over the face of the waters
bringing light and life to your creation,
pour out your Spirit on us today
that we may walk as children of light
and by your grace reveal your presence.
Blessed be God, Father, Son and Holy Spirit.
Blessed be God for ever.

Blessed are you, Sovereign God,
ruler and judge of all,
to you be praise and glory for ever.
In the darkness of this age that is passing away
may the light of your presence which the saints enjoy
surround our steps as we journey on.
May we reflect your glory this day
and so be made ready to see your face
in the heavenly city where night shall be no more.
Blessed be God, Father, Son and Holy Spirit.
Blessed be God for ever.

The Lord's Prayer and The Grace

Our Father in heaven,
hallowed be your name,
your kingdom come,
your will be done,
on earth as in heaven.
Give us today our daily bread.
Forgive us our sins
as we forgive those who sin against us.
Lead us not into temptation
but deliver us from evil.
For the kingdom, the power,
and the glory are yours
now and for ever.
Amen.

(or)

Our Father, who art in heaven,
hallowed be thy name;
thy kingdom come;
thy will be done;
on earth as it is in heaven.
Give us this day our daily bread.
And forgive us our trespasses,
as we forgive those who trespass against us.
And lead us not into temptation;
but deliver us from evil.
For thine is the kingdom,
the power and the glory,
for ever and ever.
Amen.

The grace of our Lord Jesus Christ,
and the love of God,
and the fellowship of the Holy Spirit,
be with us all evermore.
Amen.

An Order for Night Prayer (Compline)

The Lord almighty grant us a quiet night and a perfect end.
Amen.

Our help is in the name of the Lord
who made heaven and earth.

A period of silence for reflection on the past day may follow.

The following or other suitable words of penitence may be used

Most merciful God,
we confess to you,
before the whole company of heaven and one another,
that we have sinned in thought, word and deed
and in what we have failed to do.
Forgive us our sins,
heal us by your Spirit
and raise us to new life in Christ. Amen.

O God, make speed to save us.
O Lord, make haste to help us.

Glory to the Father and to the Son
and to the Holy Spirit;
as it was in the beginning is now
and shall be for ever. Amen.
Alleluia.

The following or another suitable hymn may be sung

Before the ending of the day,
Creator of the world, we pray
That you, with steadfast love, would keep
Your watch around us while we sleep.

From evil dreams defend our sight,
From fears and terrors of the night;
Tread underfoot our deadly foe
That we no sinful thought may know.

O Father, that we ask be done
Through Jesus Christ, your only Son;
And Holy Spirit, by whose breath
Our souls are raised to life from death.

The Word of God

One or more of Psalms 4, 91 or 134 may be used.

Psalm 134

1   Come, bless the Lord, all you servants of the Lord, ◆
    you that by night stand in the house of the Lord.

2   Lift up your hands towards the sanctuary ◆
    and bless the Lord.

3   The Lord who made heaven and earth ◆
    give you blessing out of Zion.

**Glory to the Father and to the Son
and to the Holy Spirit;
as it was in the beginning is now
and shall be for ever. Amen.**

Scripture Reading

*One of the following short lessons or another suitable
passage is read*

You, O Lord, are in the midst of us and we are called by
your name; leave us not, O Lord our God.

Jeremiah 14.9

(or)

Be sober, be vigilant, because your adversary the devil is
prowling round like a roaring lion, seeking for someone
to devour. Resist him, strong in the faith.

1 Peter 5.8,9

(or)

The servants of the Lamb shall see the face of God, whose
name will be on their foreheads. There will be no more
night: they will not need the light of a lamp or the light of the
sun, for God will be their light, and they will reign for ever
and ever.

Revelation 22.4,5

Into your hands, O Lord, I commend my spirit.
Into your hands, O Lord, I commend my spirit.
For you have redeemed me, Lord God of truth.
I commend my spirit.
Glory to the Father and to the Son
and to the Holy Spirit.
Into your hands, O Lord, I commend my spirit.

Or, in Easter

Into your hands, O Lord, I commend my spirit.
   Alleluia, alleluia.
Into your hands, O Lord, I commend my spirit.
   Alleluia, alleluia.
For you have redeemed me, Lord God of truth.
Alleluia, alleluia.
Glory to the Father and to the Son
and to the Holy Spirit.
Into your hands, O Lord, I commend my spirit.
   Alleluia, alleluia.

Keep me as the apple of your eye.
Hide me under the shadow of your wings.

Gospel Canticle

Nunc Dimittis (The Song of Simeon)

Save us, O Lord, while waking,
and guard us while sleeping,
that awake we may watch with Christ
and asleep may rest in peace.

1   Now, Lord, you let your servant go in peace:
     your word has been fulfilled.

2   My own eyes have seen the salvation
     which you have prepared in the sight of every people;

3   A light to reveal you to the nations
     and the glory of your people Israel.

Luke 2.29-32

**Glory to the Father and to the Son
and to the Holy Spirit;
as it was in the beginning is now
and shall be for ever. Amen.**

**Save us, O Lord, while waking,
and guard us while sleeping,
that awake we may watch with Christ
and asleep may rest in peace.**

Prayers

Intercessions and thanksgivings may be offered here.

The Collect

Visit this place, O Lord, we pray,
and drive far from it the snares of the enemy;
may your holy angels dwell with us and guard us in peace,
and may your blessing be always upon us;
through Jesus Christ our Lord.
Amen.

The Lord's Prayer (see p. 323) may be said.

The Conclusion

In peace we will lie down and sleep;
for you alone, Lord, make us dwell in safety.

Abide with us, Lord Jesus,
for the night is at hand and the day is now past.

As the night watch looks for the morning,
so do we look for you, O Christ.

[Come with the dawning of the day
and make yourself known in the breaking of the bread.]

The Lord bless us and watch over us;
the Lord make his face shine upon us and be gracious to us;
the Lord look kindly on us and give us peace.
Amen.

Reflections for Daily Prayer:
Advent 2016 to the eve of Advent 2017

Reflections for Daily Prayer returns for the 2016–17 Church year with another range of illustrious contributors! Confirmed writers so far include Steven Croft, Joanna Collicutt, Paula Gooder, Helen-Ann Hartley, Libby Lane, Graham James, Helen Orchard and Angela Tilby.

£16.99 • 336 pages
ISBN 978 0 7151 4715 3
Available May 2016

Also available in Kindle and epub formats

NEW!

Reflections on the Psalms

£14.99 • 192 pages
ISBN 978 0 7151 4490 9

Reflections on the Psalms provides original and insightful meditations on each of the Bible's 150 Psalms, from the same experienced team of writers that have made *Reflections for Daily Prayer* so successful.

Each reflection is accompanied by its corresponding Psalm refrain and prayer from the *Common Worship Psalter*, making this a valuable resource for personal or devotional use. Specially written introductions by Paula Gooder and Steven Croft explore the Psalms and the Bible and the Psalms in the life of the Church.

These two shortened editions of *Reflections* are ideal for group or church use during Advent and Lent, or for anyone seeking a daily devotional guide to these most holy seasons of the Christian year.

They are also ideal tasters for those wanting to begin a regular pattern of prayer and reading.

Reflections for Advent 2015

Monday 30 November – Thursday 24 December 2015

Authors:
Maggi Dawn, Barbara Mosse

Please note this book reproduces the material for Advent found in the volume you are now holding.

£4.99 • 32 pages
ISBN 978 0 7151 4690 3
Available August 2015

Reflections for Lent 2016

Wednesday 10 February – Saturday 26 March 2016

Authors:
Paula Gooder, Andrew Davison, Martyn Percy and Steven Croft

Please note this book reproduces the material for Lent and Holy Week found in the volume you are now holding.

£4.99 • 48 pages
ISBN 978 0 7151 4709 6
Available November 2015

Reflections for Daily Prayer
App

Make Bible study and reflection a part of your routine wherever you go with the Reflections for Daily Prayer App for Apple and Android devices.

Download the app for free from the App Store (Apple devices) or Google Play (Android devices) and receive a week's worth of reflections free. Then purchase a monthly, three-monthly or annual subscription to receive up-to-date content.

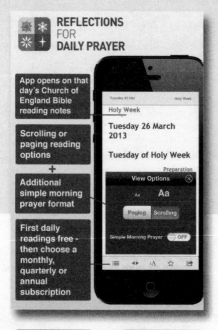

App opens on that day's Church of England Bible reading notes

Scrolling or paging reading options

+

Additional simple morning prayer format

First daily readings free - then choose a monthly, quarterly or annual subscription